SHAKESPEARE AND POLITICS

Shakespeare and Politics
What a Sixteenth-Century Playwright Can Tell Us about Twenty-First-Century Politics

Edited by
Bruce E. Altschuler
Michael A. Genovese

Paradigm Publishers
Boulder • London

Copyright © 2014 by Paradigm Publishers

Published in the United States by Paradigm Publishers, 5589 Arapahoe Avenue, Boulder, CO 80303 USA.

Paradigm Publishers is the trade name of Birkenkamp & Company, LLC, Dean Birkenkamp, President and Publisher.

Library of Congress Cataloging-in-Publication Data

Shakespeare and Politics : What a Sixteenth-Century Playwright Can Tell Us about Twenty-First-Century Politics / edited by Bruce E. Altschuler and Michael A. Genovese.
pages cm
Includes bibliographical references and index.
ISBN 978-1-61205-159-8 (paperback : acid-free paper)
1. Shakespeare, William, 1564–1616—Criticism and interpretation. 2. Shakespeare, William, 1564–1616—Political and social views. 3. Politics in literature. 4. Power (Social sciences) in literature. I. Altschuler, Bruce E., editor of compilation. II. Genovese, Michael A.
PR3017.S53 2013
822.3'3—dc23

2013011941

Printed and bound in the United States of America on acid-free paper that meets the standards of the American National Standard for Permanence of Paper for Printed Library Materials.

Designed and Typeset by Straight Creek Bookmakers.

18 17 16 15 14   1 2 3 4 5

CONTENTS

INTRODUCTION

Bruce E. Altschuler and Michael A. Genovese

The fault, dear Brutus, is not in our stars,
But in ourselves, that we are underlings.
— Cassius to Brutus, *Julius Caesar*

Yet another book about Shakespeare? With so many fine books dealing with the works of William Shakespeare already in print, why do we need another? What distinguishes this book from the others? What purpose does it serve?

We believe this book makes a valuable contribution for three reasons: first, it is always good to return to the Bard for insight, understanding, and inspiration. Second, we focus on the political contributions to our understanding made by Shakespeare. And third, we derive insights that apply to the politics of our age. In doing so, we show that the failure to consider Shakespeare a sophisticated political analyst often leads to either misunderstanding or overly naive interpretations of his plays. As Marjorie Garber has written, "In contemporary American political debates Shakespeare is often cited by lawmakers, though sometimes with scant attention to the context of the lines being quoted, and thus with occasional (and unintended) comic results."[1] What can a sixteenth-century playwright tell us about twenty-first-century politics? Plenty, but only if we pay careful attention.

Shakespeare's grasp of human nature, of greed, ambition, lust, the human psyche, power, and politics are unsurpassed. We see ourselves in his plays. He can be brutally honest in ways we find unnerving. He knows what drives us, what we fear, yearn for, how far we will go, how easily we delude ourselves. He is always modern, his insights always fresh. There is in his works a universal appeal as he speaks to what is noble and base in us all. He, more than any other, saw deep into our psyches to what moved and motivated us. He knew us—knows us—as few others have.

If human nature has not changed in the past four hundred years, we can look to Shakespeare to guide us in our understanding of how humans govern themselves. He is of the tradition of Plutarch (from whom he drew many of his characters and stories) and Machiavelli (from whom he drew insights into politics and power). He influenced the founders of the US Constitution, and he influences us today.

This book opens with an examination of Shakespeare's understanding of leadership and rulership. In that chapter, Thomas E. Cronin and Michael A. Genovese review several of Shakespeare's key leadership plays to help us understand the limits, possibilities, pitfalls, and paradoxes of power and leadership. The next chapter, by Bruce E. Altschuler, explores the dark world of *Macbeth* and how principle gives way to ambition. He then asks whether Shakespeare provides insights into better government or shows how power inevitably corrupts.

In Chapter 3, Sarah Shea presents *Hamlet* as Nietzsche's *Dionysian* man, someone unafraid to look for the essence of things, regardless of the consequences. She sees young Hamlet trying desperately to get to the core of matters, struggling to acquire the intellectual and spiritual strength to rule wisely. Shea finds hope for a modern-day leader in Hamlet's journey. Whether a head of state or simply an ordinary voter, we need to know ourselves before making reasonably passionate declarations. Chapter 4, by Paul A. Cantor, puts *Antony and Cleopatra* into context, exploring that play as a metaphor for empire, globalization, and the clash of civilizations. Rather than seeing globalization as one powerful side imposing its values on a weaker one, Cantor suggests that both today and in Shakespeare's Egypt, globalization also often works in the other direction. The play's Romans are Egyptianized not by military force but because they choose to live like Egyptians. In Chapter 5, Philip Abbott explores the complex world of decision making in *Julius Caesar*. Why do these smart men make so many poor decisions? Abbott's decision-making framework demonstrates how the rationality of each individual does not necessarily lead to overall rationality. He argues that the play can be viewed as a crisis case study, not all that different from those facing modern leaders.

Coyle Neal in Chapter 6 revisits one of Shakespeare's iconic villains, Iago from *Othello*, and asks us to reexamine the nature of evil and its role in understanding motive. Modern adaptations, such as the film *O*, illustrate the American need to understand Iago's motive even though Shakespeare created a character whose malignity defies simple explanation. In Chapter 7, Marlene K. Sokolon looks at Shakespeare's other master of evil, Richard III, and compares his behavior to modern American CEOs. She concludes that although even the most culpable of today's business elites are hardly tyrannical murderers, they share with Richard an ambitious pursuit of pure self-interest with few ethical constraints and little concern for the interests of those they are supposed to serve. David Ramsey in Chapter 8 looks at the origins of modern liberty through the lens of *Cymbeline*. He raises such still-relevant issues as the conflicts between faith and reason and between individualism and social good. In Chapter 9, John M. Parrish explores the ethics of and responsibility for war by focusing on one of Shakespeare's "successful" leaders, Henry V. The issues faced by political leaders in today's era of "wars of choice" remain remarkably similar to those that confronted Henry.

In Chapter 10, Lilly J. Goren revisits the theme of corruption by exploring the values of beauty and honor in *Troilus and Cressida*. This exploration illuminates modern issues of gender equity by examining the question of how the Greeks and Trojans in the play value the worth of Helen of Troy and Cressida. Carol McNamara in Chapter 11 looks at persuasion and deception as political tools in *Measure for Measure*. By examining three of the play's literary devices (the corrupt magistrate, the disguised ruler, and the bed trick), she is able to demonstrate the relevance of the play's scandals to those of recent American politics. And finally, Kevan M. Yenerall in Chapter 12 draws direct comparisons to modern American politics in his examination of polarization in *A Midsummer Night's Dream*. He finds that some of the 2012 presidential hopefuls bear surprising similarities to characters in Shakespeare's comedy.

Many individuals assisted in bringing this book to print. Michael Genovese wishes to thank Brian Whitaker and Mackenzie Burr, who were administrative assistants at the Loyola Marymount University Institute for Leadership Studies, and also Brianna Bruns and Katherine McGrath, research assistants. Bruce Altschuler wishes to thank the members of the APSA section on politics, literature, and film for letting us know just how important Shakespeare's plays are for so many of their courses. We both extend our great appreciation to Jennifer Knerr, our editor at Paradigm Publishers, who was kind, understanding, and professional throughout this project.

Note

1. Marjorie Garber, *Shakespeare and Modern Culture*, New York: Anchor Books, 2008: xxi.

Chapter 1

On Shakespeare's Commanders and Kings

Leadership, Politics, and Hubris

Michael A. Genovese and Thomas E. Cronin

William Shakespeare was an insightful and astute student of human nature and human behavior.[1] He lays before us the good, the bad, and the ugly of politics and power and the precarious nature of the human condition. He reaffirms that no one is perfect and that all of us, leaders especially, are a composite of good and evil inclinations. This was his genius and why we find him so relevant in our own time. His insights into leadership and the use and abuse of power by kings and commanders gives us instructive images of power and principle.

Shakespeare is not only an excellent source of drama but also compels us to reflect on leadership. He asks the fundamental questions, explores the pressures and possibilities, confronts the admixture of good and bad in us and our leaders, and squarely confronts the dilemmas and paradoxes of authority, position, and leadership. His grasp on human nature made him almost as much of a psychologist as a playwright.

Over twenty of his plays deal explicitly with politics and leadership—especially his histories and tragedies. Leadership succession, grasping the reins of power, rulership, the uses and abuses of power, manipulation and deceit, authority, and themes of the rule of law and justice reverberate in his works. Shakespeare suggests throughout that the possession of power reveals character.

We may never know with certainty what Shakespeare's political convictions were. Yale scholar Harold Bloom contends that "Shakespeare's politics, like his religion, forever will be unknown to us. I suspect that he had no politics, and no religion, only a vision of the human, or the more human."[2] Given the demands of drama, Shakespeare gives to his characters words he may or may not personally endorse yet offers for dramatic purposes. Moreover, as in *King Lear* and *Julius Caesar*, Shakespeare sometimes leaves it to his audience to decide who was right and who was wrong.

"Precisely because he was not an apologist for any single position," writes Shakespearean scholar Jonathan Bate, "it has been possible for the plays to be effectively re-interpreted in light of each successive age."[3] Shakespeare is alternately anti-war, anti-ill-informed and too-easily-manipulated people, anti–leaders with swollen egos, anti–conventional politicians, and the list goes on. He is often a contrarian, is always a splendid storyteller, and constantly asks us the reader to consider all the "what ifs" and "what fors."

Most educated people in Shakespeare's time believed in the appropriateness of hierarchical order. But this order was being challenged, and fears of potential anarchy were real. The doctrine of order and obedience to the king (or queen) was much in vogue in Shakespeare's age, and to a significant, though not complete, degree, his plays reflect adherence to this principle.

While clearly no democrat, the extent to which Shakespeare embraced a hierarchical model of society and politics is unclear. In some of his plays, the ruler clearly has a responsibility to govern with the interests of society and the people in mind. In some ways, Shakespeare seems divided politically. As W. B. Yeats notes, "Shakespeare cared little for the state."[4] He was clearly a critic of state censorship.

In Shakespeare's age, to live according to nature was to live in accordance with God's will; and if the king ruled in the name of God, one had an obligation to obey. As God ruled over us, conventional wisdom held at the time, so too must a king be God's temporal voice on earth. Elizabethan historian Sir John Hayward sums up this view: "As one God ruleth the world, one master the family ... so it seemeth no less natural that one state should be governed by one commander."[5] This concept finds its way into *Richard II* when King Richard reminds the audience:

The breath of wordly men cannot depose
The deputy elected by the Lord.
For every man that Bolingbroke hath prest
To lift shrewd steel against our golden crown,
God for his Richard hath in heavenly pay
A glorious angel. Then if angels fight,
Weak men must fall; for heaven still guards the right

If Shakespeare accepts the legitimacy of a hierarchical order, he is also concerned that the king and commander lead justly and effectively. His good leaders consult widely and are open and willing to brook criticism. Rulers who are arrogant and haughty fail of their own weaknesses. Shakespeare did not question monarchy—he was, after all, a man of his age. But he did question the ruling strategies of many of the kings and would-be emperors and commanders. If Shakespeare accepts the need for societal leaders and leadership, he gives none of them a free pass. Tyranny is derided. Only "good" rulers claim Shakespeare's approval.

Macbeth deals with kingship, *The Tempest* with power, *Julius Caesar* with individual glory and the battle for a republic versus empire, *Coriolanus* with pride and democracy, *Cymbeline* with war and peace, *Measure for Measure* with the rule of law and hypocrisy, *King Lear* with political succession and temperament, *Henry V* with what it takes to be a leader, *Hamlet* with decision making, and *Richard III* with how power is exercised and abused.[6]

Shakespeare's leading characters work within different regimes of power. How each one performs—the choices made—determine their own fortunes, and also the fortunes of the state. Leaders make choices, good and bad. Where their choices are designed for self-promotion, they often fail; when their choices are made rashly, they often fail; when they decide based on poor or faulty information, they usually fail; where they are too self-absorbed, they usually fail. It is in the choosing that Shakespeare's politics and his morality play out. Fate may play a role, but human intervention—choice—matters most. Therefore, leaders matter.

Shakespeare's view of politics was shaped in part by the age in which he lived. England was experiencing profound changes and decisive social pressures. Religious warfare, the rise of nationalism, and foreign wars characterized the era. Out of this chaos and violence, Shakespeare seemed to yearn for the politics of *order*. In this, he was somewhat conservative in his politics.

In Shakespeare's day, society was rigidly divided along class lines, and wealth was unevenly distributed. Roughly 80 percent of the English lived in small rural communities. Rulers mattered. Although society was beginning to reject the notion that the king ruled by divine right, democratic practice was still far in the future. Societies depended largely on the quality of leadership provided by a king. Like most of his contemporaries, Shakespeare was unable to envision a polity governed by the people as a viable option. Of Greek democracy, one of Shakespeare's famous characters, Roman general Coriolanus, says, "Though thee the people had more absolute power, I saw, they nourish'd disobedience, fed the ruin of the state."

Shakespeare's suspicion of democracy is evident too in *Julius Caesar* when, in the hands of Caesar, the republic begins to degenerate into a mob. Shakespeare saw the common man as fickle, irrational, and prone to manipulation. The citizens of Rome fell in love with Caesar and welcomed his autocratic rule; this invited tyranny. Equally weak is the foundation on which republican rule is built. And when the republic collapses, and Caesar is killed, a new brand of tyranny is unleashed—the tyranny of the mob.

As Shakespeare valued order, he believed order came from good leadership. What can we say of his views on what constituted good leadership? Shakespeare's focus on individual agency reinforces the conception not only that leadership matters, but that prudent leaders are crucial. This leader-centric view helps shape public and elite opinion and supports the leader-as-hero (or villain) image.

What, to Shakespeare, constitutes good and bad leadership? Military leaders do not fare well in Shakespeare's world. Macbeth, Othello, Titus Andronicus, Henry Bolingbroke, Lear, and Coriolanus come off as too quick to act, too cynical, too self-absorbed or narcissistic, hardened, and harsh, or some combination of these flaws.

Greed and ambition play a large part in Shakespeare's view of human motivation, and they lead most often to catastrophe; such rulers are presented as dysfunctional and counterproductive. Shakespeare did not question the legitimacy of the monarchy, but he cautioned against excess. In attempting to define the ideal prince, Shakespeare would have been familiar with the arguments of Desiderius Erasmus (*The Education of a Christian Prince*, 1603) as well as Niccolo Machiavelli. Shakespeare may have modeled his good princes on Erasmus, while his villains display a Machiavellian wickedness that even Machiavelli would have condemned (as not strategically useful),[7] going so far as to refer to one cad as "that notorious Machiavel!"[8] In fact, what makes Shakespeare's villains so delicious is their level of self-awareness of their crass acts. Richard III turns to his audience to persuade and enlighten them, enlisting us in his self-justifications. Shakespeare's flawed characters take their moral choices seriously, especially as they violate conventional morals in favor of self-serving expediency.

The stability of the state depends on the ability of the prince. As Hamlet's friend Rosencrantz reminds us,

The single and peculiar life is bound
With all the strength and armour of the mind
To keep itself from noyance; but much more
That spirit upon whose weal depends and rests
The lives of many. The cess of majesty
Dies not alone, but like a gulf doth draw
What's near it with it. It is a massy wheel
Fixed on the summit of the highest mount,
To whose huge spokes ten thousand lesser things
Are mortised and adjoined, which when it falls,
Each small annexment, petty consequence,
Attends the boisterous ruin. Never alone
Did the king sigh, but with a general groan[9]

Here, the prince seems to reflect the views of Erasmus, yet in *Henry V*, act 4, a more Machiavellian concept is presented by Henry:

Upon the King! Let us our lives, our souls,
Our debts, our careful wives,
Our children, and our sings, lay on the King!
We must bear all. O hard condition,
Twin-born with greatness, subject to the breath
Of every fool, whose sense no more can feel
But his own wringing! What infinite heart's ease
Must kings neglect that private men enjoy!
And what kings that privates have not too,
Save ceremony—save general ceremony?
And what art thou, thou idol Ceremony?
What kind of god art thou, that suffer'st more
Of mortal griefs than do thy worshippers?
What are thy rents? What are thy comings-in?
O ceremony, show me but thy worth!
What is thy soul of adoration?
Art thou aught else but place, degree, and form,
Creating awe and fear in other men?
Wherein thou art less happy being fear'd
Than they in fearing.
What drink'st thou oft, instead of homage sweet,
But poison'd flattery? O, be sick, great greatness
And bid thy ceremony give thee cure!

Thinks thou the fiery fever will go out
With titles blown from adulation?
Will it give place to flexure and low bending?
Canst thou, when thou command'st the beggar's knee,
Command the health of it? No, thou proud dream,
That play'st so subtly with a king's repose.
I am a king that find thee; and I know
'Tis not the balm, the sceptre, and the ball,
The sword, the mace, the crown imperial,
The intertissued robe of gold and pearly,
The farced titled funning fore the king,
The throne he sits on, nor the tide of pomp
That beats upon the high shore of this world—
No, not all these, thrice gorgeous ceremony,
Not all these, laid in bed majestical,
Can sleep so soundly as the wretched slave
Who, with a body fill'd and vacant mind,
Gets him to rest, cramm'd with distressful bread;
Never sees horrid night, the child of hell;

We turn now to six of Shakespeare's most important "leadership plays," to examine more closely or reinterpret the Bard's core beliefs about leadership. We treat them in this order: *Coriolanus, Othello, Richard III, Julius Caesar, Henry V,* and *King Lear.*

Coriolanus

Shakespeare's tragedy *Coriolanus* concerns General Caius Marcius, a fearless heroic warrior who fought on behalf of the fourth-century BCE Roman Republic and who is awarded the honorary name Coriolanus after the city where one of his major military victories took place. Most of the story is borrowed from Plutarch, and at times it shares with us a character who is a Romanized Achilles—proud, wrathful, noble, and heroic.[10]

The play raises a number of provocative, disturbing questions. It paints a cold, stern, seemingly arrogant general who is too proud and self-absorbed to become a political leader. It depicts a common people, who in the republic play at least a minor role in providing a limited form of consent of the governed, as a fickle, easily led astray, selfish, and sorry lot. It portrays Roman politicians as scheming and jealous cabalists more interested in their careers than in Rome. It suggests a time of tumult, economic and security emergencies, and conflict, all of which threaten Rome's order and stability.

We know that Shakespeare and many of his contemporaries feared both unruly democrats and ineffective political leaders. He—like Machiavelli—prized strategic, prudent, effective leaders who clearly grasped reality and who were able to devise adaptive policies for the challenges they faced.

The case of Shakespeare's (or perhaps it is Plutarch's) Coriolanus is illustrative of Shakespeare's apprehensions about war, politics, leadership, and the common people. Coriolanus is born to a patrician family. His father dies early and he is raised by a proud, patriotic, and domineering mother who inspires his military service and is, apparently, a central source of his ambition.

Coriolanus is in his early thirties, married, and the father of a son. He is much honored and justifiably decorated for his valor in war, yet he is also a loner with a prickly personality. We learn quickly that he is contemptuous of Romans who demand welfare handouts from the state but were apparently unwilling to fight Rome's frequent military foes.

Shakespeare gives us a hardened, battle-scarred military hero who has displayed excellence in war but lacks the sensibility, affability, and political tact needed to compromise and at least try to flatter the crowd of commoners. Both the art of war and the art of politics make powerful demands on their practitioners; few people can excel at both.

All this is brought to head because many Romans, especially Coriolanus's mother, believe he should be given the highest honor Rome can give—to be elected one of Rome's two consuls (a position that would be akin to copresident). His pride and his mother incline him to accept this honor should it be conferred.

But republican practices at the time required a prospective consul to curry public approval before the Roman senate would vote to elect the candidate consul. Coriolanus is reluctant and grudging about this type of politicking. Noble and prideful, Coriolanus is unwilling to fully submit his clearly superior "nature" to the humiliation of appealing to the public. (He is unwilling, in contemporary American terms, to campaign for days and days before the Iowa caucuses, or in Lincoln's words, "to take a bath in public opinion.")

Coriolanus does some "campaigning" but is unable to camouflage his disdain for the people. Meanwhile, scheming political rivals conspire to alter the people's initial favorable judgment about Coriolanus. Coriolanus becomes confused, conflicted, and increasingly contemptuous of the whole charade of republican political rituals. Who are these people and politicians who would question his integrity, his love of Rome, and his ability to serve them in the highest political leadership position?

Shakespeare hints that it was perhaps not so much arrogance that drove Coriolanus but his fear that his entire life's work defending Rome—his courage and bravery, risking his life and the lives of comrades over and over again, the many wounds he suffered—might all be in vain if Rome collapses.

Here again, Shakespeare is terrific at making his readers ask questions. One is, Wouldn't it be natural that Coriolanus would be steadfastly opposed to the fickle mob that threatens the stability of the state? Coriolanus has assumed that he, more than anyone, now "embodies" the state—but was this right? Can, or should, one person (in this case, a one-dimensional military man) embody the state? (Coriolanus, we might add, goes from "embodying" the state to becoming shortly afterward stateless and an "enemy of the state"—as we will discuss.)

Coriolanus, however, believes his honor and integrity are being questioned: *"Would you have me false to my nature? Rather say I play the man I am."* But Coriolanus's integrity is seen by the people as false pride and arrogance. Even when Coriolanus mingles with the people and reminds them of his war wounds, donning his insincere "gown of humility," he does so with such disingenuousness that it backfires, and Sicinius (one of the people's tribunes) enjoins the people to *"forget not with what contempt he wore the humble weed, how in his suit he scorned you."*

Coriolanus's unwillingness to appeal for the consent of the masses led to the people turning on their hero. Even his closest political ally worries that *"His nature is too noble for the world."* Coriolanus loses his patience and his temper, and when the people's tribunes threaten to haul him off and throw him to death over a cliff, he draws his sword in the face of his political accusers. Things calm down a bit, but soon he is formally tried for treason and banished from Rome.

As he goes into exile, the ever-proud Coriolanus declares, *"I shall be loved when I am lacked."* But, angry and bitter, he joins forces with Rome's historic neighboring enemy, the Volscians. He submits himself as a volunteer to the enemy's general, Tullus Aufidius. Aufidius accepts the offer of Coriolanus and deputizes him as a co-commander of the Volscian troops bent on destroying Rome. Thus Coriolanus, until recently Rome's greatest living legend, now becomes the enemy of his people.

With Coriolanus as one of their leaders, the Volscians now march to the very outskirts of Rome. The city is in shock. The Roman patricians entreat their former noble colleague not to attack. Coriolanus is undeterred.

Finally, Coriolanus's mother, Volumina, goes to the city gates to try to dissuade her son. She lays down in her son's path and pleads with him, trying patriotic and emotional appeals. "Too late she tried to teach him that it is not a matter of blows and rages alone; that there are softer and nobler virtues," writes commentator Isaac Asimov. Coriolanus is unmoved. Volumina rises, prepared to return to Rome and die, as the city will likely be destroyed, but "with a terrible understatement, she makes it clear that when the city is burning, she will call down a dying mother's curse upon her son."[11]

Coriolanus, who is ironically portrayed as both a mother's boy and fierce military leader, gives in to his mother's plea and gives orders to withdraw from the city. He participates in a peace-treaty exercise and then tries to return to the Volscian camp, but Aufidius accuses Coriolanus of treason and has him killed.

How could so accomplished a military leader end up as such a tragic failure? Coriolanus's military leadership, courage, skill, and strategic brilliance are indisputable and revered. Yet he was unable to adapt to the different demands posed by civilian leadership. The strength of will that aided him on the battlefield did not serve him well in the public market square.

Coriolanus is a man accustomed to wielding power, giving orders, and getting his way. The world he lived in adapted to him, not he to the world.[12]

Harold Bloom argues that "of all major figures in the [Shakespeare] plays, this one has the most limited consciousness."[13] Coriolanus appears as a "man-child," fully formed as a warrior, yet prone to the temper and emotional extremes of a child. In today's social science jargon, we would say he lacked "emotional intelligence." He sees no need to bare himself before the people: Are not his talents and contributions to the state enough? Indeed, maybe they should be enough. A noble man, who is doubtless flawed, is brought down by a lesser man.

Coriolanus does not understand or accept that the context of military leadership is different from that of societal leadership. He cannot adapt his temperament to fit the new context. Coriolanus sees such adaptation as living a lie, a betrayal of his integrity.

Coriolanus also fails to understand the fast-evolving political context he is in, especially the scheming citizen tribunes who manipulate the mob of commoners. Would appearing more humble really have satisfied these politicians? How would Coriolanus have been able to govern if he was unwilling to give more power to these politicians? Again, these are fascinating questions, and Shakespeare leaves us with more dilemmas than answers.

In his plays, Shakespeare repeatedly deals with power and its impact on those who have it and use it. Coriolanus seems to have the potential for greatness, yet he self-destructs. He does not adapt to the new civic context in which there are multiple and competing participants. The general is admirably suited for military leadership, but his temperament and disdain for the people as well as politics make him ill-suited for political leadership. Dwight D. Eisenhower was able to make this transition from military to civilian leader; Douglas MacArthur, like Coriolanus, was not.

Othello

Shakespeare's *Othello* is a complicated tragedy about power, emotions, revenge, and how, paradoxically, powerful people can be manipulated and misled. Othello, like Coriolanus, is, or so we are all led to believe, a successful military leader. He has become a much-valued Venetian general despite being an exotic foreigner—a black Moor ("The Moor of Venice" is the play's subtitle) who had converted to Christianity.

In the play, Othello falls in love with a nobleman's daughter, Desdemona, and later is the victim of a jealous officer's trickery with tragic repercussions. Othello and Desdemona secretly marry. Upon learning of the marriage Desdemona's father, a senator, is outraged. But Othello, with a quiet inner strength and apparent competence, stands firm in the face of Senator Brabantio's harsh rebukes. Othello is, writes Allan Bloom, "most impressive in his confidence in himself, an apparent sureness of his worth that nothing can shake. He bears up under abuse with a dignity that makes his attackers seem mean and small and gives the immediate impression that the right is on his side.... He is sure that his real services are appreciated by the city and that he is esteemed.... He is apparently not the uprooted foreigner unsure of his status in the world."[14]

Othello views himself as a protector of Venice, a foreigner adept at warding off Venice's alien rivals. And so it is that the Duke of Venice, ignoring Senator Brabantio's complaints about Othello, commissions Othello to sail to Cyprus (then a Venetian possession) to thwart a Turkish invasion.

The play had opened with a senior military officer, the sinister Iago, complaining to a compatriot that his commander, Othello, had passed him over and given a sought-after promotion to Cassio. Iago vows revenge for this slight.

Iago initially, together with a failed suitor for Desdemona's love, invited Desdemona's father to condemn and undo Othello's marriage. This fails, and Othello takes his bride with him as the navy sets sail for Cyprus.

Later the villainous Iago goads the promoted Cassio to get drunk and get into a brawl. For this, Othello strips Cassio of his promotion, much to the delight of Iago. But Iago's revenge is not enough. Iago next sets his sights on Othello.

His plan is to make Othello believe that Desdemona is unfaithful. As Iago coaxes Cassio to approach Desdemona and have her plead with Othello to reinstate him into his former post, Iago tries to persuade Othello that Cassio is having an affair with Desdemona.

Mad with jealousy, and trusting Iago, Othello promotes Iago and enlists his aid in a plan to kill both Cassio and Desdemona.

Othello approaches his sleeping wife, wakes her, and accuses her of adultery. While she protests, Othello smothers her. Her attendant Emilia interrupts, and Desdemona is revived, protesting that she is innocent. Desdemona dies, and as the truth of the situation emerges, Othello sees that Iago is behind it all. He tries to kill Iago, but Iago escapes, only to later be captured. Othello admits to his error and commits suicide.

Why was Othello so easily manipulated by Iago? In his defense, Othello does demand "proof" from Iago:

> Villain, be sure thou prove my love a whore;
> Be sure of it: give me the ocular proof
> Or, by the worth of mine eternal soul,
> Thou hadst been better have been born a dog
> Than answer my wak'd wrath.

Yet, the "evidence" provided is circumstantial and flimsy. Why did Othello fall for it? Iago makes a case for his claim, yet, with the stakes so high, why did not Othello probe deeper, demand more, verify his assumptions? He tragically fails to give Desdemona or Cassio any chance to provide their sides of the story. Othello lets himself be manipulated. In this, Othello probably resembles George W. Bush in the lead-up to the war in Iraq when Bush seemingly allowed himself to believe things that had not been verified and for which there was inadequate evidence. Othello, and Bush, allowed themselves to be deceived; in fact, they were compliant in their own deceit. Both should have known better. Leaders are understandably guided by emotions, yet they also have a responsibility to obtain as much valid information as possible.

Othello's suspicions become self-fulfilling prophecies. His self-doubt fed by jealousy (the "green-eyed monster") makes him irrational and ill-equipped to make the important decision he has to face. He becomes the victim, not the master, of his emotions. And once he starts down this tragic road, he serves as a self-enabler of his own destruction.

Shakespeare's Iago character is as fascinating as Othello. In fact, he is given more stage time and lines than Othello. Some writers have noted that there are Iago types everywhere, and, perhaps too, there is a bit of Iago in everyone. Does Iago mainly encourage actions and behavior already likely to happen? Perhaps, yet Iago comes off as undeniably self-serving, vengeful, and mean-spirited, not to mention inciting murders. For a partial, if strained, defense of Iago see Allan Bloom's essay "Cosmopolitan Man and the Political Community: An Interpretation of *Othello*."[15]

Leaders need to assume that there will be at least occasional Iagos in their organizations and anticipate.

Richard III

For political intrigue and sinister behavior, it is hard to top *Richard III*, Shakespeare's physically and morally deformed tragic king. Richard, the hunchback Duke of Gloucester, who conspires to become King Richard III via a web of intrigue and string of horrible acts, is one of Shakespeare's most compelling yet off-putting figures. So vile, so sinister is he, that we are drawn to him like glue, fascinated by his vile behavior yet intrigued by his rise, then fall. To get to the top, he kills enemies, relatives, his wife, and most of his "friends."

Shakespeare's Richard, misshapen and wallowing in self-pity as he systematically destroys all claimants to the throne, delights in his evil. He is blissfully, intoxicatingly evil, and like a car wreck, we know we shouldn't look, yet we can't turn away. The self-anointed villain may be a monster, yet he is a fascinating monster.

Not everyone, we should note, agrees with the power-abusing, villain interpretation of Richard III. An alternative portrait of him depicts him a worthy king, "harsh in ways that were a function of an unforgiving time," yet a king who demonstratively helped the poor, extended "protection to suspected felons," and eased bans on the printing and selling of books.[16]

But Shakespeare's pro-Tudor narrative gives us a Richard III who is consistently cussing as he acquires power by deviously evil means. The plot is merely a device for Richard to hatch his villainous schemes.

Hungry for power, ambitious beyond words, Richard signals his intentions in the opening—self-pitying—lines of the play. He is back from the war, where his family, the Yorks, have won the throne. War gave direction to Richard's ambitions. Now, with peace at hand, a new regime, a political age has arisen, one in which Richard's traits and abilities are a liability. He contrasts war and politics:

> Now is the winter of our discontent
> Made glorious summer by this sun of York;
> And all the clouds that lour'd upon our house

In the deep bosom of the ocean buried.
Now are our brows bound with victorious wreaths;
Our bruised arms hung up for monuments;
Our stern alarums chang'd to merry meetings,
Our dreadful marches to delightful measures.
Grim-visag'd war hath smooth'd his wrinkled front;
And now,—instead of mounting barbed steeds
To fright the souls of fearful adversaries,—
He capers nimbly in a lady's chamber
To the lascivious pleasing of a lute.
But I,—that am not shap'd for sportive tricks,
Nor made to court an amorous looking-glass;
I, that am rudely stamp'd, and want love's majesty
To strut before a wanton ambling nymph;
I, that am curtail'd of this fair proportion,
Cheated of feature by dissembling nature,
Deform'd, unfinish'd, sent before my time
Into this breathing world scarce half made up,
And that so lamely and unfashionable
That dogs bark at me as I halt by them;—
Why, I, in this weak piping time of peace,
Have no delight to pass away the time,
Unless to spy my shadow in the sun,
And descant on mine own deformity

"But I am not made to be a seducer," he laments. His physical deformities ("I was badly made") leave him—he argues—with no other option for satisfying his ambitions than to turn to evil: in essence, "Since I can't amuse myself by being a lover, I've decided to become a villain." And what a villain!

Richard's rise to power is swift and remarkable. In a few months he has wiped out virtually every rival and taken the throne. Once in power, he must deal with the consequences of his actions. Interested only in gaining power, once he achieves his goal he knows not how to govern. He acknowledges no limits on his authority, and though he is decisive, he lacks legitimacy and the skills of a consensus builder. He is unable to adjust to the needs of governing. All he knows is force; he is unable to use the gentile guiding hand to lead. He justifies his continued resort to force by arguing that his "kingdom stands on brittle glass," yet it is his own actions that have made it thus.

Richard goes too far, and his machinations finally backfire on him. He was well-suited to grab for power but ill-suited to use it.

Is Richard III, as some critics suggest, a "Machiavellian" leader? His cynical pursuit of power leads some to see him as a prototypical Machiavellian. But would Machiavelli really endorse such unnecessary human slaughter? Certainly not. More likely, Machiavelli would see Richard III as a psychopathically driven figure who is almost guaranteed to self-destruct. Richard gains power but can't use power; he misreads and misjudges many people and situations and is driven to excess by his self-loathing. Richard is a neither wise nor prudent pursuer of power. He is a madman.

Did President Richard Nixon fall into some of these patterns? As Richard III resented those around him who were without his deformities, so apparently did Nixon loathe various establishment elites, the Harvard educated, the rich and well born, the handsome and athletic (especially the Kennedys). Richard's physical deformities led to moral deformities, just as Nixon's negative sense of self led to his justification of a series of illegal acts.[17] Malicious, hungry for power, bitter about his physical shortcomings, Richard descends into his own personal prison, as Nixon descended deeper into isolation until his moral and personal weaknesses—like those of Richard—brought him down. Richard III and Richard Nixon enter the heart of darkness and end up destroyed.[18]

Julius Caesar

If *Richard III* shows us the high price of unbridled ambition, *Julius Caesar* shows us how ambition, crossed by jealousy, in a republic on the verge of empire, can lead to chaos and civil war.[19]

Rome's legendary general Julius Caesar returns to Rome, triumphant after another victory in battle. The Roman Republic is teetering, and strong leaders grab for power. No one is better positioned to take control than Caesar. The rise of a strong man threatens to destroy the Republic. And yet Caesar is popular, capable, a hero, ambitious, and ready to take power. Empire or republic? Rule by one strong hand, or by representatives with at least some consent of the people?

Several senators, especially Caius Cassius (who is envious of Caesar's rise) and Marcus Brutus (who is dedicated to preserving the republic), are suspicious of Caesar and his motives. They fear he will become emperor, and they fear the loss of their impressive and long-standing republican form of government. They plot to assassinate Caesar, who is warned to "Beware the Ides of March."

Caesar's wife, Calpurnia, fearing for her husband's safety, begs him not to go to the senate that day, but in the end, Caesar refuses to heed the warnings, surrendering instead to flattery and appeals to his ego. Once he is at the senate, Brutus and his coconspirators kill him.

Mark Anthony, a Caesar lieutenant who was not part of the plot, is allowed to speak at Caesar's funeral. He has his own agenda—to stir, not calm, the masses:

Antony: Friends, Romans, countrymen, lend me your ears;
I come to bury Caesar, not to praise him.
The evil that men do lives after them,
The good is oft interred with their bones;
So let it be with Caesar. The noble Brutus
Hath told you Caesar was ambitious.
If it were so, it was a grievous fault,
And grievously hath Caesar answered it.
Here, under leave of Brutus and the rest
(For Brutus is an honorable man
So are they all, all honorable men),
Come I to speak in Caesar's funeral.
He was my friend, faithful and just to me;
But Brutus says he was ambitious,
And Brutus is an honorable man.
He hath brought many captives home to Rome,
Whose ransoms did the general coffers fill;
Did this in Caesar seem ambitious;
When that the poor have cried, Caesar hath wept;
Ambition should be made of sterner stuff.
Yet Brutus says he was ambitious;
And Brutus is an honorable man.
You all did see that on the Lupercal
I thrice presented him a kingly crown,
Which he did thrice refuse. Was this ambition?
Yet Brutus says he was ambitious;
And sure he is an honorable man....
O masters! If I were disposed to stir
Your hearts and minds to mutiny and rage,
I should do Brutus wrong and Cassius wrong,
Who, you all know, are honorable men.
I will not do them wrong; I rather choose
To wrong the dead, to wrong myself and you,
Than I will wrong such honorable men.
But here's a parchment with the seal of Caesar;
I found it in his closet; 'tis his will.
Let but the commons hear this testament,

Which, pardon me, I do not mean to read,
And they would go and kiss dead Caesar's wounds,
And dip their napkins in his sacred blood;
Yea, beg a hair of him for memory,
And dying, mention it within their wills,
Bequeathing it as a rich legacy
Unto their issue.
Fourth Plebian: We'll hear the will; read it, Mark Antony.
All: The will, the will! We will hear Caesar's will!
Antony: Have patience, gentle friends, I must not read it.
It is not meet you know how Caesar loved you.
You are not wood, you are not stones, but men;
And being me, hearing the will of Caesar,
It will inflame you, it will make you mad.
'Tis good you know not that you are his heirs;
For if you should, O, what would come of it?
Fourth Plebian: Read the will! We'll hear it, Antony!
You shall read us the will, Caesar's will!
Antony: Will you be patient? Will you stay awhile?
I have o'ershot myself to tell you of it.
I fear I wrong the honorable men
Whose daggers have stabbed Caesar; I do fear it.
Fourth Plebeian: They were traitors. Honorable men!
All: The will! The testament!
Second Plebeian: They were villains, murderers! The will! Read the will!
Antony: You will compel me then to read the will?
Then make a ring about the corpse of Caesar,
And let me show you him that made the will.
Shall I descend? And will you give me leave?
All: Come down....

Antony inflames the passion of the masses and turns the tables on Brutus and Cassius. The plebians call for the blood of the traitors.

Mark Antony's speech inspires the people, and a civil war ensues. Brutus, Cassius, and the "republicans" lose, and Antony and Octavius (who later takes control of Rome as Caesar Augustus) triumph.[20]

Caesar was a demagogue, vain, imperious, and arrogant. He was a man bent on the pursuit of power. But he was also one of the most effective military leaders of all time. His individual aims clashed with the demands of the republic. Yet Cassius was no better. Only Brutus, a self-confessed stoic, is torn between betraying Caesar and preserving the republic. Indeed, much of Shakespeare's play here seems mistitled. It could well have been called "The Paradox of Brutus." In the end, Brutus strikes the deadly blow against Caesar, and his actions contribute to the demise of Republican Rome. In the end, everyone loses.

Oh how toxic the blind pursuit of power can be. Was this Caesar's blind spot? How could someone so smart, so successful, so experienced, so capable, walk into his own destruction, eyes wide open? Caesar even goes so far as to tell Mark Antony early in the play that Cassius is "dangerous ... very dangerous." Why fall so easily into his trap? Why does he not prepare for the danger he knows Cassius poses? He enters the senate without bodyguards, without an escape plan, and against the pleas of his wife as well as the warnings of danger from the soothsayer. Caesar is blinded by his own ego and selfish ambitions. With the republic crumbling around him, he sees himself as the imperial savior, as an entitled Alexander—or man/god— about to rise to the heights.

Yet Shakespeare, a monarchist at heart, concerned with preserving order, does not support just any form of monarchy. He too sees the dangers inherent in unbridled ambition, greed, arrogance, and the blind pursuit of power. In *Julius Caesar*, the "monarch"-in-waiting is killed and the civil war ends, producing Augustus as emperor.

With all his manifest skills and talents, the strutting Caesar lacks both self-knowledge and political knowledge. In fact, all the major characters fail to know themselves or know the world. Only Brutus—confused and torn apart from within—displays the human depths and possibilities that tragically also end in his death.

Through *Julius Caesar*, Shakespeare examines the drive for power and glory and its impact on personal conscience. Brutus is torn between loyalty to Caesar and loyalty to an ideal, the republic. In the end, he chooses the republic, yet all ends in tragedy.

Shakespeare wrote at a time of upheaval and social unrest in England. In 1558, Elizabeth came to the throne amid rebellion and chaos. There were several attempts on her life. By 1599, she was old and in decline. With no direct heir, the possibility of a protracted civil war over control of the state seemed likely. It is in this context that Shakespeare—who valued order—wrote *Julius Caesar*. This was not a play about some distant historical figure; rather, it spoke to the anxieties and fears as well as the aspirations and hopes of Shakespeare's age.

Elizabeth was a flexible, effective leader who at times compromised her beliefs for the greater good. By contrast, Mary Tudor was rigid and unyielding, governing in strict accordance with her religious convictions. Shakespeare hungers—as we all do—for an effective leader; one who can balance the allure of power with the skill and flexibility needed to govern effectively. Caesar is too arrogant; Cassius too ambitious; Brutus too internally torn. It is in Brutus that we see Shakespeare's central point: that a good man's private beliefs may clash with political necessity. Just as Mary Tudor's strong beliefs led to disaster, Brutus's well-intentioned and earnest act also led to disaster. Where are the wise, prudent leaders who *know themselves* and *know politics*? As William and Barbara Rosen have written,

> Personal innocence or guilt is not in question, and we are asked to feel that one man or another is "right." We are asked to see that while a just man in private life is to be praised, a just man in public life may very well bring about catastrophe. The wicked—or, like Caesar, the conceited and super-stitious—may be the genius as a ruler. Man's worth as a private individual does not necessarily ensure his value as a public ruler. Less sentimental than many of his critics, Shakespeare sees that a morally repulsive act may at times be a politically desirable one; that a man who acts from the highest of motives may be too busy keeping his conscience clean to lead well; that a man who once does evil in the expectation that good will be the final result may be forced more deeply into self-deception and impotence than a man who acts simply from expediency. But he also sees that the pursuit of expediency and lack of scruple do not in themselves guarantee ability to govern—else why not, ultimately, an Antony in command?[21]

Clearly Shakespeare prefers the wise exercise of power over the pursuit of pure virtue or power. In this he seems a bit of a Machiavellian.[22] Virtuous behavior may at times be impolitic. Wisdom, skill, and prudent judgment trump good-ness and virtue.

When Caesar dies, chaos and civil war ensue. A vacuum is created, and, at first, chaos fills that vacuum. In the end, Brutus's understandably valued republic crumbles and an emperor emerges.

Henry V

Shakespeare's tragedies are the tales of kings making what often seem to be avoidable mistakes. The playwright's flawed kings ought to know better, yet they do not see or cannot bring themselves to act prudently in a complex politi-cal arena. They overreach, overstep, hesitate too long, or can't seem to match policy to situation.

In *Henry IV, Parts I and II*, and *Henry V*, Shakespeare shows us the other side of leadership—how to prepare to assume and use power with skill.

Shakespeare gives us a reasonably clear picture not only of what makes for a good leader, but of how one can self-consciously work to become a good leader.

In *Henry IV, Parts I and II*, we are introduced to Hal (later Henry V), the son of the King, a fun-loving cad who seems ill-prepared to assume the throne. But there is method to Hal's madness, as he tells his cronies:

> I know you all, and will a while uphold
> The unyoked humor of your idleness.
> Yet herein will I imitate the sun,
> Who doth permit the base contagious clouds,
> To smother up his beauty from the world,
> That, when he please again to be himself,
> Being wanted, he may be more wond'red at
> . . . .
> By so much shall I falsify men's hopes;
> And, like bright metal on a sullen ground,
> My reformation, glitt'ring o'er my fault
> Shall show more goodly and attract more eyes
> Than that which hath no foil to set it off.
> I'll so offend to make offense a skill,
> Redeeming time when men think least I will.

Falstaff, Hal's fun-loving companion, a lecher and thief, teaches the would-be king about life and the concerns of the common man. Hal's political education is good preparation for the day when he assumes the throne. But King Henry IV is worried about his rascal son. Warwick, however, assures the King:

> The prince studies his companions
> Like a strange tongue, wherein to gain the language
> . . . .
> The prince will in the perfectness of time
> Cast off his followers, and their memory
> Shall as a pattern or a measure live,
> By which his grace must mete the lives of others,
> Turning past evils to advantages.

Hal lives the high life in the court, and the low life of a scoundrel. He is a complex and complete being. His experiences enrich and educate him, preparing him for the responsibilities of state. Yet when he becomes king, Hal, now Henry V, repudiates his old friend Falstaff, saying,

I know you not, old man....
Presume not that I am the thing I was.

Indeed, he is not the man he was. Henry is wiser for his past experiences. He has learned from his youthful indiscretions and is rich with experience and knowledge. He knows how all elements of the kingdom work and think. Henry has tasted life at all levels and is now prepared to rule. He has gained a mastery of power in all its forms. Consider his rousing Saint Crispin's Day call to battle:

We few, we happy few, we band of brothers;
For he to-day that sheds his blood with me
Shall be my brother; be he ne'er so vile
This day shall gentle his condition:
And gentlemen in England, now a-bed,
Shall think themselves accurs'd they were not here,
And hold their manhoods cheap whiles any speaks
That fought with us upon Saint Crispin's day.

Of course, we know he is being disingenuous. Henry is a master manipulator. As Harold Bloom notes, "Shakespeare does not let us locate Hal/Henry V's true self; a king is necessarily something of a counterfeit, and Henry is a great king."[23]

What lesson can we draw from Shakespeare's Henry V? Clearly Shakespeare warns us not to expect perfection in our rulers. Kings and presidents, like us, are human beings and are prone to the same drives, fears, and passions that make up human nature. We humans are complex, even contradictory, beings. We are motivated by a variety of factors, some noble, others base. We all make mistakes. Some, like Hal, learn from their pasts; others do not. Better the ruler who has sinned and learned the lesson than the would-be leader who refuses to recognize and learn from life's hardships and travails.

Shakespeare would probably also tell us to live life fully. Life is a learning process, and the good ruler, like the good person, is one who knows fully life's richness—the good and the bad. We should choose the good, but "not so fast," Shakespeare might warn us: know life, then decide.

Leaders are asked to be many things: effective leaders, ethical leaders, war-time leaders, high priests, and occasional sinners. The things we expect of our leaders are complex and often contradictory. We want our leaders to be of the highest character, yet there are times when—especially in dealing with foreign adversaries—we require them to be manipulative and deceptive, if not worse. Would a Mother Teresa make a good national leader? While she would serve as an excellent role model for individual behavior, would she, could she, stand up to the sometimes harsh world of politics and power?

We place paradoxical demands on our leaders. That being the case, we should not be surprised that on occasion they behave in ways ill-suited to life in the priesthood. Our search for the good leader should not be the search for perfection, but for the fully human person who knows good and evil, strives to bring about the good, attempts to bring out "the better angels" in all of us, knowing full well that at times he or she may have to make morally questionable decisions and life-and-death choices. Leadership is no place for the faint-hearted. It is a place where the high and low arts of politics are practiced. At its best, it produces an Abraham Lincoln and a Franklin Roosevelt, leaders who knew what was right, attempted to steer the ship of state in that direction, and on occasion, behaved in ways that were not totally virtuous.

Henry V is a multidimensional man. He knows himself, knows his world, knows how to appeal to the people, and knows politics. He also knows—and this is yet another story—why England has to go to war even if it isn't necessary. The three *Henry* plays chart Henry's growth to relative maturity. He is prepared to lead.

King Lear

King Lear is the much-revised story of a mythical noble-hearted, honest, and apparently effective British ruler. We are led to believe he was successful because he was a unifying figure who made prudent decisions and had wise advisors. He was well-intended, crafty, and politically astute. He is now, however, an octogenarian who wants a workable succession plan.

King Lear is one of Shakespeare's most sublime and powerful plays, vividly demonstrating his creative narrative abilities. It is also a play that raises compelling questions about the challenges of succession, about family politics, and about how power reveals character.

As the play opens, the aging king wants to retain his title yet divide the kingdom's land among his two older married daughters, Goneril and Regan, and his younger unmarried, yet favorite, daughter, Cordelia. He calls them to meet with him and asks them to submit to what is now commonly referred to as a "love test." He asks each of the daughters a simple question: "Which of you shall we say doth love us most?"

Goneril answers first:

> Sir, I love you more than words can wield the matter;
> Dearer than eyesight, space, and liberty;
> Beyond what can be valued, rich or rare;
> No less than life, with grace, health, beauty, and honor;

As much as child e'er lov'd, or father found;
A love that makes breath poor, and speech unable;
Beyond all manner of so much I love you.

Lear is delightfully flattered and makes Goneril Duchess of Albany. Next he calls on Regan, who replies,

I am made
Of the self-same metal that my sister is,
And prize me at her worth. In my true heart
I find she names my very deed of love;
Only she comes too short, that I profess
Myself an enemy to all other joys
Which the most precious square of sense possesses,
And find I am alone felicitate
In your dear highness' love.

The king is again well pleased, and gives to his second daughter a third of his kingdom. Finally, he turns to his youngest, and probably favorite, daughter, Cordelia:

Lear: To thee and thine hereditary ever
Remain this ample third of our fair kingdom,
No less in space, validity, and pleasure
Than that conferred on Goneril. Now our joy,
Although our last and least, to whose young love
The vines of France and milk of Burgundy
Strive to be interessed. What can you say to draw
A third more opulent than your sisters? Speak.
Cordelia: Nothing, my lord.
Lear: Nothing?
Cordelia: Nothing.
Lear: Nothing will come of nothing, speak again.
Cordelia: Unhappy that I am, I cannot heave
My heart into my mouth: I love your majesty
According to my bond, no more nor less.
Lear: How, how, Cordelia? Mend your speech a little,
Lest you may mar your fortunes.
Cordelia: Good my lord,
You have begot me, bred me, loved me. I

Return those duties back as are right fit,
Obey you, love you, and most honor you.
Why my happy sisters husbands, if they say
They love you all? Happily, when I shall wed,
That lord whose hand must take my plight shall carry
Half my love with him, half my care and duty.
Sure, I shall never marry like my sisters.
Lear: But goes thy heart with this?
Cordelia: Ay, my good lord.
Lear: So young, and so untender?
Cordelia: So young, my lord, and true.

Shocked and disappointed, Lear is outraged—how could Cordelia "only" love her father as much as is true and appropriate! Where is the flattery Lear craves to hear? In his anger, Lear disowns and curses Cordelia and divides his kingdom between Goneril and Regan. Cordelia, dowryless, leaves England and marries the King of France.

The heart-stricken Lear loses his sense of objectivity and balance. His desire for flattery blinded him to what he really needed—the truth. When the truth came, he rejected it. In fact, Lear had planned, before this "betrayal," to apportion Cordelia the largest and most important section of his kingdom and to reside with her in his remaining years. Now all was changed.[24]

Soon tragedies unfold. Lear is pushed aside by his two ambitious daughters and belatedly realizes he has been a fool. Betrayed by these two daughters, Lear goes insane, fleeing his daughters' houses to wander in the South England heath.

Lear, his wits finally returned, ends up in Dover, only to discover that the French—led by Cordelia, who is now Queen of France—are to invade England in an effort to save her father and restore him to his throne. But the English forces push back the French invaders. Lear and Cordelia are captured. A series of duels and deaths create a chaotic situation in which Goneril poisons Regan, Cordelia is executed, and Lear dies of miserable grief over what he has caused. By the time Lear recognizes his mistake, it is too late. "A great irony of this play is that Lear finds his most fully realized conception of justice in madness," during his wilderness period of insanity.[25]

When we surround ourselves with vain, ambitious flatterers and hypocrites, we should expect their advice to be skewed and often dysfunctional. Leaders are often surrounded by people who tell the leader what they think he or she *wants* to hear, not delivering the information he or she *needs* to hear. It is a structural flaw in most advising systems, one that must be overcome lest it lead to illusion and flawed decision making.

A modern example of this can be seen in President John Kennedy's efforts during the Cuban Missile Crisis to obtain fresh, contrary, outsider information before he made monumental decisions. Rather than rely merely on a few close advisors, he sought information that might prove useful. Contrast that with George W. Bush, who in the run-up to the 2003 War in Iraq apparently listened mostly to supporters of the war. Might things have turned out better had he a multiple-advocacy process and devil's advocates that encouraged him to rigorously examine and consider alternative perspectives?

One of the many messages or lessons in *King Lear* is that a president or king propped and puffed up by flatterers and true believers is an individual trapped. Lear, like so many other leaders, begins to believe the flatterers as he turns a deaf ear to the more reasonable and pragmatic (or critical) of his advisors. Leaders need "devil's advocates," critics, and those willing to speak truth to power. Leaders must *weigh and welcome* contending views, not punish and exclude them.

Conclusion

To Shakespeare, leaders matter, and in leadership, the job is hard, the path slippery, the pitfalls and paradoxes many. Most leaders fail because of their inability to control their human weaknesses: "The fault, dear Brutus, is not in our stars, / but in ourselves, that we are underlings."[26]

In his plays, Shakespeare regularly hints at the skillset "good" leaders must have. Mindful emotional intelligence is key, as are a type of Aristotelian *phronesis* to match good intentions with good judgment, a deep-seated concern for justice, and being a Machiavellian polymath who can adjust leadership style to varying contextual situations.[27]

Notes

1. A somewhat different form of this chapter appears in Thomas E. Cronin and Michael A. Genovese, *Leadership Matters: Unleashing the Power of Paradox* (Boulder, CO: Paradigm, 2012).

2. Harold Bloom, *Shakespeare: The Inventions of the Human* (New York: Riverhead, 1998), p. 113. See also the valuable Jonathan Bate, *Soul of the Age: A Biography of the Mind of William Shakespeare* (New York: Random House, 2010); and the insightful Kenji Yoshimo, *A Thousand Times More Fair: What Shakespeare Teaches Us about Justice* (New York: Ecco, 2011).

3. Bate, *Soul of the Age*, p. 315.

4. Quoted in Bloom, *Shakespeare*, p. 321, when Bloom extrapolates on Yeats's point:

> When Shakespeare thought of the state, he remembered first that it had murdered Christopher Marlowe, tortured and broken Thomas Kyd, and branded the unbreakable Ben Jonson. All that and more underlies the great lament in sonnet 66:
>
> And right perfection wrongly disgraced,
> And strength by limping sway disabled,
> And art made tongue-tied by authority.

5. Quoted in Robin Headlam Wells, *Shakespeare's Politics* (London: Continuum, 2009), p. 90.

6. See Allan Bloom and Henry V. Jaffa, *Shakespeare's Politics* (New York: Basic, 1964); and Michael Platt, *Rome and Romans According to Shakespeare* (Lanham, MD: University Press of America, 1982).

7. Hugh Grady, *Shakespeare, Machiavelli, and Montaigne: Power and Subjectivity from Richard II to Hamlet* (Oxford: Oxford University Press, 2002); and John Roe, *Shakespeare and Machiavelli* (Cambridge: D. S. Brewer, 2002).

8. William Shakespeare, *Henry IV, Part I*.

9. William Shakespeare, *Hamlet*, act 3.

10. William Shakespeare, *The Tragedy of Coriolanus*.

11. Isaac Asimov, *Asimov's Guide to Shakespeare* (New York: Gramercy, 1970), p. 249.

12. See Malcolm Gladwell, "Cocksure," *New Yorker*, July 27, 2009, pp. 24–28.

13. Bloom, *Shakespeare*, p. 577.

14. Allan D. Bloom, "Cosmopolitan Man and the Political Community: An Interpretation of *Othello*," *American Political Science Review* Vol. 54 (March 1960), p. 137.

15. Ibid.

16. Discussed in John F. Burns, "Discovery of Skeleton Puts Richard III in Battle Once Again," *New York Times*, September 24, 2012, p. A8.

17. See Michael A. Genovese, *The Nixon Presidency: Power and Politics in Turbulent Times* (Westport, CT: Greenwood, 1990); and Stanley Kutler, *The Wars of Watergate* (New York: W. W. Norton, 1992).

18. See Joseph Conrad, *Heart of Darkness*, the novella on which Francis Ford Coppola's *Apocalypse Now* is based. *Heart of Darkness* was first published as a book in 1902. It originally appeared as a three-part series in *Blackwood's Magazine* in 1899.

19. Caesar is in some ways only a supporting role to Brutus, the key figure in the play (Caesar appears in only three scenes). See Bloom, *Shakespeare*, chapter 9.

20. See Garry Wills, *Rome and Rhetoric: Shakespeare's Julius Caesar* (New Haven, CT: Yale University Press, 2011).

21. William and Barbara Rosen, eds., "Introduction," in *Julius Caesar* (New York: Signet, 1998), p. lxvi.

22. See Cronin and Genovese, *Leadership Matters*.

23. Bloom, *Shakespeare*, p. 323.

24. At least one analyst defends Lear and says his "love test" was carefully contrived to both disproportionately reward his favorite daughter and preferred successor Cordelia and ultimately prevent strife and provide for future reunification. See, for example, Harry V. Jaffa, "The Limits of Politics: An Interpretation of *King Lear,* Act I, Scene I," *American Political Science Review* Vol. 51 (June 1957), pp. 405–427. See also Yoshimo, *A Thousand Times More Fair,* chapter 8.

25. Yoshimo, *A Thousand Times More Fair,* p. 221.

26. Cassius, from *Julius Caesar,* act 1, scene 2, ll. 140–141.

27. Here, when we refer to Machiavellian, we do not mean this in a negative sense. On the contrary, Machiavelli when properly understood does not advocate "evil," he merely attempts to get the leader to understand "necessity." See Michael A. Genovese, *Me and Mach: Food Fit for "The Prince"* (New York: Amazon e-book, 2013).

Chapter 2

Macbeth and Political Corruption

Bruce E. Altschuler

Does Shakespeare's *Macbeth*, a seventeenth-century play depicting events in eleventh-century Scotland, have anything significant to tell the twenty-first century about political corruption? Traditional interpretations argue that the play is more a study of the psychology of evil than an examination of the ills of a political system. In 1930, G. Wilson Knight described the play as "Shakespeare's most profound and mature vision of Evil."[1] More recently, David Bevington argued that in *Macbeth*, "a tradition of moral and religious drama has been transformed into an intensely human study of the psychological effects of evil on a particular man."[2] Susan Snyder notes that by altering his sources to eliminate Duncan's weaknesses as a king while excluding Banquo and other coconspirators from participation in his murder, Shakespeare creates "a stark black-white moral opposition" while concentrating "on private, purely moral issues uncomplicated by the gray shades of political expediency."[3] Blair Worden similarly concludes that "Shakespeare gives little time to the machinery of politics or the workings of constitutions. His interest is in the psychological rather than the institutional basis of politics."[4]

Another common interpretation that would seem to limit the play's relevance claims that, as E. Pearlman has written, "*Macbeth* unabashedly celebrates a semi-divine monarch in terms specific to the first years of Stuart absolutism."[5] Because the play was written shortly after the 1605 Gunpowder Plot, Robert Shaughnessy believes that "the play has been seen as an extended compliment by the monarch's own company to the Scottish King whose ancestors it references and one of whose interests—witchcraft—it closely engages."[6] In this chapter I will demonstrate that these arguments grossly oversimplify Shakespeare's work. As Shaughnessy subsequently explains, whether the play endorses or subverts this traditional interpretation is very much open to question.[7] I will also look at modern stagings of the play to see whether, as Garry Wills has written, "the story is reduced to that of a murderer getting his just penalty, in place of a struggle for the soul of a nation."[8] In fact, the productions I will examine show how Shakespeare's play continues to speak to contemporary understandings of political corruption, both individual and systemic.

Defining Political Corruption

Before discussing *Macbeth*, however, we need to understand the concept of *political corruption*, which is typically defined as the abuse of public office for private benefit.[9] This contemporary definition is quite compatible with the ideas of Shakespeare's time. For example, when John Locke wrote that a tyrant, rather than using his power for the good of the governed, acts "for his own private separate advantage," he quoted approvingly from a 1603 speech to Parliament by James I, Shakespeare's king, "I will ever prefer the weal of the public, and of the whole commonwealth in making of good laws and constitutions to any particular and private ends of mine."[10] Macbeth makes clear on numerous occasions that his actions are grounded in personal ambition rather than the public good. For example, after he has Banquo killed, he tells his wife, "For mine own good, / All causes shall give way."[11]

Unfortunately, it is not always easy to determine what is abuse of public office or to distinguish clearly between public and private interests. Simply relying on laws and formal rules clarifies the terms, but, because officials seeking self-protection may be the authors of those laws, such clarity could come at the expense of legitimacy. Politicians seek to game the system by manipulating the language of corruption to make their actions appear proper. This is even more of a problem in the type of monarchy seen in *Macbeth*, where the state, rather than the public, defined the code of behavior that everyone was supposed to follow. Because the king was chosen by himself or an elite, the responsibility for these rules and the values they imposed was his. In such a system, writes Arvind Jain, corruption "reflects a failure of the political institutions within a society."[12] Thus, the key question for modern interpreters of *Macbeth* is whether it is a story of a basically good government restoring its natural order from a usurping tyrant or a more systematically flawed monarchy ripe for abuse.

Shakespeare's *Macbeth*

The plot of *Macbeth* is relatively straightforward. Returning from battle, Macbeth and Banquo encounter three weird sisters who prophesy that Macbeth will become Thane of Cawdor then king, after which Banquo's descendants, although not Banquo himself, will eventually succeed to the monarchy. The first of these predictions is quickly confirmed when King Duncan names Macbeth to succeed the traitor Macdonwald as Thane of Cawdor. However, he also names his son Malcolm Prince of Cumberland, placing him next in the line of succession. Macbeth races to his castle to prepare to host the king. Urged on by his wife, he overcomes his reservations and plots to murder Duncan and frame his grooms. After the killing, Malcolm and his brother Donalbain, fearing for their lives, flee to England and Ireland, feeding suspicion that they bribed Duncan's servants to kill him. Invited to Macbeth's coronation, Ross (a cousin of Macduff) attends while Macduff (the Thane of Fife) returns to his castle.

The insecure Macbeth commissions assassins to kill Banquo and his son Fleance, but the latter escapes. Macbeth's celebration is ruined when he—and only he—sees Banquo's ghost. Macduff travels to England to urge Malcolm to join Siward's English force to overthrow Macbeth. Although the witches warn Macbeth to "beware Macduff," they follow with the reassurance that "none of woman born / Shall harm Macbeth."[13] Learning that Macduff has left his family behind, Macbeth sends men to raid his castle and kill his wife and children. Unaware of this, Macduff is able to convince Malcolm to join forces against Macbeth. Ross then informs Macduff that his entire family has been murdered.

A guilt-ridden Lady Macbeth commits suicide as rebel forces march toward Macbeth's Dunsinane fortress. When Macduff enters with the declaration that he "was from his mother's womb / Untimely ripped," Macbeth realizes that the witches' prophecy did "palter with us in a double sense." Macduff kills him, then carries his severed head to Malcolm, proclaiming along with the others, "Hail, King of Scotland!" Malcolm's final speech calls on all exiles to return home and pledges to "make us even with you."[14]

Shakespeare made several important modifications in the history provided by his main source, Raphael Holinshead's *Chronicles of England, Scotland, and*

Ireland.[15] He transformed the weak King Duncan, whose reign was characterized by a series of military defeats, into a benevolent and popular leader. Although the events of the play seem to occur over a period of months, Macbeth actually was king for seventeen years, the first ten of which, according to Holinshead, were of good rule. He even made a pilgrimage to Rome in 1050 where he gave charity to the poor. Banquo's behavior is changed from collaboration with Macbeth to inaction, then suspicion. Despite Holinshead's account, Banquo was a fictional figure, invented by sixteenth-century historian Hector Boece to please his patron, King James V of Scotland, by providing an ancestor for the Stewart dynasty. Rather than being killed at Dunsinane, Macbeth withdrew to Moray where he continued to fight for another three years. His stepson Lulach carried on for three more months before he was killed.[16]

The standard interpretation of the play, summarizes James Calderwood, is that "in the national long run Macbeth's rule is a tyrannic interlude between the gracious reigns of Duncan and his rightful successor Malcolm, a fearsome reminder of the brutal abnormalities that befall man or nation when evil is unleashed."[17] Similarly, Alan Sinfield writes that a common reading "suggests that Macbeth is an extraordinary eruption in a good State—obscuring the thought that there might be any priority to structural malfunctioning within the system."[18] As for the succession of Banquo's heirs, in 1960 Irving Ribner wrote that it is "symbolic of a future rooted in the acceptance of natural law, which inevitably must return to reassert God's harmonious order when evil has worked itself out."[19]

The view that Macbeth was simply an aberration in an otherwise benign state has support in the text of the play. Before making his final decision to kill Duncan, Macbeth weighs the pros and cons. Not only would this mean betraying his duty as the king's host and kinsman, it would also mean murdering a benevolent monarch. "This Duncan / hath borne his faculties so meek, hath been / So clear in his great office, that his virtues / Will plead like angels, trumpet tongued, against / The deep damnation of his taking off." Against this, there is "but only / Vaulting ambition, which o'erleaps itself / And falls on th' other."[20] From the very beginning, Macbeth understands how wrong his actions are and is haunted by them throughout the play. The death of Macbeth allows Malcolm to restore the natural order, calling all those who fled tyranny to return home and ending the play with the words, "by the grace of grace, / We will perform in measure, time, and place. / So thanks to all at once and to each one, / Whom we invite to see us crowned at Scone." The stage directions then call for a "Flourish. All Exit."[21]

Shakespeare, however, defies such easy explanations. The lines of the play are so filled with ambiguities and double meanings that nearly every interpretation is instantly undercut, starting with the weird sisters' paradoxical declaration in the opening scene that "Fair is foul and foul is fair," a phrase echoed by Macbeth's first words, "So foul and fair a day I have not seen." After hearing the witches' prophecies, he comments in an aside that "nothing is but what is not."[22]

Although Shakespeare provides no reason for either Cawdor's treachery or the accompanying rebellion, Holinshead claimed it was due to Duncan's weaknesses as a ruler. In the play, Duncan is too trusting of Macdonwald, the treacherous Thane of Cawdor, explaining that "There's no art / To find the mind's construction in the face / He was a gentleman on whom I built / An absolute trust."[23] Unlike most Shakespearean kings, Duncan is an observer of the battle, depending on Macbeth and Banquo to fight to save his kingdom. Failing to learn from his error, he again places absolute trust in the new Thane of Cawdor, Macbeth. So oblivious to danger is Duncan that his first words upon entering Macbeth's home are, "This castle has a pleasant seat. The air / Nimbly and sweetly recommends itself."[24] The result is a division between Duncan's legitimacy and Macbeth's actual power.

If Macbeth's reign was illegitimate, why did the Scottish nobles select him as king rather than Malcolm? Of course, Macbeth has done his best to throw suspicion upon Duncan's sons, telling his guests that "We hear our bloody cousins are bestowed / In England and in Ireland not confessing / Their cruel parricide, filling their hearers / With strange invention,"[25] but his version is greeted skeptically. As a witness to the encounter with the witches, Banquo fears that Macbeth "played'st most foully for 't," yet, hoping that the prediction for his descendants' ascension to the throne will come true, he at least passively cooperates with the new king. Lennox sarcastically praises the official version that Macbeth was so grieved by Duncan's murder that "Did he not straight / In pious rage the two delinquents tear / That were the slaves of drink and thralls of sleep? / Was not that nobly done? And wisely too," for they could not then deny their complicity.[26] Nevertheless, he too remains with Macbeth. Perhaps they would agree with Macduff's young son, who when told by his mother that a traitor is "one that swears and lies" and that "all traitors must be hanged" by "the honest men," cynically replies that "the liars and swearers are fools, for there are liars and swearers enough to beat the honest men and hang up them."[27]

One of Shakespeare's insights is that a corrupt regime is never secure. As Macbeth puts it after becoming king, "To be thus is nothing / But to be safely thus."[28] Because the corruption must be concealed, openly legitimate methods are not adequate to preserve it. While Macbeth seeks to kill his most prominent opponents, he cannot murder everyone who might pose a problem. Speaking to Banquo's murderers, he explains that "though I could / With barefaced power sweep him from my sight / And bid my will avouch it," such overt methods would be counterproductive because they would alienate "certain friends that are both his and mine."[29] As Machiavelli wrote of "those who come to power by crime," a total reliance on violent methods will result in a ruler who is "forced to have the knife ready in his hand and he can never feel secure."[30] Such violence will only grow more intense over time.

When recruiting men to assist in his corrupt regime, Macbeth appeals to their self-interest. However, he learns that self-interest is not as reliable in retaining support as devotion to a legitimate regime. Speaking about Macbeth's troops, Angus tells other nobles that "Those he commands move only in command, / Nothing in love."[31] When self-interest fails, Macbeth resorts to spying and intimidation. His network of informers is so extensive that "There's not a one of them but in his house / I keep a servant fee'd."[32]

This forces Malcolm to resort to a different kind of deception when Macduff travels to England to urge him to return to Scotland to join the battle against Macbeth. Although Shakespeare's sources indicated that Macduff had fled Scotland after the murder of his family, the playwright reversed the order of these events so that Malcolm feared Macbeth was holding the family hostage to coerce Macduff into luring him into a trap.[33] Malcolm proves to be a less naively trusting and therefore more effective leader than his father by testing Macduff's loyalty. Confessing to a litany of faults, he declares, "Better Macbeth? Than such an one to reign." As Macduff rebuts each asserted fault, declaring "All these are portable, / With other graces weighed," Malcolm admits that his confessions were false. Having seen Macbeth's cunning attempts to win even him over, "modest wisdom plucks me / From overcredulous haste."[34] In this way, Shakespeare shows him to be a better leader than his father, even if this requires him to be less forthcoming. Only after Malcolm and Macduff agree to join Siward's English force of ten thousand does Ross tell Macduff his family has been murdered.

Do Macbeth's death and the ascension of Malcolm restore a good state? "Such natural harmony, though disrupted by Macbeth's willed choice of evil, is, according to critical consensus, restored at the end of the play," writes Carol Strongin Tufts. However, she disagrees, pointing out that the play's opening and closing deaths are "in essence, the same events seen through opposite perspectives." Malcolm will, like both his father and Macbeth, honor his friends and punish his enemies, with no mention made of the common good. His legitimacy will depend on the force supplied by Macduff and the troops supplied by England, just as his father's legitimacy depended on Macbeth's military prowess.

Malcolm's final speech says little about the regime to come, nor does the play explain the absence of his brother or how Banquo's heirs will become kings. Instead, he says, "We shall not spend a large expense of time / Before we reckon with your several loves / And make us even with you."[35] As Stephen Greenblatt puts it, "this cannot sound altogether reassuring to Malcolm's supporters."[36] To cement the loyalty of his followers, he will create new titles for those who helped him overthrow Macbeth. The historical Malcolm not only awarded these titles, he increased inequality and imported luxurious habits from England. Following his death, controversy over dynastic succession caused one son, Duncan, to be killed by another, Donalbain, whose more austere regime and return to election of the king instead of hereditary succession indicate more of a cycle of corruption and reform than a benign government.[37] Even though Malcolm's regime was a great improvement over Macbeth's, it was certainly not free of significant corruption, given our earlier definition of that term.

A good way to determine the continuing relevance of these depictions of political corruption is to look at how the play has been interpreted. We will next examine several prominent film and theatrical productions to determine more about contemporary messages of *Macbeth*.

Orson Welles's *Macbeth* (1948)

As a young director, one of Orson Welles's greatest successes was a 1936 play, a "voodoo *Macbeth*" with an all-black cast. He used an adaptation of that script for his 1948 expressionistic film, made with a more conventional cast. In 1948, the play was staged for a week in Salt Lake City, Utah, then filmed in just twenty-three days. However, as with so many of Welles's films, disagreements with the studio over editing caused a delay of three years before the movie was released. The studio's version cut Welles's already shortened version of the play by more than twenty minutes and added a prologue. In 1980 UCLA archivists discovered the original recordings, and a restored version was released a few years later.[38]

Welles told Peter Bogdanovich that "the main point of the production is the struggle between the old and the new religion."[39] Old religion is represented by the witches, whose hands are shown in the opening scene making a clay voodoo representation of Macbeth. Their line "Something wicked this way comes" is spoken as Macbeth and Banquo make their initial entrances rather than in act 4. They remain even more of a presence in the film than the play, seemingly just at the edge of camera range all the time. For example, a knife blade is shown passing in front of the voodoo doll before the vision of a dagger appears to Macbeth.

The new religion is represented by a holy father, a character of Welles's invention who is given lines from others in the play, some of whom are eliminated entirely. Thus, the holy father voices Banquo's warning that "oftentimes, to win us to our harm / The instruments of darkness tell us truths / Win us with honest trifles, to betray 's / In deepest consequence."[40] Because Duncan does not fit well into this duality, most of his scenes prior to arriving at Macbeth's castle were eliminated. When Duncan and his men arrive, the holy father conducts a service at which he asks everyone to "renounce Satan and all his works and all his pomp" at the very time that Duncan's murder is being plotted, making the thunderously positive response ring hollow. After Duncan's murder, he prays, "God's benison go with you and with those that would make good of bad and friends of foes," then joins Malcolm and the English force. He delivers Ross's lament about Scotland under Macbeth (4.3: 189–198) in front of a large, obviously symbolic cross. Malcolm's testing of Macduff is eliminated as their combined forces march forward, each man carrying a cross on a pole and wearing a cross-emblazoned helmet.

Fearing that audiences might not understand this, the studio's revisions included a prologue narrated by Welles declaring that "The cross is newly arrived here. Plotting against Christian law and order are the agents of chaos, priests of hell and magic, sorcerers and witches."[41] Fortunately, the restored version eliminated the prologue, which Welles believed "read like a trailer."[42] The film is far more ambivalent about this new religion than indicated by the prologue. Some of this ambivalence may come from Welles's conflicted feelings about the Cold War. According to now publicly available FBI files, he had been under surveillance since 1941, probably due to his outspoken support of the Popular Front. His 1945 newspaper columns had criticized "America's complacent moral superiority."[43] "Russia is wrong about a lot of things," he wrote, but, "since we carry the biggest stick in the world, we could afford to speak a trifle softly."[44]

Welles depicts the holy father as largely ineffective. His warning to Macduff's family comes too late, as his departure is followed immediately by their murder, committed directly by Macbeth rather than his agents. Pamela Mason believes that the holy father becomes passively complicit in Macbeth's actions, citing Macduff's reproof after learning his family has been slain, "Did heaven look on / And would not take their part" as being directed at him.[45] Walt Ulbricht suggests that both the witches and the holy father are "constrained by one narrow mode of action and thought."[46] Ultimately, Macbeth slays the holy father with a spear through the heart.

In the end, Macduff kills Macbeth by cutting off the clay figure's head. Malcolm's final speech is omitted, replaced by an epilogue that has the witches reciting "Peace, the charm's wound up," a line from the play's first act. Rather than restoring the natural order of good government, this is merely one battle in an ongoing struggle in which Macbeth is an early casualty. Yet, if the witches represent the temptation of corruption to which Macbeth seems fated to succumb, it is not clear that Christianity is its exact opposite. It too seems flawed, suggesting the inevitability of corruption.

Akira Kurosawa's *Throne of Blood* (1957)

In *Throne of Blood*, Akira Kurosawa transposes the story of Macbeth to feudal Japan. The movie opens with a chorus chanting about "the ruins of the castle of delusion ... never changing, now and throughout eternity. Here stood Spider's Web Castle."[47] From the beginning of the film, it is clear that the society depicted is thoroughly corrupt. According to Stephen Prince, that period of Japanese history "was marked by internecine wars among the rival clans, the absence of a national political power, and the kind of treachery, prevarication, and murder" dramatized in the film.[48] Every character is motivated by a self-interested desire for power.

Having come to power by murdering his master, the castle's lord, Tsuzuki, is now facing a rebellion against his own rule. Compelled to decide whether to strike against the rebels or fortify the castle, he chooses the latter, leaving the fight to fortress commanders Washizu and Miki (the Macbeth and Banquo equivalents), but, shortly after this decision is made, messengers report that the rebels have been defeated. A forest spirit predicts that first Washizu, then Miki's son will rule the castle. Forest and fog are so thick that Washizu and Miki ride around for hours before arriving at the castle. Washizu's wife, Asaji, argues that since Miki will surely tell Tsuzuki of the spirit's prophecy, Washizu has no choice but to act preemptively by killing the great lord. "In this degenerate age," she bluntly asserts, "one must kill so as not to be killed." J. Lawrence Guntner has accurately described Washizu as "as much a victim of a constraining feudal order and social decorum as of his personal transgression."[49]

After the murder at Washizu's North Garrison, Noriyasu (Macduff's equivalent, whose guards were framed for the murder) and the prince flee to Spider's Web Castle, where Miki has been placed in charge in the lord's absence. When Miki refuses to open the gates, Washizu allows them to escape in order to ascertain Miki's intentions. Asaji's suggestion of bringing the lord's coffin to the castle gains entrance for him and his men. Miki asks the council to name Washizu lord, as the only leader strong enough to defeat the resurgent rebels. Not coincidentally, fulfilling the prophecy that Washizu will become lord will also serve Miki's interest in having his son succeed Washizu. Lacking an heir, Washizu plans to cement Miki's loyalty by naming his son, in apparent gratitude for his support, at that night's banquet. However, when Asaji tells her husband she is pregnant, he instead solicits the murder of Miki and his son. As in *Macbeth*, dinner is ruined by the appearance, to Washizu alone, of Miki's ghost. When Washizu is told by the murderer that Miki's son has escaped, he immediately kills the assassin.

Soldiers are then shown skeptically discussing the official version of Miki's death, noting that his son, the prince, and Noriyasu have all joined the rebels. So rotten have things become that even the rats are leaving the castle. "Rats," the soldiers say, "flee a house before it burns." After Asaji suffers a miscarriage, she has a breakdown. Although Washizu temporarily bolsters his troops' confidence by telling them of the spirit's prophecy that he will not be defeated until the forest rises up, this confidence is quickly dissipated as the rebels, carrying tree branches to provide cover in the open field directly in front of the castle, seem to be a mass of trees on the march. Washizu's panic-stricken troops then kill him with a volley of arrows, after which the film indicates that this is simply part of a cycle of corruption as it ends with the same chant it began with.

Kurosawa's warlords are men of action, lacking the articulate self-reflection and poetic language of Shakespeare's characters. In their society, self-preservation forces them to subordinate all considerations to self-interest. Even though there is a council to ratify succession, there seems no institutionalized method of transferring power. None of the leaders appears to have any interest in the common good. The chorus's chant at film's end suggests a repetition of this pattern. Although some critics believe that this represents Japanese disillusionment with the American occupation and even the ideals of western liberalism and democracy, more consistent with the film is Erin Suzuki's argument that it reflects a stage in which Japan was "caught between the hard-learned lessons of its militaristic past and the unfulfilled promise of a democratic future."[50]

By changing Shakespeare's ending, Kurosawa provides a measure of democratic hope. Unlike Macbeth, who is killed by others in the elite, Washizu is killed by his own men, suggesting the possibility that future governments will have to consider the public good rather than their own. Such a check on corruption would be more reliable than hoping for leaders like Malcolm, who utilize their own personal checks and balances to root out corruption.

Barbara Garson's *MacBird!* (1966)

While speaking at a 1966 rally against the Vietnam War, Barbara Garson inadvertently referred to Lady Bird Johnson as Lady MacBird. Soon after turning this slip of the tongue into a fifteen-minute skit, she expanded it into a satirical play. The first-time playwright transformed the leading politicians of the day into the characters of *Macbeth* while also borrowing lines from other Shakespearean plays. Her characters include MacBird and his wife (corresponding to Lyndon and Lady Bird Johnson); John, Robert, and Teddy Ken O'Dunc (the Kennedy brothers); the Egg of Head (Adlai Stevenson); the Wayne of Morse (Senator Morse); the Earl of Warren (Chief Justice Earl Warren); and Lord (Defense Secretary Robert) MacNamara.

Despite what some of those offended by the satire said, the play does not directly implicate MacBird in John Ken O'Dunc's assassination. Instead, by inviting him to visit MacBird's ranch, then parade through the streets, he will be put in danger. As Lady MacBird suggests, *"expose him to the fury of his foes ... just expose him. Nothing more."*[51] As in *Macbeth*, the actual assassination occurs offstage, after which a newspaper diagram is projected onstage. However, the play strongly implies that MacBird himself kills the assassin.

Unfortunately for MacBird, a rebellion in Viet Land, a country he had never heard of, hampers the implementation of his Smooth Society program. Efforts by Lord MacNamara to defeat the rebellion prove unsuccessful as the continuing war unites the president's domestic foes around Robert Ken O'Dunc. MacBird's attempts to kill the remaining two brothers fail.

In the end, MacBird's heart fails just as Robert aims his spear. Garson then turns Shakespeare's ending on its head. Rather than vowing to reverse his predecessor's policies and make all even with him, Robert instead repeats the exact words used by MacBird when he succeeded John, then promises to "follow my great predecessor's path." Holding aloft MacBird's fallen banner, he leads his followers in a procession bearing the body while waving their banners side by side.[52]

Garson, who was the Socialist Party candidate for vice president in 1992, presents all leading governmental officials of the time as corrupt. As she told the *Washington Post* when the play was revived in 2006, President Johnson "was as bad as the other guys in this play ... but he wasn't worse."[53] The O'Duncs are selfish power seekers whose father replaced their human hearts with mechanical devices and their blood with antiseptic brine in order "to free his sons from paralyzing scruples."[54] Warren agrees to lead an inquiry into John's murder that he knows will be a whitewash. Not even religious leaders escape ridicule. MacBird hopes to divert public attention from political issues by declaring a national day of prayer for which "we'll get the biggest preacher in the country / You know the one I mean—the guy's got class."[55]

For Garson, the elites who governed the United States at the time, whether Democratic or Republican, were corrupt because their goal was gaining and retaining power rather than the good of the broader public. As she wrote when running for vice president, "although *MacBird!* is often remembered as an attack on Lyndon Johnson, it in fact presented the scorned president and his glowing Kennedy rivals as all-too-similar top-down politicians."[56] Marjorie Garber's comparison between *Macbeth* and *MacBird!* seems particularly apt. For her, one of the most powerful aspects of Shakespeare's play is its "insistence upon the return of the repressed," while "what is repressed and returned in *MacBird!*" consists of "the underlying issues: inequity, poverty, rage, corruption, deceit, and war. What makes the witches' prophecies come true is the anger in the streets and the cynicism of political education."[57] Although the mechanisms for changing government are very different for Shakespeare's Scottish monarchy and 1966 America's elected representatives, the framework provided by Shakespeare allowed Garson to skewer corrupt political leaders for failing to act in the public interest.

The play's impact can be seen from the polarized reactions to it.[58] The establishment bitterly attacked it. FBI director J. Edgar Hoover denounced it in his agency's monthly *Law Enforcement Bulletin*. The publisher of *Showcard* refused to print the program. Critics such as the *New York Times*'s Walter Kerr not only criticized the play as "tasteless and irresponsible" but also personally attacked Garson as "a woman who seems to have started talking and couldn't be stopped."

Other critics, such as Robert Brustein, admired what had made the play so tasteless to Kerr, especially its "power to provoke, energize, and even upset its audiences." The play was a success with audiences, running off-Broadway for 386 performances.

Roman Polanski's *Macbeth* (1971)

When Roman Polanski's wife was murdered, he was filming *The Day of the Dolphin* in London. Abandoning that project, he flew home to Los Angeles, where he decided to direct a film adaptation of *Macbeth* instead. Having always wanted to film a Shakespeare play, he chose *Macbeth* due to his belief that of all the major tragedies, its film versions had been the least successful.[59] The film substitutes visual depictions for much of Shakespeare's language because, as Polanski explained, "If you use the screen as a medium, then what you tell has to be told by visual means."[60] One result was that more of the play's violence was depicted on screen. For example, Polanski not only shows Macbeth killing Duncan but also has the awakening king resist, forcing Macbeth to stab him numerous times as his crown rolls along the ground.

One way in which Polanski depicts political corruption is to substantially expand the role of Ross, who becomes an opportunist, siding with whoever seems to be winning and will benefit him the most. It is he who turns out to be Shakespeare's unnamed third murderer of Banquo. After the deed, he throws the other two into a well. Upon leaving Macduff's castle, he leaves the door open to allow the family's murderers to enter. When Lennox leaves Macbeth's service to join Macduff and Malcolm, it is Ross, hoping to replace him, who brings his medallion to Macbeth. Passed over for this promotion, he defects to the other side. In order for Ross to then appear in England in the next scene, Polanski had to move act 5, scene 3 to precede act 4, scene 3 as well as remove the crucial testing of Macduff by Malcolm entirely, but the result is to show that, according to Kenneth Rothwell, "Ross has donned new robes as malevolent witness to dreadful events to come."[61] It is Ross who, after Macduff kills Macbeth, picks up the decapitated head and crown, then hands that crown to Malcolm, proclaiming, "Hail, King of Scotland." Polanski emphasizes the view that self-interest is the key determinant of power by replacing Malcolm's final speech with an epilogue showing his brother Donalbain seeking out the witches, undoubtedly in the hope of restarting the cycle of violence in order to become king himself.

E. Pearlman believes that Polanski's alterations convert Malcolm into "just another politician, tainted by both his henchmen and his own ambition."[62] Even if some kings are better than others, all are ultimately corrupt because they and those who assist them place gaining and retaining power above the public good. Like most of the other adaptations we have examined, however, the result is, as Rothwell has concluded, that "for so equivocal a play, the film becomes curiously unequivocal."[63]

Rupert Goold's *Macbeth* (2007–2010)

Rupert Goold's production of *Macbeth*, starring Patrick Stewart, began at the Chichester Festival, successfully transferred to London's West End then to New York, and ultimately was shown throughout the United States on Public Broadcasting.[64] The setting was transformed into a state akin to Stalinist Russia with echoes of George Orwell's *1984*. Rosie Millard describes it as "an inhumane world where nurses turn into sorceresses and no one trusts anyone."[65]

The production opens with a video of battle followed by the play's "bleeding captain" as a wounded sergeant on a hospital gurney who recounts Macbeth's heroics. In the text (act 1, scene 2), a stage direction says that "the Captain is led off by attendants," but here, nurses, who turn out to be the weird sisters, instead kill him with a lethal injection and rip out his heart after the other soldiers have left. Duncan is a uniformed military leader; Ross a trench coat–clad bureaucrat with a briefcase.

Goold depicts a society where brutality and torture are so routine that they are accompanied by the most mundane activities. The witches are omnipresent, appearing not only as nurses but also as cooks, maids serving dinner, and morgue workers. Lady Macbeth decorates pastry as she urges her husband to kill Duncan. While planning Banquo's murder, Macbeth makes and eats a sandwich. Much of this occurs on a stage dominated by a larger-than-life poster of Macbeth, much like Stalin or Big Brother.

No one is exempt from becoming complicit in this corrupt society. Ross tries to be a neutral technocrat until he is brutally interrogated to reveal Macduff's whereabouts. This alteration of the play requires him to speak dialogue Shakespeare used in a conversation between Lennox and an unnamed lord, but without Lennox's sardonic commentary on the official version of events.[66] After the murders, at which Macbeth is present, a guilt-ridden Ross is shown cowering and crying.

Nor does the play suggest that Malcolm's reign will be a great improvement. After killing Macbeth, Macduff hands the severed head to Malcolm, who holds it high in triumph while delivering his final speech, suggesting that his rule will be characterized more by vengeance and another cycle of violence than by any consideration of the public good.

The constant presence of violence and torture gives the production considerable contemporary resonance. In addition to the examples already mentioned, Macbeth's predecessor as Thane of Cawdor is shown hooded and shot in the head. Banquo is murdered on a crowded train rather than on a lonely ride with his son. Preparations for a luxurious dinner at Macbeth's castle are intercut with videos of people interrogated and tortured in the search for Fleance, who is hunted using bloodhounds. It is hardly surprising that one critic described Goold's interpretation as "a *Macbeth* for the age of [George W.] Bush."[67]

Although Goold's production is more than simply a critique of the Bush administration's use of coercive interrogation, like so many of the interpretations we have examined, it views the society it depicts as hopelessly corrupt. As Stephen Greenblatt has written, "the Stalinist setting does something more than provide an instance of modern tyranny; it closes off the vistas of hope that might otherwise have been glimpsed in such characters as Banquo, Malcolm, and Macduff."[68] If corruption is inevitable and the public's choices are only between bad and worse, it's difficult to see any reason for political involvement at all, save for those who seek to join in the selfish battle for power.

Conclusion

One of the most striking aspects of our examination of corruption in *Macbeth* is how Shakespeare defies straightforward interpretations. This often frustrates those looking for a moral to *Macbeth*. Is it an apolitical play that shows the psychology of a heroic soldier giving in to the evil temptations of power? Is it the story of a benign monarchy temporarily interrupted by a usurping tyrant until restored to its rightful order? As we have seen, Shakespeare is too great a playwright to be so didactically interpreted. *Macbeth* has considerable insight into political corruption—what it is, how it takes effect, and what can be done about it—yet it defies readings that see either those who overthrow Macbeth as heroes or the Scottish monarchy as enlightened. The same violence that made Macbeth a hero later turned him into a tyrant. Duncan's faults include being too honest and trusting while his son promises to be a better king because he knows when to dissemble. The question of whether Malcolm will be as dependent on Macduff's military prowess as his father was on Macbeth's is not fully answered by the play's ending. What does seem implicit in that ending and the entire play is that unless force, legitimacy, and concern for the public are united, corruption is likely. Actual Scottish history subsequent to the play's ending supports this view.

While the text of the play has allowed interpretations that take account of governments very different from either Macbeth's or Shakespeare's time, these interpretations often lose sight of Shakespeare's ambiguities in order to make their points more directly. Orson Welles's attempt to see the play as a clash of two religious views of the world proved less than convincing. Although like so many modern interpretations, Akira Kurosawa's transposition of *Macbeth* to feudal Japan portrays its society as led by power-seeking warlords with no interest in the good of the public, the ending supplies hope in its empowerment of ordinary soldiers. If political leaders are too corrupt to consider the public interest, it is up to the people to make things right.

Macbird! makes a surprisingly similar point. Because it is set in a society that allows leadership change through elections, Garson argues that corruption is inevitable as long as the public simply rotates high office among the leaders of the Democratic and Republican parties, both tainted by their subordination of the good of the less privileged to the maintenance of power by whatever means are necessary. Although *MacBird!* was seen as scandalous in 1966, when it was revived forty years later, critics found its satire relatively mild in an age of *Saturday Night Live* and *The Daily Show.*[69]

Polanski's and Goold's versions also see their societies as corrupt and violent. By seeming to eliminate the possibility of real change, however, they gain relevance at the cost of hopelessness. If all leaders are corrupt and government is a cycle of one self-serving leader replacing another, what are we to do? Unfortunately, at a time when the American public's trust in government and faith in its political institutions are at a low point, these interpretations of *Macbeth* tell us a lot about the state of contemporary society.

For example, a 2011 CNN survey found that an all-time low of 15 percent of the American public trusts the federal government to do what is right all or most of the time.[70] In another poll, taken shortly before the 2008 election, more than two-thirds of likely voters "strongly agreed" that corruption is a "significant problem" for the federal government, and 62.6 percent "strongly agreed" that "political corruption played a major role in our nation's recent financial crisis."[71] Nor does Shakespeare's own country fare better, as when asked in 2009 to "rate the standards of honesty and integrity of elected politicians in Britain today," 65 percent ranked them "very or somewhat low," compared to 6 percent who chose "very or somewhat high."[72]

Japan shows similar trends. Soonhe Kim summarizes scholarly literature as indicating "that politicians' corruption scandals and their misuse of public money for private and party gain have been significant predictors of citizen confidence in government" in Japan.[73] Kim notes that one response to the shrinkage of trust in government was the 1999 enactment of ethics reform. Support for this view can be seen in surveys such as one that found in 1998 that 2 percent trusted and 14 percent somewhat trusted "high-ranking government officials."[74] Reforms such as these have failed to arrest the erosion of public confidence, as demonstrated by a recent poll finding that 85 percent of those questioned believe that elected officials favor special interests over the people they represent, essentially accusing their leaders of corruption.[75]

It is not surprising that the Polanski and Goold *Macbeth*s, produced after this deterioration of trust was well under way, lack the faith in possible democratic change seen in Kurosawa and Garson's versions.[76] Garson and Kurosawa's adaptations suggest that an informed and active public can be a check on self-serving leaders. Supporting their view is Kim's conclusion, after citing studies indicating an inverse relationship between Japanese citizens' perception of corruption and trust in government institutions, that "citizen participation positively influences public trust in administration," in such areas as fairness and honesty.[77]

Although not ranking corruption at the top of their agenda, American voters have some faith that their ballots can be used to improve ethics in government. In a 2007 CNN poll, 41 percent said that "corruption and ethical standards in government" would be "extremely important" in their presidential vote, while another 36 percent said they would be "very important."[78] Americans might be considered cynical yet hopeful, or as the title of a recent article put it, using Ronald Reagan's well-known maxim about arms control, they seek to "trust but verify."[79] In a way they are emulating Malcolm by questioning potential leaders in order to choose those who are the least likely to prove corrupt after gaining power. This would support Mlada Bukovansky's belief that in both developed and developing countries, the most effective approach to reducing corruption is "reasoned public debate and discourse" rather than externally imposed governmental standards.[80] Shakespeare may not give us a road map to change, but he does provide an ambiguous hope that change can be for the better.

Notes

1. Quoted in Carol Strongin Tufts, "Shakespeare's Conception of Moral Order in *Macbeth*," *Renascence* 150 (Spring/Summer 1998): 169.

2. David Bevington, "*Macbeth*: Introduction," in William Shakespeare, *Four Tragedies*, New York: Bantam Books, 1980: 598.

3. Susan Snyder, "*Macbeth*: A Modern Perspective," in William Shakespeare, *Macbeth*, Folger Shakespeare Library Edition, New York: Simon & Schuster, 1992: 197–198.

4. Blair Worden, "Shakespeare and Politics," in Catherine M. S. Alexander (ed.), *Shakespeare and Politics*, Cambridge, UK: Cambridge University Press, 2004: 30.

5. E. Pearlman, "*Macbeth* on Film: Politics," in Alexander, *Shakespeare and Politics*: 236.

6. Robert Shaughnessy, *The Routledge Guide to William Shakespeare*, New York: Routledge, 2011: 249.

7. Ibid., 250.

8. Garry Wills, *Witches and Jesuits: Shakespeare's Macbeth*, New York: Oxford University Press, 1995: 146.

9. For example, see Michael Johnston, "Democracy without Politics? Hidden Costs of Corruption and Reform in America," in Michael A. Genovese and Victoria A. Farrar-Myers (eds.), *Corruption and American Politics*, Amherst, NY: Cambria Press, 2010: 10–35.

10. John Locke, *Two Treatises of Government*, London: J. M. Dent, 1993: 216.

11. *Macbeth*, act 3, scene 4: 167–168. All references to the play are from the Folger Shakespeare Library Edition, cited in note 3.

12. Arvind K. Jain, "Power, Politics, and Corruption," in Arvind K. Jain (ed.), *The Political Economy of Corruption*, New York: Routledge, 2001: 3.

13. *Macbeth* 4.1: 82, 91–92.

14. *Macbeth* 5.8: 19–20, 24, 70–71, 74.

15. The Oxford University text of the *Chronicles* is at www.english.ox.ac.uk/holinshed/.

16. This summary is based on the more detailed accounts in David Norbrook, "*Macbeth* and the Politics of Historiography," in Kevin Sharpe and Steven N. Zwicker, *Politics of Discourse*, Berkeley: University of California Press, 1987: 78–116; and Nick Aitchison, *Macbeth: Man and Myth*, Gloucestershire, UK: Sutton, 2000. Aitchison, however, finds no evidence to confirm the common portrayal of Macbeth "by both medieval chroniclers and modern historians as a wise and good king and his reign as a prosperous one" (95).

17. James L. Calderwood, *If It Were Done: Macbeth and Tragic Action*, Amherst: University of Massachusetts Press, 1986: 72.

18. Alan Sinfield, "*Macbeth*: History, Ideology, and Intellectuals," *Critical Quarterly* 28 (1986): 67.

19. Quoted in ibid.: 74.

20. *Macbeth* 1.7: 16–20, 26–29.

21. *Macbeth* 5.8: 85–88.

22. *Macbeth* 1.1: 12, and 1.3: 39, 155.

23. *Macbeth* 1.4: 13–16.

24. *Macbeth* 1.6: 1–2.

25. *Macbeth* 3.1: 33–36.

26. *Macbeth* 3.1: 2–3, and 3.6: 12–15.

27. *Macbeth* 4.2: 53–64.

28. *Macbeth* 3.1: 52–53.

29. *Macbeth* 3.1: 135–137.

30. Niccolo Machiavelli, *The Prince*, New York: Penguin, 1961: 66.

31. *Macbeth* 5.2: 22–23.

32. *Macbeth* 3.4: 163–164.

33. Wills, *Witches and Jesuits*: 115–116.

34. *Macbeth* 4. 3: 78–79, 105–106, 138–139.

35. *Macbeth* 5.8: 72–74.

36. Stephen Greenblatt, "In the Night Kitchen," *New York Review of Books* 55 (July 17, 2008): 28.

37. This account of the historical Macbeth is based on Norbrook.

38. Although this film has never been released on DVD in the United States, a Korean edition of the restored version is available and can be easily watched in English with the Korean subtitles turned off.

39. Simon Callow, *Orson Welles, Volume 2: Hello Americans*, New York: Penguin, 2007: 387.

40. *Macbeth* 1.3: 135–138.

41. For the full text of this prologue, see Wendy Rogers Harper, "Polanski vs. Welles on *Macbeth*: Character or Fate?" *Literature Film Quarterly* 14 (1986): 204.

42. Pamela Mason, "Orson Welles and Filmed Shakespeare," in Russell Jackson, *The Cambridge Companion to Shakespeare on Film*, Cambridge, UK: Cambridge University Press, 2000: 188.

43. Geoffrey Green, "'There Is No Logic in This': Orson Welles's Transgressive Challenge to Cold War Paranoia in *Mr. Arkadin* (1955)," *Interdisciplinary Humanities* 26 (Spring 2009): 6.

44. Callow, *Orson Welles, Volume 2*: 251.

45. *Macbeth* 4.3: 263–264; Mason, "Orson Welles and Filmed Shakespeare": 183–198.

46. Walt Ulbricht, "Orson Welles' *Macbeth*: Archetype and Symbol," *University of Dayton Review* 14 (1979): 25.

47. The film is available on DVD as part of the Criterion Collection.

48. Stephen Prince, "*Throne of Blood*: Shakespeare Transposed," essay accompanying the Criterion Collection DVD, 2003.

49. J. Lawrence Guntner, "*Hamlet, Macbeth,* and *King Lear* on Film," in Jackson, *The Cambridge Companion to Shakespeare on Film*: 126.

50. Erin Suzuki, "Lost in Translation: Reconsidering Shakespeare's *Macbeth* and Kurosawa's *Throne of Blood*," *Literature/Film Quarterly* 34, 2 (2006): 93–103.

51. Barbara Garson, *MacBird!*, New York: Grassy Knoll Press, 1966: 11.

52. Ibid.: 56. MacBird's speech is on p. 27.

53. Jane Horwitz, "She Hopes 'MacBird' Flies in a New Era," *Washington Post*, September 5, 2006: C5.

54. Garson, *MacBird!*: 55.

55. Ibid.: 40.

56. Barbara Garson, "The Stealth Socialist: I'm Running Too—So Won't Somebody Ask Me about NAFTA?" *Washington Post*, November 1, 1992: C5.

57. Marjorie Garber, *Shakespeare and Modern Culture*, New York: Anchor, 2008: 103.

58. Discussion of reaction to the play is based on Bruce E. Altschuler, *Acting Presidents: 100 Years of Plays about the Presidency*, New York: Palgrave Macmillan, 2010: 65–67.

59. Roman Polanski, *Roman by Polanski*, New York: William Morrow, 1984: 331.

60. Larry DuBois, "The *Playboy* Interview: Roman Polanski," *Playboy* 18 (December 1971): 98.

61. Kenneth S. Rothwell, "Roman Polanski's *Macbeth*: The 'Privileging' of Ross," *CEA Critic* 46 (1983): 54.

62. Pearlman, "*Macbeth* on Film": 241.

63. Rothwell, "Roman Polanski's *Macbeth*": 55.

64. A DVD of the PBS program is commercially available.

65. Rosie Millard, "Bloody, Bold, and Resolute," *New Statesman* 137 (October 8, 2007): 42.

66. *Macbeth* 3.6.

67. Scott Horton, "*Macbeth* for the Age of Bush," *Harper's Magazine*, October 4, 2007. Accessed at http://harpers.org/archive/2007/10/hbc-90001349.

68. Greenblatt, "In the Night Kitchen": 29.

69. For example, see Peter Marks, "60s Satire *MacBird!* Lays a MacEgg," *Washington Post*, September 13, 2006: C2.

70. "CNN Poll: Trust in Government at All-Time Low," September 28, 2011. Accessed at http://politicalticker.blogs.cnn.com/2011/09/28/cnn-poll-trust-in-government-at-all-time-low/.

71. "New Judicial Watch/Zogby Poll: 81.7% of Americans Say Political Corruption Played a 'Major Role' in Financial Crisis," Reuters, October 21, 2008. Accessed at www.reuters.com/article/2008/10/21/idUS209746+21-Oct-2008+MW20081021.

72. Sara Birch and Nicholas Allen, "How Honest Do Politicians Need to Be?" *Political Quarterly* 81 (January–March 2010): 50.

73. Soonhe Kim, "Public Trust in Government in Japan and South Korea: Does the Rise of Critical Citizens Matter?" *Public Administration Review* 70 (September/October 2010): 802.

74. *Asahi Shimbun* poll, December 16, 1998, archived in the Roper Center's JPOLL.

75. Malcolm Foster, "AP-GfK Poll: Japanese Distrust Government after Disaster," Associated Press, September 1, 2011.

76. In contrast to the more recent surveys, according to the 1958 American National Election Study, 73 percent trusted government to do what is right all or most of the time.

77. Kim, "Public Trust in Government in Japan and South Korea": 803–804.

78. CNN/Opinion Research Corporation Poll, May 4–6, 2007.

79. Paul Gronke, James Hicks, and Timothy E. Cook, "Trust but Verify: Three Lenses on Americans' Trust in Government," in Barbara Norrander and Clyde Wilcox (eds.), *Understanding Public Opinion*, 3rd ed., Washington, DC: CQ Press, 2010: 197–214.

80. Mlada Bukovansky, "The Hollowness of Anti-Corruption Discourse," *Review of International Political Economy* 13 (May 2006): 204.

Chapter 3

A Dionysian Hamlet[1]

Sarah A. Shea

As Hamlet deeply mourns the loss of his father and struggles to make sense of the world around him, his soul becomes intoxicated by his unruly emotions, pushing him to the edge of madness. Truly in this Dionysian state of pure ecstasy, Hamlet transcends the natural and ordinary bounds of existence. By immersing himself in anger, confusion, and harbored contemptuousness toward his uncle-turned-king, Claudius, and the injustices surrounding the legitimacy of his kingship, Hamlet desperately searches for order and truth in the world around him but is left disappointed and without a spirit-satisfying answer. The young Nietzsche's profound insights into the dark and wild nature of Hamlet's soul in *The Birth of Tragedy* tastefully characterizes Hamlet as courageous in his willfulness to glance into the nauseating and unsettling truth of reality, but in spite of his willful bravery, there is also a will-negation, hence Hamlet's inability to move to action because he cannot distance himself from his melancholy. "In this sense," writes Nietzsche,

> the Dionysian man is similar to Hamlet: both have at one time cast a true glance into the essence of things, they have acquired *knowledge*, and action

is repugnant to them; for their action can change nothing in the eternal essence of things, they feel that it is laughable or shameful that they are expected to repair a world which is out of joint.[2]

To authentically glance into reality to the point at which the ground of the soul, that once found its solace in comfort and familiarity, is unsettled and jolted, is to move the soul in a peculiar and gripping way that illuminates in terror and grief, the absurdity of existence. When the soul is imperiled in this way and finds itself at a juncture, ironically churned by its lethargic state, this is where art bewitches the soul and serves as a redemptive and healing "enchantress." Art alone for Nietzsche has the power to transform these horrible reflections on the terror and absurdity of existence into "notions" in which living becomes palatable. For Nietzsche, "these are the representations of the *sublime* as the artistic conquest of the awful, and of the *comic* as the artistic discharge from the disgust of the absurd."[3] The conquest of Hamlet's soul to transform his gut-wrenching experiences is necessary if he is ever to become fit to take his rightful place as the one true King of Denmark. It so happens that in the bittersweet gift of madness, Hamlet wrestles his demons into disciplined action and puts his disordered soul back into its proper order, opposed to being ruled by his inordinate passions and emotions, and despairing over his initial juvenile submission. Hamlet does not merely feign madness, other than the single instance where he pretends to be mad for the gross, empty laughter of Rosencrantz and Guildenstern.[4] Even then, Hamlet's soul is still muddled with confusion—sick with resentment, stricken with grief, bereft of all common sense; his soul is inflicted by a thousand tugs and pulls, this way and that, making "driving" quite impossible in his inebriated state.[5]

Beginning with Nietzsche's exalted description of Hamlet as a "Dionysian man" in *The Birth of Tragedy* as the scaffolding for further study into Hamlet's character and his battle with madness, we journey with his soul from a dark and befuddled wilderness of untamed emotions, irrational thoughts, and world weariness consequential to his inability to manipulate nature to his will, to the luminous moment after he returns from sea a changed man equipped with the necessary intellectual discipline and spiritual fortitude endowing him with a "readiness" that is "all," which finally pushes him to act, albeit to a tragic and devastating end.[6] Since politics begin in the *agon* (contest) of the individual soul and radiate outward to the larger city, it is imperative that the soul of the ruling man is healthy. In this way, our study of Hamlet's character is twofold: on the one hand, we trace the movement of Hamlet's soul in order to understand what drives it, but on the other hand, we are analyzing the relation of the individual soul to political practice. The reader will note that the lessons derived from the tragedy of *Hamlet* are historically timeless and that its context is transferable to everydayness. In investigating Hamlet's character, we address central themes of the play as they become manifest in his soul—madness, friendship, appearances and reality, death, and tragedy, to argue that not only may Hamlet be Nietzsche's "Dionysian man," but he is every man and every woman who has ever faced reality in all seriousness, while "breathlessly" attempting to "catch up" to it.[7]

As Hamlet accepts death as the inevitable lot of humankind, we, the readers, celebrate the rebirth of tragedy again and again, amid the nihilistic-superficiality of contemporary literature, praising Shakespeare for his exquisite insights into the raw nature of the human condition and his existential wanderings of his tragic heroes, and how these all-too-human things translate into his political prowess. While Hamlet frantically battles against himself to come to terms with the inner abyss of his soul, the reader will note that his pains are not solely unique to him, but shared among all humankind in solidarity—Horatio, his loyal friend and Apollonian, who helps balance his disproportioned emotions with sound advice and an open ear; the Dionysian and Apollonian come together in a final, epic crescendo where Hamlet gladly welcomes death, and Shakespeare's disciples rejoice in witnessing a political act of immeasurable value while gawking at its nobility, as something almost foreign to politics as they are practiced in the twenty-first century. Essentially, Shakespeare's *Hamlet*, a play about the dark politics of the soul, teaches us the most important lesson of life and politics: "know thyself," or in the words of Hamlet, "to know a man well were to know himself."[8]

Either Philosophical or Political: Hamlet as Shakespeare's Political-Philosopher Par Excellence

The first "rule" of the political philosopher, and one of the main points Shakespeare articulates in *Hamlet*, is that the individual must first learn to govern his or her self if ever he or she is to accept responsibility in governing over others. The internal politics of Hamlet's soul is complicated to say the least, without jumping head-first into interpreting the external political facts of the play. As Colin McGinn claims that *Hamlet* is about "the constitution of the self" and must be studied "philosophically" as the "best way" of understanding Hamlet's madness because he is a "victim of his own formlessness," we can begin to comprehend the brave willfulness behind Hamlet's self-examination.[9] McGinn addresses the paradoxical and "inextricably interwoven[ness]" of Hamlet's character in phenomenological terms, asking either-or questions like, "Is [Hamlet] a comedian or tragedian? Does he love life or hate it? Is he likable or detestable? Is he the hero of the play or one of its villains?" while attempting to account for the obvious schizophrenic nature of Hamlet's soul.[10] "He is poet and philosopher, a man of high ideals and a sensitive soul," writes McGinn, but at the same time, Hamlet is also "a soldier and a man of action, capable of unreflective acts of violence.... He lives by language, but can be contemptuous of words."[11] Therefore, according to McGinn, merely "speak[ing] of Hamlet's 'character' is already to misrepresent him," but is it? In daring to speak of Hamlet's "character," are we reducing the complexity of his inner turmoil? Does Hamlet "elude" our understanding of him as McGinn suggests? If the answer to any of these questions is yes, then McGinn undermines his own argument for *Hamlet* being about the "constitution of the self" as ironically there can never really be an underlining definitive "self," but only self that mirrors the Heraclitean flux of nature as inconsistent, temperamental, unpredictable, irrational, and formless—the self harkening of Nietzschean "becoming" and everything contrary to the idea of "constituting" as a kind of grounding—*essence preceding existence*. It so happens that like the paradoxes inherent to Hamlet's character, the answers to these questions are paradoxical too insofar as in attempting to constitute a self, the premise which must be accepted is that there is no single, discernible self but a multitude of drives and impulses that make up a self that is continually creating it-*self*, and in the process of becoming—"formlessness" based on existence, lived experience, and the freedom of our consciousness and our choices. We therefore "become" who we are, as we are not born who we are, and this process repeats itself ad infinitum. Though I agree that Hamlet does "approximat[e] to the condition of the paradox," in McGinn's terms, it is seems rather obvious that he is driven in one direction more so than the other as recognized by Nietzsche, betwixt madness and melancholia, action and passivity, doing the right thing or acting on the wrong; undoubtedly, Hamlet responds more passionately in his outbursts more so than he appropriates an epistemological framework for his decision making. In this way, Hamlet is more Dionysian than he is Apollonian, much more emotional than rational; his madness, as we will learn, is a response to attempting to wrestle with these driving forces while at the same time striving for self-betterment and clarity.

Following McGinn, our investigation is philosophical, but it must also be political in order to appreciate Hamlet as Shakespeare's political philosopher par excellence. In Zdravko Planinc's essay "'It Begins with Pyrrhus' (2.2.451): The Political Philosophy of *Hamlet*," he examines the political anthropology of the play as he argues that the external politics—that is, the tension between Denmark and Norway, Hamlet and Fortinbras—echoes the internal politics of Hamlet's inner struggles as it becomes manifest in the players' telling of the story of the Trojan horse in act 2. What is most noteworthy of Planinc's observations is that in over four hundred years of scholarship on *Hamlet*, he is the first to draw a parallel linking the significance of the Trojan horse story with the external-internal politics of the play. Consequently, for Planinc, Shakespeare's choice to have the form of the play reflect in its contents on various planes suggests a Platonic influence:

> The political philosophy of *Hamlet* is distinctly Platonic in content as well as form. Like Plato, Shakespeare examines several related questions: What is the nature of politics? What is the nature of a human being? And what is the relation between them? The study of politics is conventionally divided into internal and external affairs: the order of the polity, or the regime, on the one hand; and war, on the other. Philosophic anthropology is similarly divisible into internal and external affairs: it studies the order of the soul, broadly understood; and the place of the human soul in a greater or transcendent order.[12]

Though I agree with Planinc's emphasis on the Trojan horse story as more than a strong literary device, it seems that the Platonic influences are not as rich and obvious as Planinc attests aside from act 2. According to Planinc, even though Hamlet falls short of being Plato's philosopher-king, he nonetheless returns from his voyage at sea a changed man who restores reason to its proper place, finally combining the contemplation and action adherent to Plato's philosopher-king. The point Planinc makes, however, is that in spite of Hamlet's coming up short of Platonic ideals, Shakespeare nevertheless "endowed" Hamlet with "the greatness of mind to become Plato's philosopher-king."[13] But why is it that Hamlet never fully becomes the philosopher-king? Though the ideal image is not fully actualized in the play for Planinc, is it only because Hamlet dies? Does harsh reality not allow for such ideals? It may be important to pose a further question to Planinc: if Hamlet was in fact endowed with a greatness of mind, how is it that he initially falls short of the Platonic ideal but at the same time "goes beyond" it? Planinc writes,

> The Hamlet who returns to Denmark and announces himself "the Dane" is not only a true contemplative, but also a true king. His spiritual "readiness" is not resignation, but rather a spiritual dispensation that combines the *vita contemplativa* and the *vita activa* perfectly: Plato's philosopher-king; but also *something else*.[14]

What is this "something else" for Planinc? The paradoxical image of Hamlet as a political ruler who is both "dove" and "serpent" implies a powerful militant Caesarean-esque tone but also places an emphasis on appearance, drawing the reader's attention to the outward impression of Hamlet's character—his madness as a type of intentional aesthetical approach to politics, but not like the Hamlet of *Saxo Grammaticus* or the Brutus of Shakespeare's *Rape of Lucrece,* as Planinc observes, rather "something else" that retains a certain ambiguity.[15] What I derive from Planinc's ruminations on Shakespeare's politics as Platonic in structure and content is that he is correct to argue that understanding politics is about understanding the self. It is therefore impossible to view this study as either strictly philosophical, as McGinn does, or solely political in terms of external political factors because the two concepts are inseparable from the complex character of Hamlet, which Planinc does a fine job illuminating in his essay. Hamlet is as much a self as he is a political animal. Politics is one avenue of human experience that promotes self-expression and self-realization, but also participation in one's society.

Here the political and philosophical work together to form an interpretation of not only the *character* of Hamlet but the *character* of politics. We shall now closely examine the nature of Hamlet's madness so that we may understand the significance behind his spiritual change and how he finally becomes fit to rule.

Melancholia to Madness: The Transformative Character of Hamlet

McGinn suggests that Michel de Montaigne could have been speaking of Hamlet when he asks, "Is it not true that the soul can be most readily thrown into mania and driven mad by its own quickness, sharpness and nimbleness—in short by the qualities which constitute its strength? Does not the most subtle wisdom produce the most subtle madness?"[16] Why would McGinn turn to this quote from Montaigne? What does it reveal about the nature of Hamlet's madness? Undeniably there is a conglomeration of causes that can disturb and disorder the soul, causing madness or mania—which are not negative in themselves but rather negative or positive depending on how they are interpreted and then acted upon. Clearly the concept of madness is not a simple condition like Polonius in his sophistry believes it to be, "to define true madness, / What is't but to be nothing else but mad?" but madness in a more meaningful sense—not a madness of the mind, but of the soul. The disharmonious state of Hamlet's soul is no secret from his friends or enemies; in fact, as Hamlet's disposition is so "horridly" shaken, it is impossible for him to hide his feelings. Any authentic experience that is powerful enough to move the soul in the first place makes "wearing one's heart on one's sleeve" less of a cliché than it is a living reality and authentic expression. The spiritual condition of humankind, especially men and women whose souls are particularly attuned to their surroundings, is that their souls are perpetually longing—whether they long for answers, justice, forgiveness, or hope for a better world. For the Dionysian, like Hamlet, these longings are exceptionally loud, violent, and can even be dangerously erotic, but also creative and destructive. What makes the Dionysian man like Hamlet stand out among his peers is that in the midst of spiting his fate, he also loves and accepts it: "O cursèd spite, / That ever I was born to set it right!"[17] Dancing to the rhythm of the dithyrambic dramatist, Hamlet immerses himself in his emotions, emitting the appearance of madness because he knows he must put on an act in the time it will take him to formulate a plan of action:

> Here as before, never, so help you mercy,
> How strange or odd some'er I bear myself
> (As perchance hereafter shall think meet
> To put an antic disposition on),
> That you, at such times seeing me, never shall
> With arms encumb'red thus, or this headshake,
> Or by pronouncing of some doubtful phrase,
> As "Well, well, we know," or "We could, an if we would,"
> Or "If we list to speak," or "There be, an if they might,"
> Or such ambiguous giving out, to note
> That you know aught of me—this do swear,
> So grace and mercy at your most need help you.[18]

Hamlet's madness is not just an act; while he is feigning madness, he is also still wrestling with accepting the truth. The "antic disposition" is ironic because as Claudius, Gertrude, Polonius, Ophelia, Rosencrantz, and Guildenstern are convinced of Hamlet's decline into mental illness, and use his weariness and "strange behavior" as factual proof of it, Hamlet does not need to put on a disposition because the feelings he is experiencing in his soul emit unintentional strange behavior because of the force at which the truth has made itself heard to Hamlet. Once Claudius suspects that Hamlet may know of the truth, he calls Rosencrantz and Guildenstern to "draw [Hamlet] on to pleasures, and to gather / So much as from occasion you may glean, / Whether aught to us unknown afflicts him thus, / That opened lies within our remedy."[19] What a strange remedy to cure a mental illness with another affliction in drawing Hamlet to pleasures! In noticing a "transformation" in Hamlet, Claudius acknowledges that "nor th' exterior nor the inward man / Resembles that it was," he begins to fear that he may get caught and therefore wants to distract Hamlet because "Madness in great ones must not unwatched go."[20] Claudius sends Hamlet out to sea because of "this fear, / Which now goes free-footed."[21] If Claudius and Gertrude were genuinely concerned for Hamlet's mental health, why would they insist on sending him out to sea, especially with such haste? It is because the guilty party members, that is, those who helped calculate murdering the King or knew of it, do not ever fully believe Hamlet is mentally ill for two reasons: their own guilt eating away at their rational faculties, and the perpetual fear of being exposed for their wrong actions and losing the luxuries of royalty. Claudius never wanted to become king to accept the responsibilities inherent to being a king and properly governing over his countrymen, which is evident by his continual poor judgment in personal and political matters.

Hamlet's madness is an outer manifestation of an inner spiritual strength; a strength that, if left unwatched, has the potentiality of overturning Claudius's rule by unveiling the sickening truth to Denmark, which would perpetuate an honest rebellion in the name of justice and nobility. While madness can manifest itself either negatively or positively in the individual, it is never ambivalent; rather, it is the "all or nothing" attitude that Hamlet takes as his personal gospel. The *truth of the truth*, as it were, is that prior to Hamlet's full acceptance of the truth, his "nothing" attitude made action of any sort—positive or negative in kind—impossible. By accepting the truth, Hamlet's attitude changes to the "all" and understands that he must act because it is right to do so, but also because the cause is greater than his own; a political rebellion, if it is to be honest, must be founded in solidarity, compassion, and a desperate, unified cry for the restoration of justice. In a certain sense, Hamlet's rebellion (as well as his madness) begins at the moment in which the truth makes itself known to Hamlet, startling his spirit to madness—movement, the "all" he needs to eventually commit himself to action, though not without its serious difficulties. We now turn to the nature of harsh truths and their effect on the soul, in particular, how the truth makes itself heard to Hamlet and why Shakespeare craftily chose a ghost to reveal the truth to Hamlet. As we shall see, the ghost represents the young prince's admiration for his deceased father and his intellect, placing Hamlet in a hypothetical conversation; if he could speak to his father, what would his father say? What advice would he give Hamlet?

The Ghostly Appearance of Harsh Truths

In the words of Horatio, truth "harrows" with both "fear and wonder" the same way seeing a ghost startles us with terror and curiosity.[22] Regardless of the form in which harsh truths penetrate the soul, it is unnerving to have our dispositions so "horridly" shaken, but it is also commanding, crudely demanding utterance.[23] The precise moment in which the soul is moved, each person is entirely free to interpret and respond as he or she so desires, yet he or she may also be content to allow the moment to pass him or her by and lose his or her nerve to the wind. In determining what an appropriate response is, contemplation and self-examination are of the utmost importance; each person must make reason the central ruling force and guiding counsel, otherwise he or she may become overwhelmed by the intensity with which external forces penetrate the soul, leaving him or her befuddled, face-down in self-pity, and fumbling for meaning in the damning, stifling trenches of the abyss. Experience alone is saturated in meaning and commanding—men and women must teach themselves the good habit of conforming to these commands if ever they are to retain meaning in and for itself. Perhaps this is where Nietzsche's reading of Hamlet falls short; defining Hamlet as the Dionysian man is to read Hamlet in a way that seems to conclude the book at the point in which Claudius is on his knees confessing his sins in act 3, scene 3 and Hamlet merely contemplates murdering him but does not follow through on his thirst for blood: "Now might I do it pat, now 'a is a-praying, / And now I'll do't. And so 'a goes to heaven, / And so am I revenged. That would be scanned. / A villain kills my father, and for that / I, his sole son, do this same villain send / To heaven."[24] At the highest peak of madness, Hamlet does not want to murder Claudius while he prays because he believes there is a chance that Claudius may go to heaven, and so he resigns himself—which is a strong indication that Hamlet still has a sense of culpability and measure. Nietzsche's spiritual diagnosis of the descent of Hamlet's soul to the blackened depth of madness cannot fully account for Hamlet's total transformation—the precise moment when the Dionysian and Apollonian aspects of the self fuse together in cadenced synchronization. Even though Hamlet's soul, to a great extent, responds to the dithyrambic song of the Dionysus, to the contrary, the concept of measure that lingers as a result of his meditation curbs his vengeful appetite.

Truly Hamlet is divided against himself—his worst enemy is not Claudius but his own unruliness and confusions. In this way, we may engage in discussing the dual nature of Hamlet; on the one hand, there is Hamlet's musical lyricism, which is duly articulated through Nietzsche's artful description of the Dionysian man whose madness ultimately leads to his salvation in art as transformative happening within the soul (though Nietzsche argues Hamlet falls short of wholly possessing this part of himself and, as a consequence, is unable to create or produce art as action due to his melancholic state). On the other hand, we may also speak of Hamlet as Apollonian, though lacking in the necessary maturity to be able to clearly articulate and digest his situation for a large majority of the play (perchance a mark of his youthful heart forced to suddenly mature), when he comes to terms with his madness and melancholia—in contemplation. Sadly, Nietzsche does not account or wish to completely acknowledge the divide in Hamlet's soul and therefore cannot account for the final transformation in Hamlet's spirit when he arrives home from his voyage to England, ready to declare himself as the Crowned King.

Hamlet's madness begins at the moment in which the ghost, in the "questionable shape" of his deceased father in "complete steel," appears to him.[25] However, prior to the ghost revealing itself to Hamlet, Hamlet anticipates the effect it will have on him, "My father's spirit—in arms? All is not well. / I doubt some foul play. Would the night were come! / Till then sit still, my soul. Foul deeds will rise, / Though all the earth o'erwhlm them, to men's eyes."[26] Hamlet's loyal companions, Marcellus, Francisco, Bernardo, and Horatio, are already acquainted with the dark truth of the night behind the former king's death in act 1, scene 1, which "bodes some strange eruption to [their] state" as Horatio describes it and also makes them "sick at heart" because they know how accepting this truth will be unsettling for Hamlet and they are genuinely concerned for their friend and their country.[27] Given the unsettling nature of the souls of Hamlet's companions, Horatio knows full well how Hamlet will respond, especially considering his current state of melancholy. Before Hamlet's soul is jolted by the ghost, he is unable to form cohesive thoughts or move to action because he is frozen by the "trappings and suits of woe," which are direly mistaken by Gertrude and Claudius as symptoms of madness.[28] Claudius has the gall to tell Hamlet not to take his father's death "to heart" and that mourning his death is to show "unmanly grief."[29] Hamlet explains to both Gertrude and Claudius, however, that the "cloud [that] still hang[s] on [him]" is "common" for someone who has just experienced a profound loss; but moreover, and rather boldly, Hamlet tells them that he is "not alone in his inky cloak."[30] Though melancholy can turn into madness, that is not the case with Hamlet.[31] The ghost penetrates his soul, churning its sluggish, weary state by revealing to Hamlet the terrible truth of his father's "foul, strange, and unnatural murder" and his mother's infidelity—seducing Claudius, whom she "won to his shameful lust."[32] Knowing the impact the truth will have on Hamlet, the ghost provides positive momentum in sound advice:

> If thou hast nature in thee, bear it not.
> Let not the royal bed of Denmark be
> A couch for luxury and damnèd incest.
> But howsomever thou pursues this act,
> Taint not thy mind, nor let thy soul contrive

Against thy mother aught. Leave her to heaven
And to those thorns that in her bosom lodge
To prick and sting her.[33]

The ghost perceives Hamlet as more than "apt" in his ability to accept this thorny truth.[34] In this gruesome momentary experience of lucidity, even in his current state of disorder, he reminds himself to "remember" this moment, "Remember me" the ghost tells Hamlet; an "eruption" to the soul such as this cannot be forgotten, otherwise all momentum and attempts at restoring order will be lost:

Ay, thou poor ghost, whiles memory holds a seat
In this distracted globe. Remember thee?
Yea, from the table of my memory
I'll wipe away all trivial fond records,
All saws of books, all forms all pressures past
That youth and observation copied there,
And thy commandment all alone shall live
Within the book and volume of my brain,
Unmixed with baser matter. Yes, by heaven![35]

The "honest ghost" as Hamlet decides to call him, stirs Hamlet's soul to examine itself. The "eruption" is sudden, "nimble" in Montaigne's words, "sickening" Hamlet's heart; he abandons his rationality to blind vengeance with the same potency of love he has for his father and the sadness in mourning the loss of him. Hamlet cannot keep up with the pace at which life is unfolding.[36] Still "There needs no ghost, my lord," says Horatio, "come from the grave / To tell us this"—what is the ghost but nothing more than Hamlet's soul coming to terms with the truth? The ghost cannot be a physical appearance of his father's death because that would contradict Hamlet's philosophy on dying as "The undiscovered country, from whose bourn / No traveler returns, [that] puzzles the will, / And makes us rather bear those ills we have" is a truth, an elephant in the room, so to speak; a truth that his companions have already accepted and are patiently waiting for Hamlet to "see" for himself, "In [his] mind's eye."[37] The ghost is representing the terrifying essence of truth. Horatio and the others take it to be their "duty" to let Hamlet "know of it," but once the truth is revealed, they band "together" to "swear" their secrecy and also loyalty to their fellowship while Hamlet restores order to his soul so time no longer feels "out of joint."[38]

The Importance of Friendship and Solidarity for Proper Livelihood

The initial feeling of doubt that Hamlet experiences surrounding the "eruption" in his soul caused by the ghost is an insecurity about the commanding nature of his rational faculties.[39] If Hamlet can abandon his conscience entirely, his feelings alone can justify murdering Claudius out of pure revenge, "Making night hideous" and Hamlet a "fool" of nature in satisfying his immediate need for justice: "Now could I drink hot blood / And do such bitter business as the day / Would quake to look on."[40] Nonetheless, Hamlet also tells his heart to "lose not thy nature; let not ever / The soul of Nero enter this firm bosom. / Let me be cruel, not unnatural," revealing the extent of the fight between his mind and soul for sole driving force; his mind still has some power over his passions. If Hamlet gives in to his desire for revenge, he knows that his interpretation of the ghost would be a "devil" because "Out of [his] weakness and [his] melancholy" he would be "damn[ing] himself."[41] Hamlet's conscience knows that he needs to "have grounds / More relative than" selfish revenge.

Before Hamlet's departure out to sea, the reader will note that only when he is without Horatio by his side do his passions overtake his mind. This is because Horatio represents, and as his "wounded name" symbolizes, "Roman" rationality—and in keeping with Nietzsche's distinction between the Dionysian and Apollonian, the wisdom of Apollo.[42] Horatio balances Hamlet's extremities with his calming presence and reliable counsel. "Think" and "Be ruled," Horatio advises Hamlet, because "while men's minds are wild, lest more mischance / On plots and errors happen," though Hamlet responds to him, "There are more things in heaven and earth, Horatio, / Than are dreamt of in your philosophy."[43] The constant back-and-forth play between Hamlet and Horatio, betwixt their souls and minds, the interplay and mingling of passions and governance, balances out each other in physical approximation throughout the play—a friendship Nietzsche would rightfully acknowledge as *agonic*—as both men push the other to continually strive for self-betterment. As a good companion, Horatio sees it as his "duty" to "acquaint" Hamlet further with the ghost as needful to Hamlet's spiritual health but also worries that the ghost "might deprive [Hamlet of his] sovereignty of reason" and "draw [him] into madness."[44] Marcellus also tells Hamlet to "Look with courteous action" because the ghost "waves [him] to a more removèd ground."[45] Neither Horatio nor Marcellus wants Hamlet to "go with" the ghost because they foreshadow that if Hamlet submits himself to the ghost completely, in his melancholy, he may be "tempt[ed] toward the flood" or "the dreadful summit of the cliff," self-annihilation.[46] Shakespeare understands the importance of friendship for proper livelihood, but also as a structure that can withstand the injustices and cruelties of the world—in solidarity with others, but also in understanding the full implications of needing solidarity, for no experience is entirely unique to man.[47] In his most fragile state, in the few seconds before Hamlet's "fate cries out" and he is "called" by the ghost, his companions do not let him face it alone. "Nay, let's follow him," suggests Marcellus. A spiritual "readiness," a renaissance of the lamenting spirit, is what Hamlet chooses as an alternative to the limitations set by reason alone. Neither following reason alone nor our soul alone leads to impotence or bestiality. Hamlet must embrace reason as manifested by Horatio, but he must also sort through his passions under the influence of reason in order to overcome his madness and turn it into an absolute affirmation of right action, for indeed, "There are more things in heaven and earth" than Horatio's "philosophy" can account for.[48] Reason alone cannot be the sole arbitrator for decision making for Hamlet; his powerful rejection is a result of his Dionysian spirit—the "Dane" in him that he does not become fully cognizant of until his head is almost "struck off."[49]

Death, Dying, and the Making of a "Noble Heart"

Hamlet confesses to Horatio that before going out to sea "in [his] heart [there] was a kind of fighting / That would not let [him] sleep. [He thought he] lay / Worse than the mutinies in the bilboes."[50] While Hamlet is at sea, however, he is presented with an opportunity to intercept the letter, which commissioned a "royal knavery!—an exact command, / Larded with many several sorts of reasons / Importing Denmark's health, and England's too"; his "fears forgetting manners," he unsealed it, and wrote in its place:

> An earnest conjuration from the King,
> As England was his faithful tributary,
> As love between them like the palm might flourish,
> As peace should still her wheaten garland wear
> And stand a comma 'tween their amities,
> And many sucklike as's of great charge,
> That on the view on the knowing of these contents,
> Without debatement further more or less,
> He should those bearers put to sudden death,
> Not shriving time allowed.[51]

By "heaven['s] ordinant" Hamlet was able to seal the letter with his "father's signet," which he was carrying in his "purse," further, the "changeling was never known."[52] The next day, as Hamlet retells his encounter with death to Horatio, was the "sea fight" that Hamlet survives.[53] Does Hamlet's close encounter with death at sea force him to truly self-examine the "do or die"? Does a particular kind of clarity come when one is faced with death? Clearly Hamlet reestablishes his priorities; as the rightful King of Denmark, he puts the livelihood of his people before his own need for justice.

There is another possibility for interpreting Hamlet's transformation at sea; Shakespeare's use of the sea as creating contemplative distance between Hamlet and the ensuing anarchy of Denmark is also an image that can be applied as a metaphor to articulate Hamlet's inner struggles—for what is the sea but unruly itself? What calms the sea in the midst of a storm? As things are happening with such brute quickness around Hamlet, his soul is dizzy and ill-prepared, leaving him to drown in muddied water. As distance provides perspective for Hamlet, and an opportunity to set things right, he is able to calm his "peturbèd spirit" naturally and reach the required clarity to transform, allowing him to create a new order within himself, restoring reason to its lawful place.[54]

In either reading, the crucial point is that Hamlet restores reason. The "readiness" Hamlet returns to Denmark with is the result of a more balanced relation between his mind and soul. Prudence is gained in understanding that the mind aids the soul in sorting through a multitude of intense emotions, while simultaneously the soul provides the mind with the strength it needs from intense passion. Even so, the spirit proves itself much more potent when it comes to Hamlet, hence his Dionysian drive; ultimately, though he restores reason to its proper place of governance, his spirit is what primarily drives his "readiness."

Hamlet returns from sea a transformed man; he undergoes a profound psycho-spiritual change that makes him wiser and calmer than before, ready to fight for what is rightfully his. Instead of spiting the way the world is, he now accepts it as something he cannot change, as a "divinity that shapes our ends," but holds to the idea that it is up to the individual to "hew [our ends] how we will."[55] As Horatio recognizes the change in Hamlet, he trusts his judgment; in the captivating dance of rhyme and reason, rhyme takes the lead and bravely leaps into destiny undaunted by what pains may strike the body. Horatio resides in the "core" of Hamlet's "heart of hearts," prepared to follow Hamlet anywhere, even to hell, if Hamlet were to ask it of him.

Lingering in the graveyard upon Hamlet's return, the truth Hamlet previously feared and the difficulties therein pass as he looks to death unafraid and willfully acknowledges what is at stake. His experience would be rendered inauthentic if he were not ready and willing to sacrifice himself for a greater good. In more colloquial terms, it can't all be about Hamlet. But if that is true, what is it all about then? According to Hamlet, what is the greatness of Alexander the Great when compared to his fond childhood memories of Yorick, a "fellow of infinite jest, of most excellent fancy" who had "borne [him] on his back a thousand times"?[56] What makes a human being excellent? What makes a man or woman noble of heart? If all men and women "returneth to dust; the dust is earth; of earth / we make loam," then the questions we ask about death and dying are only answered in how a life is lived.[57] The tragedy of Hamlet is that he dies precisely at the moment where he restores order to his country and countrymen—not being able to celebrate his just victory with his people is unquestionably a sad loss. But the tragic tone of the play hits its lowest note not in the legacy of nobility Hamlet leaves behind, because Horatio will speak on "How these [tragic] things came about," but because of the joy that remains unquenched because of a death that came too soon.[58] Surely "angels [sung Hamlet] to [his] rest" as Horatio laments the death of his dear friend, the true King of Denmark, "noble heart" and spirited "Dane," since this play of "woe and wonder" continues to capture the "common consciousness," as remarked by Allan Bloom, because it compels its readers to seriously glance into his or her own unsettling truth and experience a sense of solidarity with Hamlet.[59]

Conclusion

Nietzsche's instinct about the young Prince of Denmark creates an opus of interplay between Hamlet's unruly drives and Horatio's soundness of mind, unraveling the necessity of cultivating both aspects of the self, body talk aside. What makes *Hamlet* a particularly poignant read for the young or old political philosopher in this century is that if ever we want to engage in political practice honestly, whether running for office or voting in an upcoming election, we must be courageous enough to know our self first, before making a reasonably passionate declaration of any kind. In reading the tragic story of Hamlet, we come face-to-face with our own horrifying ghosts, but we also learn from the mistakes made by Hamlet and also from the things that he does right. Reading cultivates our judgment and gives birth to prudence. Because we are living in a time where "rushing the clock" is an all-too-familiar philosophy we seem bound to, breathlessness has become a sad mark of our culture. Contemplation provides perspective and an openness to discuss these things freely, uniting us in our experiences—our struggles, failures, victories, and in our madness—helping us to grow as individuals, and as individuals within a society that is boundless in its potential. Finally, as Shakespeare's *Hamlet* ends in the sudden death of a political philosopher par excellence with the noblest of hearts, we may shed worthy tears for him, but only hope that our fate is far less tragic.

Notes

1. An early version of this chapter was given at the annual McGill-CREOR (Center for Research on Religion) Graduate Students' Conference at McGill University in the fall of 2011. I am grateful to the participants for the opportunity to share my ideas and receive excellent constructive criticism, which has been taken into consideration here. In particular, I thank Dr. Torrance Kirby, founder of CREOR and a fellow appreciator of Shakespeare's philosophy. My gratitude goes to my friend Dr. Rouven J. Steeves and his melodic writings of Nietzsche, which continue to inspire me to write with unapologetic passion.

2. Friedrich Nietzsche, "The Birth of Tragedy," in *The Nietzsche Reader*, trans. Douglas Smith, ed. Keith Ansell Pearson and Duncan Large (Malden, MA: Blackwell Publishing, 2006), §7, 61.

3. Ibid.

4. William Shakespeare, *The Tragedy of Hamlet Prince of Denmark*, ed. Sylvan Barnet (Toronto: Penguin, 1998), 2.2, 40–60.

5. In employing Socrates's analogy of the horses and charioteers in the *Phaedrus* as an effective metaphor to describe the character of the soul, it further illuminates the difficulty in attempting to "take the reins" and discipline our passions, which makes it compatible with Nietzsche. For Plato, these passions are almost always dangerously erotic in nature. This analogy, however, is not to contradict Nietzsche's understanding of the various drives but to focus on the nature of them, their sharp movements, and the difficulty in ruling over them. For the reference to the *Phaedrus* see 246a–246b, also the *Republic* 434d–441c, and the *Timeas* 69cff. for the physiological basis for Plato's understanding of the soul as tripartite.

6. Shakespeare, *Hamlet*, 5.2.223–224, 137.

7. I invoke the phrase "breathlessly attempting to catch up" from two important sources. The first is Zdravko Planinc, "'It Begins with Pyrrhus' (2.2.451): The Political Philosophy of *Hamlet*," *Hamlet Studies* 20, 1/2 (Summer/Winter 1998): 35–49, 40, whereby Planinc brilliantly describes Hamlet's soul as "breathless" in his attempt to come to terms with the ugly truths that face him. The second source is from a series of lectures given at the University of Sudbury on *Hamlet* by Dr. Ron Srigley in 2007, who, like his former teacher Planinc, used "breathless" to articulate the youthfulness of Hamlet's soul for the majority of the play, but also to compare Hamlet's breathlessness with a spiritual maturity recognizant of coming of age. I am deeply indebted to both sources, whose interpretations are undeniably present throughout this chapter.

8. Shakespeare, *Hamlet*, 5.2.140–141, 134.

9. Colin McGinn, *Shakespeare's Philosophy* (Toronto: Harper Perennial, 2007), 32.

10. Ibid., 40–41.

11. Ibid., 41.

12. Planinc, "'It Begins with Pyrrhus' (2.2.451)," 35.

13. Ibid.

14. Ibid., 49, author's emphasis.

15. To no surprise, Planinc turns to Plato's understanding of "mania" to describe Hamlet's madness to avoid Freudian interpretations and to emphasize the character of the soul, and how various external factors can contribute to waking and jolting the spirit from basking in familiarity. See ibid., 41. Madness or mania, according to Planinc via Plato, is "fine," that is, "when it comes from divine dispensation," rather a "god-sent madness," which Planinc argues that Hamlet longs for in his soliloquies prior to his sea-change; Plato *Phaedrus*, trans. Robin Waterfield (New York: Oxford University Press, 2002), 244c, 26; 245b, 27.

16. Michel de Montaigne, *Michel de Montaigne: The Complete Essays*, trans. M. A. Screech (London: Penguin, 1991), 548, from McGinn, *Shakespeare's Philosophy*, 46.

17. Nietzsche, *The Birth of Tragedy*, §7, 61.

18. Shakespeare, *Hamlet*, 1.5.169–180, 34. For a more in-depth look at Nietzsche's "dithyrambic dramatist" see Friedrich Nietzsche, *Untimely Meditations*, trans. R. J. Hollingdale (New York: Cambridge University Press, 2007), §7, 223, 225–226, 231–232. The quote that in my opinion best expresses Hamlet as the dithyrambic dramatist is the following: "His art conducts him along this twofold path, from a world as an audible spectacle into a world as a visible spectacle enigmatically related to it, and the reverse; he is continually compelled—and the beholder is compelled with him—to translate visible movement back into soul and primordial life, and conversely to see the most deeply concealed inner activity as visible phenomenon and to clothe it with the appearance of a body. All this constitutes the essence of the dithyrambic dramatist, this concept extended to embrace at once the actor, port and composer: as it must be, since it is necessarily derived from the only perfect exemplar of the dithyrambic dramatist before Wagner, from Aeschylus and his fellow Greek artists," ibid., §7, 223. Transferring Nietzsche's quote to Hamlet, who also portrays the role of "actor, port and composer," further elucidates the transformative yet simultaneously artistic aspect of Hamlet's character.

19. Shakespeare, *Hamlet*, 2.2.15–18, 40.

20. Ibid., 2.25–27, 40; 3.1.191, 67.

21. Ibid., 3.3.25–26, 83.

22. Ibid., 1.1.44, 5.

23. Cf. Planinc, "'It Begins with Pyrrhus' (2.2.451)," 42–43.

24. Shakespeare, *Hamlet*, 3.3.73–77, 85.

25. Ibid., 1.4.43, 26; 1.1.52, 26.

26. Ibid., 1.3.225–228, 19; 1.1.8, 4.

27. Ibid., 1.1.69, 6.

28. Ibid., 1.2.869, 13.

29. Ibid., 1.2.101, 13; 1.2.94, 13.

30. Ibid., 1.2.66, 12; 1.2.74, 13; 1.2.77, 13.

31. A. C. Bradley in "From Shakespearean Tragedy" argues that melancholy is an immobile state for Hamlet. Bradley says that Hamlet's "melancholy is something very different from insanity, in anything like the usual meaning of that word. No doubt it might develop into insanity. The longing for death might become an irresistible impulse to self-destruction; the disorder of feeling and will might extend to sense and intellect;

delusions might arise; and the man might become, as we say, incapable and irresponsible" in *Hamlet*, 189–190. Bradley retains the notion that the character of Hamlet is melancholy and not truly mad at all (aside from feigning madness); nonetheless Bradley's insight about the difference between the state of madness and melancholy is to be noted.

32. Shakespeare, *Hamlet*, 1.5.28, 29; 1.5.45, 29.

33. Ibid., 1.5.81–88, 30–31.

34. Ibid., 1.5.32, 29.

35. Ibid., 1.5.96–104, 31.

36. Ibid., 1.1.7–8.

37. Ibid., 3.1.79–81, 64; 1.2.185, 16.

38. Ibid.; 1.2.220, 17; 1.5.190, 33; 1.5.181, 34; 1.5.188, 34.

39. See Planinc, "'It Begins with Pyrrhus' (2.2.451)," 43.

40. Shakespeare, *Hamlet*, 1.439–441; 3.3.398–399, 82.

41. Ibid., 2.2.611, 60; 2.2.613, 60; 2.2.615, 60.

42. Ibid., 5.2.345, 142; 5.2.343, 142, also see Planinc, "'It Begins with Pyrrhus' (2.2.451)," 42.

43. Shakespeare, *Hamlet*, 1.4.74, 27; 1.4.81, 27; 5.2.395–396, 144; 1.5.166–167, 34.

44. Ibid., 1.4.73–74, 27.

45. Ibid., 1.4.60–61, 27; 1.4.61, 27.

46. Ibid., 1.4.69–70, 26.

47. For an excellent discussion of friendship in Shakespeare's writings, see Allan Bloom, *Shakespeare: On Love and Friendship* (Chicago: University of Chicago Press, 2000). Bloom also has an exceptional book on Shakespeare's political thought whereby he analyzes a number of plays emphasizing the brilliance behind Shakespeare's political philosophy as it relates to common moral problems. See Allan Bloom and Harry V. Jaffa, *Shakespeare's Politics* (Chicago: University of Chicago Press, 1981).

48. Shakespeare, *Hamlet*, 1.5.166, 34.

49. Ibid., 5.2.342, 142; 5.2.24, 131.

50. Ibid., 5.2.4–6, 130.

51. Ibid., 5.2.38–47, 131.

52. Ibid., 5.2.48, 131; 5.2.49, 131.

53. Ibid., 5.2.54, 131.

54. Ibid., 1.5.182, 34.

55. Ibid., 5.2.10, 130; 5.2.11, 130.

56. Ibid., 5.1.186–187, 125.

57. Ibid., 5.1.211–213, 126.

58. Ibid., 5.2.381, 143.

59. Shakespeare, *Hamlet*, 5.2.361, 143; 5.2.360, 143; 5.1.259, 128; Allan Bloom, *Shakespeare: On Love and Friendship*, 2.

Chapter 4

Antony and Cleopatra

Empire, Globalization, and the Clash of Civilizations

Paul A. Cantor

And we are here as on a darkling plain
Swept with confused alarms of struggle and flight,
Where ignorant armies clash by night.
> —Matthew Arnold, "Dover Beach"

Ben Jonson's famous tribute to William Shakespeare—"He was not of an age, but for all time"—has often been taken as a measure of his greatness.[1] Generation after generation has kept coming back to his plays as a font of wisdom. Shakespeare has been praised for the universality of his genius—the fact that even after four centuries his insights remain relevant to our world. But is it really true that Shakespeare has something to say about our problems today? Are there some issues that are uniquely modern, which Shakespeare, as an Elizabethan playwright, could not possibly have comprehended or even been aware of?

Take, for example, the issue of globalization, arguably the central concern of the contemporary world. Many contend that globalization, especially the clash of civilizations it generates, is a phenomenon unique to the late twentieth and early twenty-first centuries. Samuel P. Huntington, for example, writes, "In the post–Cold War world, for the first time in history, global politics has become multipolar *and* multicivilizational. During most of human existence, contacts between civilizations were intermittent or nonexistent."[2] Modern technological advances, above all in high-speed communication and transportation, are often said to explain why the globalization of the modern world constitutes an entirely new and unprecedented development. With no knowledge of jet aircraft or the Internet, how could Shakespeare have anything to tell us about globalization?

But perhaps the globalization of the contemporary world is not entirely without precedent. Globalization in the twentieth century developed out of the great era of European imperialist expansion in the nineteenth century. Indeed, many have viewed some aspects of globalization as a form of neocolonialism. If the concept of empire is intertwined with the concept of globalization, then there is at least one historical precedent for the integration of the modern world—the Roman Empire. In its self-understanding, the Roman Empire was a globalizing force. It sought to create one world out of the vast territory Roman armies had conquered over the centuries. Modern geographers would be quick to point out that even at the peak of its expansion, the Roman Empire never came close to encompassing the whole of the Earth. But of course the Romans themselves were aware of this fact. They knew that they traded—and sometimes warred—with people outside the borders of their empire. Nevertheless, in very important ways the Romans chose to regard the Roman world as *the* world simply, and worked to integrate it into a whole in a manner that is very similar to what we now call globalization. For example, in their massive road-building projects, the Romans understood full well the central importance of rapid transportation in creating an integrated world. Above all, in putting together their empire, the Romans created exactly the situation of clashing civilizations that Huntington regards as unique to the contemporary world. Under Roman rule, the Mediterranean world offers fascinating case studies of what happens when widely divergent civilizations come into contact, interact, and transform each other, often in unpredictable and surprising ways.

When people speak of globalization today, they often have in mind the Americanization of the globe, the relentless expansion of American economic and cultural power and influence. For many, the chief form globalization takes is the spread of McDonald's, Coca-Cola, KFC, and other American brands and franchises all around the world. The corresponding phenomenon in antiquity was the Romanization of the Mediterranean world.[3] People from the Iberian peninsula to the Middle East suddenly found themselves confronted by the strange spectacle of Roman temples, statues, aqueducts, and amphitheaters springing up in their midst. But globalization is not now, and was not then, a one-way street.[4] Even as the globe today is being Americanized, America is being globalized. Its identity is being profoundly transformed by its encounter with alien civilizations, as witness significant changes in its eating habits, clothing fashions, musical taste, and even its religious beliefs, as well as other cultural phenomena subject to foreign influences. Ancient Rome was also profoundly changed by its encounter with alien civilizations and its attempt to bring them within its cultural orbit. The presence of Cestius's pyramid to this day in downtown Rome is a monument to the way Rome was Egyptianized, even as it was Romanizing Egypt.[5] The complex intermixture and fusion of cultural forms that the Roman Empire generated is the principal reason why it provides a precedent for contemporary globalization.

From this perspective, Shakespeare did have access to the kind of phenomena we label "globalization" because he was a deep student of Roman history and politics. His interest in Rome is evident throughout his career, from his earliest to his last plays, and can be found even in his poetry (*The Rape of Lucrece*, for example). Shakespeare's Roman plays trace the development of Rome from a republic to an empire, culminating in *Antony and Cleopatra* as his portrait of the nascent imperial regime.[6] The play explores the connections between empire and what we call globalization. It shows that the desire for empire is a drive toward universality, an urge to demolish existing borders and create one world. In Shakespeare's portrayal, the Roman Empire aspires to become "the universal landlord" (3.13.72).[7] The play contains many references to Rome's efforts to defeat the last of its viable enemies on its eastern frontier, the Parthians (see, for example, act 3, scene 1). Once its borders are secure, Rome can go about the task of imposing its rule on the whole Mediterranean world. That is why Octavius Caesar speaks optimistically about the emergence of what came to be known as the *Pax Romana*:

> The time of universal peace is near.
> Prove this a prosp'rous day, the three-nook'd world
> Shall bear the olive freely. (4.6.4–6)

Uniting three continents in peace—Europe, Asia, and Africa—Rome will create a universal community, a unified world.

Roman rhetoric in *Antony and Cleopatra* is emphatically "global." Shakespeare's Romans refer to themselves and to each other in terms that call to mind one world united under their rule. The triumvirs are presented as dividing the whole world among themselves. Antony is called "the triple pillar of the world" (1.1.12); he regards himself as "the greatest prince o' th' world" (4.15.54). Lepidus is referred to as "the third part of the world" (2.7.92). Antony says to Octavius, "The third part o' th' world is yours" (2.2.63). Pompey speaks of the triumvirs as "the senators alone of this great world" (2.6.9), and Menas calls them "these three world-sharers" (2.7.70). Once Octavius triumphs over both Lepidus and Antony, he becomes "sole sir o' th' world" (5.2.120). The Romans are acutely conscious that they are performing on a world stage, that their actions have global consequences, and the whole world is watching what they do. Proclaiming the grandeur of his love with Cleopatra, Antony wants "the world to weet / We stand up peerless" (1.1.39–40). Octavius knows that people throughout the empire will pass judgment on how he treats Cleopatra. Speaking through a subordinate (Proculeius), he calls upon her to act accordingly: "let the world see / His nobleness well acted" (5.2.44–45). Time and again in *Antony and Cleopatra* words and deeds make it clear that what is at stake in the play is nothing less than the fate of the world as a whole.

When the pirate Menas offers to kill the triumvirs for Pompey, his speech is saturated with language that points to the fact that Rome has brought all the world under one yoke:

> *Menas:* Wilt thou be lord of all the world?
> *Pompey:*   What say'st thou?
> *Menas:* Wilt thou be lord of the whole world? That's twice.
> *Pompey:* How should that be?
> *Menas:*   But entertain it,
> And though thou think me poor, I am the man
> Will give thee all the world.
> *Pompey:*   Hast thou drunk well?
> *Menas:* No, Pompey, I have kept me from the cup.
> Thou art, if thou dar'st be, the earthly Jove;
> Whate'er the ocean pales, or sky inclips,
> Is thine, if thou wilt ha't. (2.7.61–69)

Menas understands that in the new era of imperial politics, a truly ambitious man must aim at global hegemony. Having triumphed militarily over all rival regimes, Rome seems poised to impose its way of life on the entire Mediterranean world. With everyone acknowledging the authority of Rome, the Romanization of Egypt seems to be the order of the day. When Cleopatra thinks of committing suicide in the wake of Antony's death, she claims to be following a Roman model: "Let's do't after the high Roman fashion" (4.15.87). More generally,

Roman religion has evidently begun to permeate Egyptian society at all levels, from the lowest to the highest. The Egyptian eunuch Mardian talks of "what Venus did with Mars" (1.5.18), while Cleopatra's speech is filled with references to Roman deities:

> Though he be painted one way like a Gorgon,
> The other way's a Mars. (2.5.116–117)

> Had I great Juno's power,
> The strong-wing'd Mercury should fetch thee up
> And set thee by Jove's side. (4.15.34–36)

This is exactly what one would expect to see in a *Roman* empire. The Roman gods begin to take the place of local deities, even in a land as old as Egypt, whose religious traditions antedate those of Rome by centuries.

But Shakespeare seems more interested in the Egyptianizing of Rome than in the Romanizing of Egypt.[8] Rome has conquered Egypt militarily, but Egypt seems to be conquering Rome culturally.[9] In postcolonial studies today, this process is often cleverly labeled "The Empire Strikes Back," as conquered people pursue subtle strategies of raising doubts about and even subverting the way of life of their ostensible masters.[10] In *Antony and Cleopatra* the Romans are inordinately fascinated by the exotic world of Egypt.[11] They want to hear about its strange customs and listen avidly to tales of its pyramids and crocodiles (2.7). Above all, they are entranced by stories of the fabulous Cleopatra, Antony's "Egyptian dish" (2.6.126). Rumors of her erotic conquests arouse their senses; she threatens to overturn their hierarchy of values:

> Other women cloy
> The appetites they feed, but she makes hungry
> Where most she satisfies; for vildest things
> Become themselves in her, that the holy priests
> Bless her when she is riggish. (2.2.235–239)

The breakdown in Roman discipline is evident in their excessive interest in "Egyptian cookery" (2.6.63). A new Roman tendency toward indulgence in food and drink has been inspired by Egyptian models. When the triumvirs banquet with Pompey, their celebration "ripens towards" an "Alexandrian feast" (2.7.96–97). At this feast, the formerly restrained Romans end up abandoning their moderation and dancing "the Egyptian bacchanals" (2.7.104).[12] Even the normally sober and temperate Octavius admits that he grows drunk

(2.7.125–126). The Egyptians have begun to talk of Roman deities, but the Romans have undergone a more fundamental transformation: they have begun to behave like Egyptians. Their firm Roman identity is shaken as they become increasingly open to foreign influences. After centuries of martial discipline under the republican regime—the very source of Rome's ability to triumph over its enemies—imperial Rome becomes decadent, partially as a result of encountering the luxury and idleness of the Egyptian way of life. Rome's success in militarily defeating its enemies allows the Romans to relax and rest on their laurels. In the process, they grow soft and self-indulgent, and become the mirror image of the decadent people they conquered. Shakespeare's Rome illustrates a general principle about empire—the country that dominates the world is often altered just as much in the process as the world it tries to dominate.

In *Julius Caesar*, Shakespeare portrays Rome breaking with its long-standing republican traditions and moving toward one-man rule. *Antony and Cleopatra* portrays the working-out of this imperial logic, and Rome's encounter with Egypt, with its centuries of imperial rule behind it, accelerates the corruption of traditional Roman institutions. Octavius professes shock at the way Antony blatantly adopts decadent Egyptian customs in his public behavior with Cleopatra:

> I' th' market-place, on a tribunal silver'd,
> Cleopatra and himself in chains of gold
> Were publicly enthron'd. At their feet sat
> Caesarion, whom they call my father's son,
> And all the unlawful issue that their lust
> Since then hath made between them. Unto her
> He gave the stablishment of Egypt, made her
> Of lower Syria, Cyprus, Lydia,
> Absolute queen....
> His sons he there proclaim'd the kings of kings:
> Great Media, Parthia, and Armenia
> He gave to Alexander; to Ptolemy he assign'd
> Syria, Cilicia, and Phoenicia. She
> In th' abiliments of the goddess Isis
> That day appear'd. (3.6.3–11, 13–18)

When Maecenas chimes in "Let Rome be thus / Inform'd" (3.6.18–19), he shows that he is aware of how un-Roman Antony's imperious behavior must seem to anyone steeped in the city's republican traditions.

In *Julius Caesar*, Antony had seen how reluctant his master Julius Caesar was to adopt the ways of a king in public in Rome (precisely what is at issue when

ANTONY AND CLEOPATRA 71

Antony offers him a crown in act 1, scene 2). Ever the shrewd politician, Caesar knew that the very name of king was anathema in republican Rome. But now in Egypt, Antony embraces kingly grandeur, openly proclaiming his sons "kings of kings" and displaying an unseemly (and un-Roman) interest in founding a dynasty. In the republic, he was the leader of a citizen-army, and at least professed to treat the Roman populace as active participants in the regime. Now Antony elevates himself above the common people, treating them as passive subjects who must bow down and worship him. He assumes the role not just of a king, but of a god-king, accompanied by Cleopatra in the guise of Isis (an Egyptian goddess, not a Roman one). All the silver and gold are characteristic of oriental luxury and ostentation, the antithesis of the simplicity and moderation characteristic of republican Rome. Although nominally the conqueror of Egypt, Antony has gone over to the Egyptian side. More generally, in the clash of Roman and Egyptian civilization he has surrendered to the exotic East. In addition to pharaonic models of oriental despotism, the names of "Alexander" and "Ptolemy" call to mind the Hellenistic god-kings who came to power in the wake of Alexander the Great and his imperial conquests.[13] Octavius sees the propaganda value of making Antony's un-Roman actions known to the Roman public. And yet these actions are un-Roman only by the standards of the now defunct republic. They are perfectly suited to the new imperial regime. Ironically, Octavius condemns in Antony a public pose that he was soon going to adopt himself. As the first established emperor in Rome, Octavius as Augustus Caesar went on to become a god-king himself and founded his own dynasty.[14] Representations of Augustus as a god sprung up throughout the empire.

Images of oriental despotism are basic to a broader pattern in *Antony and Cleopatra*, its evocation of stereotypes of the East. Discussions of contemporary globalization and the clash of civilizations are often cast in terms of East versus West, and a frequently debated question is, after centuries of the West dominating the East and the rest of the world, will the positions be reversed, and the East—such nations as China, Japan, and India—come to dominate a globalized world? *Antony and Cleopatra* portrays a world strongly polarized in terms of East versus West, with Egypt representing the former and Rome the latter. The sense of Egypt as the exotic East is emphasized in the play. Of Cleopatra, Alexas reports that Antony says, "All the East, / . . . shall call her mistress" (1.5.46–47). Thinking of Egypt and Cleopatra, Antony says, "I' th' East my pleasure lies" (2.3.41), and later he reiterates the point: "The beds i' th' East are soft" (2.6.50). And as Cleopatra is dying, her maid Charmian thinks of her as the "eastern star" (5.2.308). With all this talk of the East as an exotic, sensuous realm, presided over by the female Cleopatra, *Antony and Cleopatra* provides a classic example of what is known as orientalism.[15] The play constructs its world in terms of a whole series of binary oppositions that define the West (Rome) by contrast with the East (Egypt).[16] The West is presented as rational, disciplined, active, busy, emotionally restrained, moderate, and masculine, while the East is presented as irrational, undisciplined, passive, idle, emotionally self-indulgent, luxurious, and feminine. Cleopatra's court is a textbook example of an orientalist fantasy, complete with the eunuchs who help to stamp the Orient as effeminate. Her wild swings of mood and violent outbursts of anger—her inability to control her emotions—identify her as the archetype of the oriental despot. In terms of another stereotype, she is also the oriental seductress, who tempts the European hero away from his Western way of life, subverting his allegiance to his homeland and introducing Antony to exotic customs and decadent pleasures that unfit him for command of his armies and himself.[17]

Orientalism is usually thought of as presenting the West as simply superior to the East, but Shakespeare complicates the picture in *Antony and Cleopatra* by blurring the lines between East and West, specifically by portraying a heavily orientalized Rome. As we have seen, in the clash of civilizations the Rome of *Antony and Cleopatra* has succumbed to Egyptian influence and adopted many elements of the Egyptian way of life. Indeed, the Rome that traditionally represents the West seems to be largely a thing of the past in *Antony and Cleopatra*, the Rome of the recently vanquished republic. Antony provides the best measure of how far the orientalization of the Rome of *Antony and Cleopatra* has proceeded. When Octavius speaks of Antony's military discipline—his traditional Roman ability to endure long marches without ordinary nourishment—he is referring to Antony's power in the past, in the waning days of the republic, when there were still republican consuls to fight (1.4.55–71). As for the present moment in Roman history, as is evident in Antony's appearance with Cleopatra in Alexandria, he has become an oriental despot himself, indulging in the pleasures of the flesh and presiding over a lavish and decadent court.

Above all, in terms of the imagery of the play, Antony has become feminized and thus gone over to the other side in the West-East polarity.[18] This transformation in Antony is emphasized throughout the play, from its very opening lines (1.1.1–10). He is always threatening to change places with Cleopatra, as she becomes the more masculine of the two. She makes the point herself:

> Ere the ninth hour, I drank him to his bed;
> There put my tires and mantles on him, whilst
> I wore his sword Philippan. (2.5.21–23)

The blunt soldier Enobarbus dwells upon the effeminization of Antony under Cleopatra's influence; he tells her,

'tis said in Rome
That Photinus an eunuch and your maids
Manage this war. (3.7.13–15)

Octavius says of Antony that he

is not more manlike
Than Cleopatra; nor the queen of Ptolemy
More womanly than he. (1.4.5–7)

The spectacle of Antony subordinated to Cleopatra—"the triple pillar of the world transform'd / Into a strumpet's fool" (1.1.12–13)—epitomizes the weakness of Rome's military strength when faced with exotic Egyptian culture and its "infinite variety" (2.2.235). Shakespeare portrays the Roman imperial regime as ultimately hollow. Spiritually empty and having lost its former strong sense of purpose, Rome becomes prey to all sorts of foreign influences, such as soothsayers and other purveyors of mysteries and mystifications who make the claim, "In Nature's infinite book of secrecy / A little I can read" (1.2.9–10).

The Rome of the republic, especially as Shakespeare portrays its early days in *Coriolanus,* is a self-contained and decidedly finite world, one of fixed horizons with the city narrowly focused on its military affairs. The newly globalized world of *Antony and Cleopatra* has much broader horizons, bordering on the infinite. The opening up of horizons is the keynote of the play, voiced by Antony and Cleopatra in their first exchange:

Cleopatra: If it be love indeed, tell me how much.
Antony: There's beggary in the love that can be reckon'd.
Cleopatra: I'll set a bourn how far to be belov'd.
Antony: Then must thou needs find out new heaven, new earth.
(1.1.13–18)

Antony's contempt for the bounded and the finite, the local and the particular, is characteristic of the empire. This pattern becomes typical of Antony and Cleopatra and the new world they live in and preside over. Any boundary is established only to be crossed; any limit is set only to be transcended. That is the fundamental principle of life in an empire that aspires to universality. It is also the principle of globalization and its aspiration for a borderless world. In their drive to go beyond all boundaries, Antony and Cleopatra become in effect the patron saints of both empire and globalization.

The imperial urge to universality is especially evident in the realm of religion in *Antony and Cleopatra*. The old pagan religions, specific to particular countries such as Rome or Egypt with their local deities, seem inadequate in the new imperial order. Characters repeatedly feel compelled to call on "all the gods" (1.3.99), not just one particular deity. Scarus appeals to "Gods and goddesses, / All the whole synod of them!" (3.10.4–5). As one of the rulers of the imperial world, Antony, as we have seen, tries to play the role of a god—perhaps a new universal form of divinity. His servant Eros sees in Antony's "noble countenance" "the worship of the whole world" (4.14.85–86). After Antony's death, Cleopatra's dream of him seems like an attempt to conjure up a universal deity suitable to the global dimensions of the new Roman Empire and its increasingly cosmopolitan culture. Cleopatra's Antony is more like a cosmic god than the city gods of the old pagan religions:

> His face was as the heav'ns, and therein stuck
> A sun and moon, which kept their courses and lighted
> The little o' th' earth....[19]
> His legs bestrid the ocean: his rear'd arm
> Crested the world. (5.2.79–81, 83–84)

Here finally is an image of divinity appropriate to a global empire; as J. L. Simmons writes, "Bestriding the ocean, Antony unites Egypt and Rome into one world."[20] In the Roman Empire only a trans-Mediterranean god is adequate to the religious needs of people who have developed new universal concerns.

Everywhere one looks in *Antony and Cleopatra*, the characters are seeking to break out of the narrow limits of the local and the particular. Cleopatra says of her love with Antony, "Eternity was in our lips and eyes" (1.3.35), and as she contemplates her death—in pagan terms the ultimate instance of human finitude—she refuses to accept it as a limit and insists upon her "immortal longings" (5.2.281). Several references to Herod of Jewry in the play (1.2.28, 3.3.3–4, 3.6.73, 4.6.13), together with other Biblical allusions, suggest that Shakespeare was very much aware that the events he portrayed in the early days of the Roman Empire were roughly contemporaneous with the birth of Christianity—a transpolitical religion that ultimately aspires to universality.[21] The orientalizing of the Roman Empire culminated in its being Christianized. If one seeks an illustration of the law of unintended consequences at work in empire and globalization, one could find no better example than the way Rome's imperialist incursions into the East ultimately resulted in the transformation of this pagan community into the center of worldwide Christianity.

Obviously, *Antony and Cleopatra* does not portray all the facets of what we think of as globalization today. Shakespeare does not show Antony and Cleopatra gazing upon each other in loving adoration via Skype. But Shakespeare does draw upon all his skills as a dramatist to suggest the global dimensions of the new imperial world taking shape in the play. He took advantage of the fluidity of Elizabethan staging; given the absence of scenery, he is able to change scenes effortlessly to suggest how swiftly things move in the world of *Antony and Cleopatra* and what vast distances can be covered in the blink of an eye. In the divisions editors make in modern texts, the play contains an exceptional number of scenes (thirteen in act 3 and fifteen in act 4 alone), as it moves over much of the Mediterranean world with sometimes dizzying speed. The characters themselves remark on how quickly things happen; armies turn up before they are expected, and news of their movements arrives even faster. As the crucial battle of Actium develops, Antony is shocked by the speed with which Octavius's forces move:

> Is it not strange, Canidius,
> That from Tarentum and Brundusium
> He could so quickly cut the Ionian Sea
> And take in Toryne? (3.7.20–23)

When a messenger arrives with more military bad news, Antony marvels at Octavius's mobility: "Can he be there in person? 'Tis impossible" (3.7.56). We may think of Roman means of transportation as slow, but Shakespeare's Antony is already voicing the typical response to globalizing forces today: "This speed of Caesar's / Carries beyond belief" (3.7.74–75).

Given the size of the Roman Empire portrayed in *Antony and Cleopatra*, communication between its widely dispersed seats of power is remarkably easy and dependable. The Mediterranean world of the play is crisscrossed by apparently tireless messengers. Indeed, "mail delivery" in the Roman Empire seems more frequent than it is today in the United States. Octavius receives messages many times a day from the imperial frontiers:

> Thy biddings have been done, and every hour
> Most noble Caesar, shalt thou have report
> How 'tis abroad. (1.4.34–36)

Cleopatra is just as determined to stay in daily communication with Antony:

> Get me ink and paper.
> He shall have every day a several greeting,
> Or I'll unpeople Egypt. (1.5.76–78)

The imperial messenger service may not be quite as fast as the Internet, but it evidently gets the job done. Rome is technologically primitive by comparison with the contemporary world, but Shakespeare shows it already aspiring to a kind of global integration via rapid transportation and communication.

As different as the Roman Empire is from the modern world, we might draw many lessons from *Antony and Cleopatra* that apply to contemporary globalization, but one stands out. The experience of the Roman Empire suggests that military power does not simply translate into cultural power, and that the ostensible winner in the contest to dominate the world may end up being the loser in the resulting clash of civilizations.[22] More generally, Shakespeare stresses the sheer unpredictability of what happens when rival civilizations clash. Because no one is fully in control of the process, it may go in unexpected directions and generate seemingly contradictory responses. Many people today think of globalization as the product of a single centralizing force, a matter of one government or an international organization imposing order on the whole world. The Roman Empire offers a model of this conception of globalization. It used its military force to gain control of the whole Mediterranean world and to exercise hegemony over the many lands it conquered. This tendency to create a new administrative order is evident in Octavius Caesar, as he issues commands to his captains:

> Do not exceed
> The prescript of this scroll. (3.8.4–5)

Here in a nutshell is the dream of worldwide Roman rule—a single Roman emperor tells his subjects exactly what to do, scripting their lives for them down to the smallest details.

Although this vision of the perfectly administered world would seem to be the new order of the day in *Antony and Cleopatra*, Shakespeare shows that, in Hamlet's terms, this is a custom "more honor'd in the breach than the observance" (*Hamlet*, 1.4.16). Things do not happen exactly according to the imperial script in Rome, and Octavius is faced with many surprises. Above all, Antony and Cleopatra refuse to play the roles that he has in mind for them on the Roman stage. They kill themselves to thwart Octavius's plans to humiliate them in public. For a realm that is supposed to be firmly under Roman control, the world of *Antony and Cleopatra* is strangely chaotic and unpredictable. Things mysteriously transform into their opposites; as Antony says,

> The present pleasure
> By revolution low'ring, does become
> The opposite of itself. (1.2.124–126)

Even more ominously in *Antony and Cleopatra*, the world keeps threatening to dissolve into oblivion and nothingness. The play is filled with images of instability, of melting and dissolution, of a world of solid things suddenly losing their clear shape:

> Let Rome in Tiber melt, and the wide arch
> Of the rang'd empire fall! (1.1.33–34)

> Melt Egypt into Nile! (2.5.78)

> Sink Rome! (3.7.15)

This pattern culminates in Antony's haunting vision of the clouds, in which the whole world dissolves into one vast blur:

> That which is now a horse, even with a thought
> The rack dislimns, and makes it indistinct
> As water is in water. (4.14.9–11)

In moments such as this, Shakespeare conveys a sense of how unnerving and uncanny globalization can seem, with the globe threatening to dissolve even at the moment it is supposedly being integrated into a whole. This passage calls to mind the words with which Karl Marx and Friedrich Engels famously characterized the revolutionary disruptions in consciousness created by global capitalism: "All that is solid melts into air, all that is holy is profaned."[23] This sense of global disorientation has been offered as the defining experience of modernity, and yet Shakespeare shows his imperial Romans already in the grip of the same malaise.[24]

Indeed, as imaged in *Antony and Cleopatra*, Roman power seems to dissipate and threatens to dissolve at the moment of its greatest triumph. That explains the widely divergent moods that sweep through the play. What is presented by some characters as the beginning of a new world order strikes others as the end of an era:

> *Antony:* The long day's task is done,
> And we must sleep. (4.14.35–36)

> *Guard 2:* The star is fall'n
> *Guard 1:* And time is at his period.[25] (4.14.106–107)

As is evident today, globalization is both a creative and destructive force; indeed, it creates new orders only by destroying old ones.[26] In particular, as an economic process, globalization sets in motion the force Joseph Schumpeter called "creative destruction."[27] Given a wider range of global options, new forms of production and consumption supplant traditional patterns. Shakespeare does not dwell on the economics of the Roman Empire, but he does show in *Antony and Cleopatra* that one order has to die to bring a new order into life. One of the most pervasive patterns of imagery in the play is the ambivalence of life and death, specifically of dying things coming to life and living things dissolving into death.[28]

That is why empire and globalization generate such contradictory responses. In *Antony and Cleopatra*, Shakespeare captures perfectly the blend of millennial hopes and apocalyptic fears generated when a new world order is coming into being. That is perhaps the deepest point of contact between the world he creates in *Antony and Cleopatra* and our globalizing world today. Thus one might apply to the play the words of a modern poet confronting a global apocalypse and the ultimate clash of civilizations:

> Turning and turning in the widening gyre
> The falcon cannot hear the falconer;
> Things fall apart; the centre cannot hold;
> Mere anarchy is loosed upon the world,
> The blood-dimmed tide is loosed, and everywhere
> The ceremony of innocence is drowned;
> The best lack all conviction, while the worst
> Are full of passionate intensity.[29]

Many analysts view globalization as an external force, imposed upon people from above. Indeed, they treat globalization as in effect indistinguishable from empire, a hegemonic power exercised from a colonizing center on a colonized periphery. But Shakespeare offers a bottom-up model of globalization as an alternative to the simple top-down model. He dwells on the way the globalizing impulse wells up from within people because he shows it to be driven by *desire*.[30] If the Romans in *Antony and Cleopatra* are Egyptianized, the reason is not that Egyptian armies impose this result on them. Shakespeare shows that the Romans *want* to live like Egyptians. They gaze upon Egyptian luxury and crave it for themselves. The driving force behind the Egyptianizing of the Romans as portrayed in *Antony and Cleopatra* is a complex of very human qualities, an amalgam of curiosity, envy, and desire—all epitomized by the infinitely seductive image of Cleopatra. When Antony wishes that he had never seen the Egyptian queen, Enobarbus replies in the spirit of the true global tourist: "O, sir, you had then left unseen a wonderful piece of work, which not to have been blest withal would have discredited your travel" (1.2.153–155).[31] Shakespeare's

Romans have indeed become world travelers, actively seeking out the alien and the exotic. Deep down, they crave to be globalized—they long to merge with what appears to them to be their antithesis among clashing civilizations. Many critics of globalization today treat it as a wholly artificial process, imposed upon people against their will by remote and hostile forces. In fact, as Shakespeare suggests, many aspects of globalization—not all—correspond to perfectly human needs and desires. Ever since the first caveman wondered if things might be better in the cave across the valley, the world has been marching toward globalization. Because globalization is rooted in the "infinite variety" of human desire, it inevitably takes unpredictable and kaleidoscopic forms. Recall Enobarbus's paradoxical image of Cleopatra:

> Other women cloy
> The appetites they feed, but she makes hungry
> Where most she satisfies. (2.2.235–237)

The same might be said of globalization: it constantly awakens new desires in the process of satisfying old ones; it dissolves old orders even as it brings new ones into being.[32]

Conclusion

Antony and Cleopatra thus does offer food for thought about our contemporary issue of globalization. One might turn elsewhere in Shakespeare's plays for more insight into the subject. *The Merchant of Venice*, for example, takes place in the increasingly globalized world of the Italian Renaissance, and its horizons truly stretch across the Earth, even as far as the New World. In this play, Shakespeare explores the economic aspects of globalization, specifically the ways that commerce both facilitates and complicates the process. Encompassing a wide range of nationalities and ethnic types, and especially the conflict between Christians and Jews, *The Merchant of Venice* is another study in the global clash of civilizations. Perhaps Ben Jonson was right after all—Shakespeare *is* a writer for all ages, even our age of globalization.

Notes

1. The line appears in Jonson's poetic tribute to Shakespeare in the original First Folio of his plays (1623).

2. Samuel P. Huntington, *The Clash of Civilizations and the Remaking of World Order* (New York: Simon & Schuster, 2003), 21.

3. For a study of this subject, with wide-ranging geographic reference, see Ramsay MacMullen, *Romanization in the Time of Augustus* (New Haven, CT: Yale University Press, 2000).

4. Looking at Rome and its colonies, MacMullen speaks "of the currents of influence flowing in both directions across the ancient world" (*Romanization*, 16).

5. MacMullen discusses at length a parallel development: the Hellenizing of Rome as it expanded into the eastern Mediterranean; see *Romanization*, 1–29.

6. I discuss this subject at length in my book *Shakespeare's Rome: Republic and Empire* (Ithaca, NY: Cornell University Press, 1976).

7. All quotations from *Antony and Cleopatra* and other Shakespeare plays are taken from G. Blakemore Evans, *The Riverside Shakespeare* (Boston: Houghton Mifflin, 1974); citations are incorporated into the body of the essay, giving act, scene, and line numbers.

8. On this subject, see Geraldo U. de Sousa, *Shakespeare's Cross-Cultural Encounters* (Basingstoke, Hampshire, UK: Palgrave, 1999), 129–130.

9. MacMullen makes a similar point about Rome's encounter with Greek civilization: "The Romans, to no one's surprise, won out where arms, administration, and practical technology were in question. As to the rest, in familiar words, captive Greece took Rome captive" (*Romanization*, 29).

10. On this subject, see Bill Ashcroft, Gareth Griffiths, and Helen Triffin, *The Empire Writes Back: Theory and Practice in Post-Colonial Literatures* (London: Routledge, 1989).

11. See Sousa, *Cross-Cultural Encounters*, 152–155.

12. For a good analysis of this scene, see John Michael Archer, *Old Worlds: Egypt, Southwest Africa, India, and Russia in Early Modern English Writing* (Stanford, CA: Stanford University Press, 2001), 51–54.

13. On the adopting of the model of Hellenistic god-kings in Rome, see Ronald Syme, *The Roman Revolution* (Oxford, UK: Oxford University Press, 1960), 54.

14. Archer notes that "Antony is scapegoated for Rome's own covert Egyptianism and current decadence" (*Old Worlds*, 61).

15. The classic study of this subject is Edward W. Said, *Orientalism* (New York: Vintage, 1979).

16. See Sousa, *Cross-Cultural Encounters*, 136, 140; and Ania Loomba, *Shakespeare, Race, and Colonialism* (Oxford, UK: Oxford University Press, 2002), 116–118.

17. One archetype of this kind of seductress is Dido in Vergil's *Aeneid*, who tries to prevent Aeneas from completing his divine mission of founding Rome. Shakespeare has Antony refer to Dido and Aeneas at 4.14.53. For the relevance of the *Aeneid* to *Antony and Cleopatra*, see my comments in the "virtual roundtable" in Sarah Spence, ed., *Poets and Critics Read Vergil* (New Haven, CT: Yale University Press, 2001), 188–189.

18. For a good analysis of this process, see Loomba, *Shakespeare*, 120–127. Loomba is correct to speak of Antony as "going native" (130). The way the Roman general

succumbs to the charms of Egypt anticipates a pattern that recurs in nineteenth- and twentieth-century British fiction of empire, story after story of colonial officers and officials on the imperial frontier losing their European discipline through fraternization with the natives (often specifically women). Among the classic "going native" narratives are Rudyard Kipling's "The Man Who Would Be King," Robert Louis Stevenson's *The Beach of Falesá*, Joseph Conrad's *Heart of Darkness* and *Lord Jim*, and Rider Haggard's *She*, perhaps the wildest of orientalist fantasies. Haggard's exotic queen Ayesha is partly modeled on Cleopatra, and the novel is filled with Egyptian and ancient Greek lore. All these details point to *Antony and Cleopatra*, providing a link between Shakespeare's play and fiction of empire—a reminder of the way the British Empire provides the middle term between the Roman Empire and modern globalization.

19. I have restored the original wording as it appears in the First Folio. All modern editions I have seen accept a preposterous emendation proposed by the eighteenth-century editor Lewis Theobald, with the line reading "the little *O*, th' earth." This bizarre phrase then requires glossing, whereas the original wording makes perfect sense as it is. Indeed, Shakespeare seems to be creating a deliberate contrast between the colossal Antony and the worshipful subjects who now stand beneath him, "the little o' th' earth." The apotheosis of the Roman emperor reduces ordinary human beings to underlings, a point Cassius originally made about Julius Caesar: "Why, man, he doth bestride the narrow world / Like a Colossus, and we petty men / Walk under his huge legs" (*Julius Caesar*, 1.2.135–137). The Theobald emendation has the effect of downplaying the way Cleopatra's dream of Antony as a Colossus echoes Cassius's complaint about Julius Caesar. For the standard editorial position on this phrase, see Michael Neill, ed., *Anthony and Cleopatra* (Oxford, UK: Oxford University Press, 1994), 308, note 81. Neill says that the Folio's "little o' th' earth " "makes no sense as it stands," even though in note 82, he draws the parallel with the Colossus passage in *Julius Caesar*, in which Cassius explicitly states that Caesar's status as a god makes ordinary Romans feel like little men.

20. J. L. Simmons, *Shakespeare's Pagan World: The Roman Tragedies* (Charlottesville: University Press of Virginia, 1973), 159.

21. For a brief overview of the Biblical allusions, see my *Shakespeare's Rome*, 220–221, note 18.

22. On this point, see Sousa, *Cross-Cultural Encounters*, 152.

23. From "The Manifesto of the Communist Party," in Lewis S. Feuer, ed., *Marx and Engels: Basic Writings on Politics and Philosophy* (Garden City, NY: Anchor, 1959), 10. Right after these words, Marx and Engels give one of the earliest descriptions of economic globalization: "The bourgeoisie has through its exploitation of the world market given a cosmopolitan character to production and consumption in every country.... [I]t has drawn from under the feet of industry the national ground on which it stood. All old-established national industries have been destroyed or are daily being destroyed. They are dislodged by new industries ... whose products are consumed not only at home, but in every quarter of the globe.... In place of the old local and national seclusion and self-sufficiency we have intercourse in every direction, universal interdependence

of nations.... National one-sidedness and narrow-mindedness become more and more impossible" (10–11).

24. See, for example, Marshall Berman, *All That Is Solid Melts into Air: The Experience of Modernity* (New York: Penguin, 1988).

25. As a prime example of the way *Antony and Cleopatra* subtly refers to the rise of Christianity, these lines amount to quotations from the Revelation of John (cf. Rev., viii:10, x:6). The verbal parallels are clearer if one looks at the Geneva translation of the Bible, rather than the King James (the Geneva Bible was evidently the English translation Shakespeare was familiar with). These parallels were first noted in Ethel Seaton, "*Antony and Cleopatra* and the Book of Revelation," *Review of English Studies* 22 (1946): 219–224.

26. On this subject, see Tyler Cowen, *Creative Destruction: How Globalization Is Changing the World's Cultures* (Princeton, NJ: Princeton University Press, 2002).

27. Joseph A. Schumpeter, *Capitalism, Socialism, and Democracy* (New York: Harper, 1975), 81–86.

28. Cleopatra, for example, uses the words "die / With looking on his life" (1.5.33–34) and later says, "My desolation does begin to make / A better life" (5.2.1–2). Her whole encounter with the rustic clown who brings her the figs in act 5, scene 2 turns on the ambivalence of life and death.

29. William Butler Yeats, "The Second Coming," *The Collected Poems of W. B. Yeats* (New York: Macmillan, 1956), 184–185. Yeats was fascinated by the theme of apocalyptic violence at the great turning points of history; see also his poems "Leda and the Swan" and "The Mother of God." Yeats saw parallels between the violent events in the twentieth century and those at the time of the founding of the Roman Empire and the birth of Christianity. See especially his play *Resurrection* and Book V of his *A Vision*.

30. MacMullen raises the question whether Romanization should be understood as a "push" or a "pull" phenomenon. He contrasts the idea that Roman authorities pushed Roman civilization on conquered people with the idea that the pull (the allure) of Roman civilization is what led people to imitate it. For example, he writes of the unified Roman monetary system: "the fact that at the end of Augustus's reign the whole region had come under a single precious-metal currency system ... arose out of no central pressure or policy at all. It was a result rather of unhurried market behavior and the realities of power expressed in numberless situations ad hoc" (*Romanization*, 6). Studying multiple examples of Romanization, MacMullen does not find "a Roman will to unify all subjects under a single set of regulations" (11). In the case of the imitation of Roman architecture around the Mediterranean, MacMullen says that we need to resist "the temptation to infer a push from the center in explanation of all the copying, that is, the Romanization, that so plainly went on in the provinces of Augustus's time. For 'push' read 'propaganda,' for 'center' read 'regime,' and the next word out is 'ideology.' No term is more prominent in recent treatments of Augustan art and architecture, importing quite anachronistic assumptions, quite unsupported by evidence, into the discussion. The emperor had no interest at all in how people decorated the walls of their homes. What explains the rapidity of imitation was pull, not push" (113). MacMullen

stresses "the intrinsic attractiveness of the Roman way of life seen through the eyes of the indigenous population.... Baths and wine and so forth recommended themselves to the senses without need of an introduction. They felt or they looked good.... The natives ... *pulled* Roman civilization to them—to their homes, their families, their world. It used to be supposed that acculturation was more a matter of push.... [But] what determined choice were local tastes, not imperial 'ideology.'... It was the eagerness particularly of the urban well-to-do, the pull of that rich class, that so greatly accelerated the process" (134–137). My contention is that Shakespeare develops a similar understanding of the Egyptianizing of Rome. His Romans feel the "pull" of Egyptian civilization; it is not "pushed" on them. In understanding globalization today, we need to bear in mind that it may be more a matter of "pull" than of "push." Much of what we call globalization takes place through channels of trade and other normal forms of interaction between individuals, which do not require governmental apparatus or other forms of central planning.

31. Archer perceptively speaks of Antony as "a European sightseer in Egypt" and even "a travel writer" (*Old Worlds*, 54–55).

32. Cf. what Marx and Engels say about economic globalization: "In place of the old wants, satisfied by the productions of the country, we find new wants, requiring for their satisfaction the products of distant lands and climes" (Feuer, *Marx and Engels*, 11). It is remarkable how well these words characterize the world of Shakespeare's *Antony and Cleopatra*.

Chapter 5

Decisions, Decisions, Decisions

Tyrannicide in Julius Caesar

Philip Abbott

While Shakespeare's *Julius Caesar* has been analyzed primarily as an examination of tyrannicide, critics have been divided about whether the playwright intended to portray the assassination of Caesar as "the foulest crime in secular history" or as a justifiable action against a "monstrous tyrant."[1] Was Brutus an exemplar of republican virtues or an "intellectually dishonest," self-righteous traitor? Even allowing for intentional ambiguity in Shakespeare's account, a clearer answer to whether assassination is justified can be found by examining the figures in *Julius Caesar.* Together they are engaged in a classic example of crisis decision making in which the consequences of an action are far-reaching and irrevocable and accompanied by high risk and under conditions of limited knowledge and under time constraints. This chapter examines the decision to assassinate Caesar, but like many crisis situations one central decision is surrounded by many related ones. Brutus, the putative tragic hero, makes more than ten fateful decisions.

Cassius, Antony, and even Caesar himself, as well as several minor figures, also make clusters of major decisions. If *Julius Caesar* is viewed as a crisis case study, not dissimilar from those undertaken by twentieth- and twenty-first-century leaders and those who later analyze them, the rationality and ethics of the decision makers can only be assessed by carefully calibrating the totality of their actions.

I

Despite the title of Shakespeare's play, it is Brutus, not Caesar, who is the central figure of the tragedy. It is Brutus's decisions that propel the conspirators to assassinate Caesar, and it is his decisions that lead to civil war and the defeat of the "Liberators." Brutus decides to (1) join the conspiracy; (2) lead the conspiracy; (3) refuse to include Antony as an assassination target; (4) refuse to require oaths by the conspirators; (5) refuse to invite Cicero to join the conspiracy; (6) perform the assassination as a religious rite; (7) permit Antony safe passage to the capitol; (8) permit Antony to deliver a funeral oration; (9) permit Cassius to raise an army by any means necessary; (10) meet the Triumvirate's army at Philippi; and (11) commit suicide. Except for (9), which leads to a bitter quarrel with Cassius, and (11), in which several of his associates refuse to assist him, all of Brutus's momentous decisions are met without any major resistance.

Brutus's decisions, however, are intertwined with Cassius's, for it is Cassius who decides (12) to recruit Brutus into the conspiracy. In order to close the deal, Cassius decides to (13) plant forged letters of support for Brutus as a conspirator. Despite Cassius's successful manipulation, he continually defers to Brutus's decisions (3–8). Cassius's deference is especially noticeable in his decision to accept Brutus's military decision (10) despite the fact that it is he, not Brutus, who has combat experience. Cassius's precipitous decision (14) to commit suicide is puzzling as well.

The decisions of Caesar himself seem to inadvertently encourage his own political murder. He decides (15) to celebrate his victory over Pompey and sons, his own countrymen; (16) to silence the tribunes for their attempt to halt the celebrations; and (17) to consider kingship of Rome. Despite the recent civil war and his stated concerns about the motives of Cassius, Caesar seems remarkably oblivious to threats to his own safety. He (18) ignores the pleas of the soothsayer and his wife not to attend the capitol, and he (19) pushes aside a letter from Artemidorus, who has uncovered the conspiracy.

Antony, the loyal friend of Caesar, oddly (20) rejects Caesar's concerns about Cassius. While one of his most effective arguments for Caesar's benevolence in his funeral oration is his will, Antony quickly (21) plots ways to renege on its provisions to the populace. Antony was invited by Brutus to join the new government. Instead, he decides (22) to speak at Caesar's funeral; (23) to urge civil war; (24) to assassinate 100 senators, including Cicero and his own nephew; and (25) to betray Lepidus, one of the Triumvirate.

One defense of the inconsistencies among these figures is the fact they must make high-risk decisions that are irrevocable under severe time constraints. All the conspirators expect Caesar to accept the crown at the next session of the Senate. To await the outcome, which appears inevitable, is to be confronted with dealing with Caesar when he is king and surrounded by his legions in his upcoming expedition, scheduled to begin in eighteen days. After the assassination, the Triumvirate too does not know how much support the Liberators enjoy in the Senate and among the populace. They must act before a new government is formed and before they themselves become targets. Given these time constraints, discussion of decisions in *Julius Caesar* is almost always relatively brief. When, for example, Antony states that Lepidus is not fit to share in the "threefold world divided," Octavius objects that he is a "tried and valiant soldier." Antony replies, simply, "so is my horse, Octavius," and the discussion immediately changes to dealing with Brutus and Cassius.[2]

Nevertheless, many decisions undertaken by these figures appear so obviously bad, even under conditions of stress, that commentators have searched for explanations in the character of the participants. Brutus is often portrayed as an idealistic figure motivated by his conception of the public good, much like, according to L. C. Knight, the "liberal young men in the 1930s" who joined the Communist cause.[3] In some interpretations, Brutus would never have engaged in the assassination had his patriotic sentiments not been manipulated by Cassius. The view of Brutus as an "upright man" who thought too much of the "common good without regard to the complexities of the world" provides plausible explanations for decisions (1), (3), (4), (6), (8), and (11). This view is reiterated by his adversaries at the very end of the play. Antony declares over Brutus's body that he was the "noblest Roman of them all," and Octavius orders he be given "all respect and rites of burial." Even (9) fits with this interpretation. Brutus is unprepared to face the kind of methods necessary to defend himself. But why must Brutus lead the conspiracy and declare who be allowed to join, especially when he is a late participant? Is Brutus perhaps too full of himself, too fixated on his own virtue? One view, even harsher, concludes that Brutus's virtuous motives are a facade for his own incipient Caesarism: "We may say that Brutus's faults are seated at the very heart of his character. Although his behavior, even to himself, is clothed in his habit (both dress and custom) of virtue, his basic motivation is egotistical satisfaction of his will, for he rules or overrules on all occasions, with brandished virtue if possible, without it, if he must."[4]

Cassius, too, appears to be a self-interested schemer in decisions (12) and (13). Brutus later recognizes Cassius on these terms in his quarrel over his methods in recruiting an army, and Caesar identifies him as such just before his assassination. But Cassius fails to play the part consistently. His deference to Brutus begins at the moment that he joins the conspiracy, and at the close of the play his decision to commit suicide, using the same sword with which he struck Caesar, appears to be prompted by Brutus's own intentions.[5] Some critics attempt to resolve this contradiction by suggesting Cassius, perhaps under the influence of his Brutus, underwent a transformation of character.[6] But if Brutus's motives are problematic, what really explains the source of this "growth"?

The depiction of Caesar is as ambiguous as that of his assassins. In an examination of tyrannicide, Shakespeare seems systematically unclear as to whether Caesar was in fact a tyrant. There certainly is ample evidence in the play that he was. Caesar did silence those tribunes who questioned his decision to celebrate the defeat of the Pompeys, and he unquestionably was poised to make himself king. Brutus is, however, uncertain that Caesar is a tyrant but is concerned rather that he will shortly become one, comparing him to a "serpent's egg, which hatched would as his kind grow mischievous."[7] Cassius's arguments, which appear more motivated by personal envy than republican concerns, are not in themselves persuasive except that they prompt Brutus's decision.

These are certainly instances of royal arrogance when Caesar himself is on stage. When Decius asks him why he will not come to the Senate, Caesar replies, "The cause is my will. I will not come: That is enough to satisfy the Senate."[8] But the predominant image of Caesar is one of a conceited leader with a weakness for flattery and prone to physical disabilities. Cassius plays upon the latter when he describes to Brutus Caesar's appeal to him in the Tiber: "Help me, Caius, or I sink!"[9] When Caesar describes his concerns about Cassius to Antony, he reminds him, "I rather tell thee what is to be feared / Than what I fear: for always I am Caesar." His next line is, "Come to my right hand, for this ear is deaf."[10] Decision (18) can thus be explained by Caesar's vanity. He does not wish to be seen as under the influence of his wife. Caesar must appear to be fearless. Decius's mission to convince Caesar to attend the Senate (to be assassinated) is a relatively easy task. He merely reinterprets Calpurnia's vision of his death as a celebration of his achievements and suggests that in his absence the Senate might change its mind about offering him the crown, mock him for fearing his wife's dreams. Vanity, ambition, and fear of ridicule quickly lead to a reversal of Caesar's decision. He is "ashamed" for even considering his spouse's pleas. On the basis of these examples and others, many observers have endorsed H. N. Hudson's view that Caesar "is indeed little better than a grand strutting piece of puff-paste; and when he speaks it is very much in the style of a glorious vapourer and braggart, full of lofty airs and mock-thunder."[11] Caesar as a tyrant poseur would explain disregard for the possibility of threats to his life. He is so infatuated with himself, with his achievements and imminent honors ("I in conquest stretched mine arm so far"),[12] that he is oblivious to discontent, let alone assassination. This interpretation of Caesar's decisions, however, creates two problems. On the one hand, it makes the case for tyrannicide a weak one. Republican paranoia and envy are not sufficient grounds for political murder. On the other, it conflicts with Antony's portrayal of Caesar in his funeral oration. Here Caesar's many achievements are recited along with his affection and generosity.

Perhaps, however, the key to these events lies in Antony's decisions. Antony appears to be the most consistently Machiavellian figure in the play. He duplicitously implies sympathy for the assassination, apparently in order to gain with the public for revenge (23). Unlike the conspirators, who under Brutus's leadership restrict the number of people to be "touched" by political murder, Antony initiates a post-assassination reign of terror that includes his own nephew and Cicero, who was not involved in the conspiracy. His description of how he intends to use his fellow member of the Triumvirate, Lepidus ("Let us not talk of him, but as property"), is one worthy of one of Shakespeare's major villains, Richard III.

Here, too, problems of consistency emerge. At various points Caesar, Brutus, and Cassius each underestimate Antony, who they see as a playboy. Caesar compares Cassius, who unlike Antony does not go to plays, "reads much," and "looks quite through the deeds of men." Brutus argues against including Antony as an assassination target in part because he is "given to sports, to wildness, and much company." Cassius repeats this characterization to Antony before the battle at Philippi. It is certainly possible a character transformation occurs after Caesar's death, but if so it is an extremely quick and radical one. The playboy turns his attention from wine, women, and song to civil war. If Antony is such a ruthless opportunist, can we believe his second eulogy, his honoring of Brutus's body at the end of the play?

Because a focus on the character of the decision makers does not resolve ambiguities, many commentators have sought cohesion in the larger forces. For John Uhler, Julius Caesar is "not a tragedy of person but Respublica." The "enterprise of Brutus is hopeless; days of the Republic are done" no matter what decisions are made.[13] In this interpretation, the inconsistencies in the major figures are the result of their situation. Neither Cassius's scheming nor Brutus's nobility is able to halt the inexorable march to Caesarism. Even the portrait of Caesar as a "slightly ridiculous" figure does not alter the determined outcome, for it is the spirit of Caesarism that survives. Brutus himself says so at Philippi: "O Julius Caesar! Thou art mighty yet / Thy spirit walks abroad and turns our swords / In our own proper entrails."[14] There is much to be said for this perspective, for it not only resolves the issue of the discrepancy between Caesar's vanity but also Brutus's, Cassius's, and Antony's views of him. However ridiculous the character of Caesar himself might be, he has altered the republic in ways that cannot be repaired. Caesarism thus emerges full blown in Antony (24, 25) and makes its appearance in Cassius and even Brutus (9).

Yet this determinist interpretation glides over instances in which human agency does seem relevant. Had Brutus included Antony as an assassination target, the Liberators might have been successful and even their own "Caesarism" problematic. After all, (3) is reached by Brutus in part (unless it is a complete feint) because he does not wish to be a "butcher" and the Liberators to "be called purgers."

Is it possible, however, to include the insights of both these perspectives, one acknowledging the impact of human agency in the decision makers as well as historical contingency and larger forces that reduce and alter their actions? One way to accommodate both is to identify the two simultaneous developments outlined by Shakespeare in *The Tragedy of Julius Caesar*. In one, each figure is in the process of constructing and maintaining a narrative of his behavior. For Brutus, it is a narrative of republican restoration. As a senator whose ancestors founded republican Rome, he announces that he "loves the name of honor more than I fear death."[15] In pre-assassination scenes with his spouse and servant, Brutus is presented as the model republican in his private life. He is a sensitive husband to his wife, who reminds him she is the daughter of the young Cato— who committed suicide rather than serve Caesar. He is a kind master. Brutus is troubled by Caesar's ascendancy even before his conversation with Cassius. After Cassius's plea for his support, he asks for more time but signals his sympathy for the cause: "Till then, my noble friend, chew upon this: Brutus had rather be a villager / Than to repute himself a son of Rome / Under conditions as this time / Is like to lay upon us."[16]

While Cassius frames his case for tyrannicide to Brutus in republican terms, it is impossible to ignore that his primary motive is envy. Cassius's jealousy of Caesar melds well with republican equalitarianism. He deftly compares Caesar's current exalted status to each of them: "the fault, dear Brutus, lies not in our stars / But in ourselves that we are underlings."[17] When he asks why Caesar's name "be sounded more than yours" we know that it is Cassius who has asked himself this question. Proof of Cassius's resentment is given just after he makes his case for tyrannicide. After Brutus leaves, Cassius notes that he "doth bear me hard, but he loves Brutus."[18] If the positions were reversed, "he should not humor me." Cassius feels entitled to forge letters urging Brutus to take action (13) because he knows envy is not a convincing ground for assassination from Brutus's viewpoint, but pleas based on his sense of virtue are. The effect of the entreaty, "Awake, and see thyself!" may be as self-regarding as Cassius's envy, but both are based on Caesar's affront to their dignity.

Brutus and Cassius are reacting to a narrative constructed by Caesar, who is in the midst of revising the concept of republican leadership. In Roman terms, dictatorship did not challenge republican values. It was not only a method for preserving the republic in moments of emergency but also signified confidence in the leader's republican virtue. Only a reliably republican person could be given vast powers, even temporarily. It is true, of course, that repeated resorts to dictatorship were already wearing down this ideal. Caesar was now prepared to overturn this model.[19] He planned to exchange his title as dictator for king (or some more permanent form of rule). In doing so, he needed a different persona than the Cincinnatus model. Caesar was exceptional, a man who vanquished every foe both foreign and Roman. In the timeline of the play, Caesar had already established many of the features required to make this transition. He had created a court atmosphere among his supporters and signaled the price of opposition both by the celebration of his victory over Pompey's son and silencing the tribunes. Caesar's relationship with the Senate was already more imperial than collegial. "The cause is my will," he tells Decius, who asks what to tell the Senate about his absence.[20] According to Casca, at least, Caesar had prepared the populace for the transformation by arranging the spectacle of multiple rejections of the crown offered by Antony. Still Caesar had not yet had the crown. As the conspirators operated under a deadline, so too did Caesar. Until he obtains it, Caesar must act strictly in terms of the grandeur narrative he fashioned. Just before his death, he haughtily rejects Cassius's plea for his brother with the declaration, "I am as constant as the northern star."[21]

Antony's narrative, of all the figures, is most under construction during the events surrounding the assassination. Before the murder, Antony is at best a loyal friend to Caesar. Less sympathetically, he is his crony, a young competent military aide but a less effective administrator, and one who, according to Caesar himself, "revels long a-nights." At least by the sight of Caesar's corpse, whose spirit is "ranging for revenge," Antony sets a different course. Antony attempts to frame his subsequent actions in terms of his promise to avenge Caesar. He apologizes before Caesar's corpse for seeming to seek conciliation with "butchers" and pledges civil war. He shows the crowd Caesar's wounds to evoke the same reaction he experienced. Before the battle of Philippi, he repeats his vow.

Even before these roles are tested by multiple decisions, one can see strains and tensions in each figure's narrative. Brutus is aware that he is betraying his friendship with Caesar and finds the necessary duplicity of the conspiracy itself, which hides in "smiles and affability" beneath the dignity of virtuous Romans. Even at the onset of the conspiracy, Cassius finds Brutus less malleable as he, in quick succession, rejects his advice about taking oaths, inviting Cicero to join and including Antony as an assassination target. In Caesar's grandeur narrative he has already established himself as a military and political figure so exceptional that the gift of the crown is a foregone conclusion. Yet in the dress rehearsal of the coronation, he suffers from a seizure at the close of the spectacle. Antony discovers that his revenge narrative requires sharing power with two other figures, one of whom is Caesar's designated successor.

The more severe problem with these narratives, however, is that none are powerful enough to always dominate the others. On occasion, one does appear to overwhelm another both before and after the assassination. Cassius, for example, is able to formulate his envy narrative in republican terms, although later he seems to succumb to the very narrative he seeks to colonize. Antony quickly reverses the motivation of Brutus in his funeral oration.

The primary reason for the inconsistencies in the actions of each figure is the fact that they are involved in a complex political game requiring continual trade-offs under intense pressure and time constraints. Neither Brutus, Cassius, Caesar, nor Antony is the only player in this game although each strives to be so. Each participant is able to identify his own narrative, and for the most part, those with whom he is dealing. The most revealing example of this behavior occurs just before the battle of Philippi, when Shakespeare gathers the leaders of the Liberators and the Triumvirate. Here we see each figure attempting to expose another's narrative. When Brutus attempts to confirm the nature of the meeting ("Words before blows, it is so my countrymen?"), Octavius mocks his aristocratic erudition and Antony shouts for revenge. Cassius returns to the speech theme by suggesting that Antony is the verbal seducer who stole the honey of the Hybla bees. The bee metaphor is thrown back and forth. Antony then focuses on the deception of the conspirators, who "bowed like bondsmen, kissing Caesar's feet" only to strike him from behind. Cassius characterizes Octavius as a "peevish schoolboy" who is "joined with a masker and reveler." The republican narrative devised by Brutus, in which the assassination is framed as a religious rite, is exposed as a cowardly act. In fact, it is this charge that moves Cassius to remind Brutus these words would not have been spoken had "Cassius ruled." Antony's revenge narrative is interpreted as an opportunist act. The twin insults, Antony's demagoguery and his status as "masker," converge. He is only "playing" the part of the avenger. Octavius ends the exchange of insults with a call to arms.

Collective verbal battle is one way in which the political game requires revisions and exposes narrative conflicts, but in most instances the game is played on the field of action. Cassius skillfully manipulates Brutus's republican commitments to force his entry into the conspiracy; but, as we noted, observers have been perplexed by his subsequent subservience. Can we conclude, however, that

Cassius's envy narrative is completed with the assassination because the act has satiated Cassius's anger or because it is simply no longer operational? Without any independent motivations, Cassius, with increasing intensity, adopts Brutus's narrative. Because he has convinced Brutus of his key role in rescuing republicanism, Cassius has little choice but to accept his leadership, including decisions (2–8) as well as the question of recruiting an army and military strategy at Philippi (9, 10). The finale of this absorption of Brutus's narrative is Cassius's deferential farewell at the close of their quarrel and reconciliation:

> *Brutus:* Everything is well.
> *Cassius:* Good night, *my lord*.[22]

Cassius's suicide may be precipitous in part because Brutus has signaled to him his decision never "to go bound to Rome." The change of Cassius the schemer to Cassius "the last of all Romans" can be explained as growth in character, but if so, it is under the tutelage of Brutus's narrative.

Brutus's decision to lead the conspiracy (1), including his decisions to exclude Cicero as a participant (5) and to determine the targets and mode of assassination (6) as well as his post-assassination decisions regarding Antony (7, 8), can be explained less in terms of the conflicting assessments of naiveté and narcissism than as the result of Cassius's successful use of flattery, which intensifies his own narrative. If Brutus is the ancestral link to republican Rome, as the forged letters indicate, then he is forced to assume leadership if he joins the conspiracy. Fellow conspirators Cassius, Casca, Cinna, and Metellus all argue for Cicero's inclusion on the grounds that his age will balance the youth of the other assassins. Is Brutus's objection simply that Cicero would be a competitor, or is it based on Brutus's assessment that he is unreliable ("For he will never follow anything / That other men have started"[23])? Casca's own report on Cicero's reaction to Antony's offer of the crown to Caesar suggests he could be an unreliable coconspirator and that Brutus's assessment is correct. Few understood Cicero's remarks, delivered in Greek, and those who did "smiled at one another and shook their heads."[24] Similarly, Brutus's insistence to attack rather than defend at Philippi can be seen as a politically adept strategy to establish the point that it is the Triumvirate who is the treasonous party. The decisions (3), (7), and (8) can also be explained less in terms of the demands of his republican narrative than a simple underestimation of Antony's talents. If Antony was only a Caesarian sycophant and a "masker and reveler," he posed no danger to the Liberators. Brutus, in fact, bristles later at what he regards as Antony's subterfuge in the meeting before the battle.

It is true that Brutus consistently misjudges the republican commitments of the Roman citizenry. He might be defended for ignoring the enthusiasm of the crowd for crowning Caesar since he believed his death would eliminate his spirit. When the same crowd offers him the crown after the assassination, Brutus would come to see his role as savior of republicanism as futile, hence his loss of control with Cassius (9).

Caesar's pomposity, which has led many critics to doubt his designation as tyrant, is also the result of his own narrative and leads directly to his assassination. The incipient king is not unaware that he has enemies. He is suspicious of Cassius and has the tribunes silenced. Still, he must not appear fearful for his safety. Moreover, his exceptional status is based in part on his magnanimity in victory. Both Cassius and Brutus fought on Pompey's side. To regard Brutus, the exemplary republican, as a threat would be to acknowledge his own role in subverting the republic.

Antony must find ways to cast off his reputation for frivolity and sycophancy in order to make his case as an avenger. He initiates this new narrative of himself brilliantly in his funeral oration for Caesar. As Brutus was troubled by his outward friendship with Caesar, Antony regrets the hypocrisy of feigning accommodation with the Liberators. Clearly, too, the brutality of the assassination has shaken Antony as it had Brutus and the conspirators. The latter have walked from the Forum to the crowd with Caesar's blood "up to their elbows"; Antony appears before them with Caesar's body in his arms. The agreement he has made with Brutus not to blame the Liberators is technically kept by repeating the refrain of their own narrative that they are "honorable men." Once Antony has adopted the avenger narrative, his subsequent decisions can be evaluated on these terms. His post-assassination reign of terror, as well as the betrayal of Lepidus, establishes his new gravitas. The young Octavius is the official heir of Caesar. For Antony to capture that role, he must assume the position of the primary avenger and hence the true successor. The eulogy to the dying Brutus as the only conspirator that acted from honorable motives—a revision of his funeral oration—can be seen as an attempt to acknowledge and to honor the republican tradition. Both Caesar, the generous servant of the people, *and* Brutus, their conscience, are now his predecessors.

Thus taken from the perspective of character alone these alterations lead to the conclusion that Cassius is a jealous manipulator; Caesar, a blowhard; Antony, an opportunist; and Brutus, a sanctimonious, willful leader. Assessed from another vantage point, one concludes however much each of these actors struggles, their fate has already been set. In fact, these inconsistencies and apparently questionable decisions are the result of accommodations in a complex, high-risk political game.

II

Shakespeare's insight, and his relevance to contemporary politics, lies in his exploration of the fundamental antagonism between these two projects: the narrative game and the political-bargaining one. No figure can abandon either to obtain his objectives, nor can he make them fit perfectly. Political action becomes unpredictable and problematic, hence the tragedy of Julius Caesar. Gary Wills uses an apt analogy to characterize the action in the play: "The characters rotate around each other like the plates of a Calder mobile. Touch one and it affects the decision of all the others. Raise one, another sinks."[25]

Contemporary political scientists have struggled to explain high-risk decisions much like those made in *Julius Caesar*. Like Graham Allison's analysis of the actors in the Cuban missile crisis, the multiple decisions made by Caesar, the Liberators, and the Triumvirate cannot be explained solely in terms of rational calculations. According to Allison, additional models (organizational and political) offer new insights. Each serves as a "search engine in a larger effort to identify all the causal factors that determine an outcome."[26] Yet some political scientists are reluctant to abandon a rational-choice approach while others claim that even more models are needed to explain crisis behavior.[27] Even additional information does not seem to have resolved differences in analyses. Multiple international conferences have actually made the fog of crisis decision making even more dense. Did Khrushchev really send missiles to Cuba to defend an ally? Had Kennedy really given orders to remove Jupiter missiles from Cuba before the crisis? Had the KGB officer who spoke to journalist John Scali about the terms of a deal acted on his own? As Len Scott and Steve Smith have concluded, the reason for the added confusion is that "the motivations and intentions" of participants "are rarely revealed and usually inconsistent across time if not at each specific moment. Policy-makers in the crisis acted for a variety of reasons, and spoke and wrote for different purposes and audiences at different times. They may not have even been aware of what motivated their actions."[28]

Shakespeare's contribution to this discussion can help in resolving these issues by introducing an additional perspective: a narrative model of analysis. The struggle among competing narratives and evolving political circumstances permits us to identify and understand the multiple decisions made in crisis situations, some reached by the demands of the actor's own narrative and others reached by political necessity. Applied to the missile crisis, President Kennedy struggles to demonstrate the plausibility of his statecraft and resolution in the face of challenges that he is a young and inexperienced man of privilege (Khrushchev) or, like his father, an appeaser (Joint Chiefs of Staff) under conditions of imminent nuclear war.[29] Numerous decisions are made in the context of this effort, not only in terms of the level of responses to the installation of the missiles but also in the decision-making structure utilized to determine them.

Conclusion

If Shakespeare demonstrates that crisis decision making leads to outcomes that are problematic, so does his analysis of the particular case of tyrannicide. Each of the participants does make decisions that are rational within his own narrative constructions. Without a narrative of republican restoration, Brutus would not have resisted Caesar, nor would Cassius have been able to convince him to join the conspiracy. However, Brutus's republicanism, if it does not doom the success of the enterprise, certainly increases the chance of failure. There is a poignant irony in Antony's eulogy before Brutus's body at the end of the play. For if indeed he is the noblest Roman of them all, then there is a justification for tyrannicide. Yet there is the surmise that Brutus's actions accelerated Rome's departure from republican governance.[30] The numerous assassinations and attempted assassinations, direct and indirect, during the Cold War and the War on Terror rely on arguments for tyrannicide advanced in *Julius Caesar*. They too have been justified in the name of freedom, with the same concessions to political necessity and with the same paradoxical results.

Notes

1. For reviews of differing assessments, see Ernest Schnazer, "The Problem of Julius Caesar," *Shakespeare Quarterly* 6 (Summer 1955), pp. 297–308; and Mildred E. Hartsock, "The Complexity of Julius Caesar," *PMLA* 8 (March 1966), pp. 56–62.

2. *Julius Caesar*, Marvin Spevik, ed. (Cambridge: Cambridge University Press, 1988), 4.1, pp. 117–118. All citations are from this edition.

3. "Personality and Politics in Julius Caesar," in Peter Ure, ed., *Shakespeare: Julius Caesar* (London: Macmillan, 1969), p. 138.

4. Gordon Ross Smith, "Brutus, Virtue, and Will," *Shakespeare Quarterly* 10 (Summer 1959), p. 378. Smith bases his assessment on fourteen decisions made by Brutus.

5. Cassius asks Brutus before if he would be "content to be led in triumph / Through the streets of Rome" if the battle is lost. Brutus replies that he will not, and both appear to agree on suicide as the only option in defeat. *Julius Caesar*, 5.1, p. 137.

6. For example, Mildred E. Hartsock states that "the Cassius of Act V represents the emotional peak of the play. His suffering, his death, the response to it of those who loved him—these involve us more emotionally than anything else on the play." See Hartsock, "The Complexity of Julius Caesar," p. 61.

7. *Julius Caesar*, 2.1, p. 75.

8. Ibid., 2.2, p. 90.

9. Ibid., 1.2, p. 59.

10. Ibid., 1.2, p. 63. Caesar's deafness anticipates the miscommunication and incomplete information that surround the tyrannicide decisions later in the narrative.

11. H. N. Hudson, *Shakespeare: His Life, Art, and Characters* (1872) (New York: Timeless Classic Books, 2010), vol. II, p. 234.

12. *Julius Caesar*, 2.2, p. 89.

13. John Uhler, *Studies in Shakespeare* (Miami: University of Miami Press, 1964), p. 120.

14. *Julius Caesar*, 5.3, p. 142.

15. Ibid., 1.2, p. 59.

16. Ibid., 1.2, p. 62.

17. Ibid., 1.2, p. 62.

18. Ibid., 1.3, p. 67.

19. See Franklin L. Ford's discussion on this point: *Political Murder: From Tyrannicide to Terrorism* (Cambridge, MA: Harvard University Pres, 1985), pp. 47–67. Michael Parenti revises this position to argue that Caesar was a democratic reformer assassinated by corrupt senators; see Parenti, *The Assassination of Julius Caesar: A People's History of Ancient Rome* (New York: New Press, 2003).

20. *Julius Caesar*, 2.2, p. 90.

21. Ibid., p. 97.

22. Ibid., p. 130. Emphasis added.

23. Ibid., p. 80.

24. Ibid., p. 66.

25. Gary Wills, *Rome and Rhetoric: Shakespeare's Julius Caesar* (New Haven, CT: Yale University Press, 2011), p. 117.

26. Graham Allison and Philip Zelikow, *The Essence of Decision*, 2nd ed. (New York: Longman, 1999), p. 392.

27. Jonathon Bendor and Thomas H. Hammond, "Rethinking Allison's Models," *American Political Science Review* 86 (June 1992), pp. 301–322. Barbara Kellerman has offered three additional models as adjuncts to Allison's: see Kellerman, "Allison Redux: Three Decision-Making Models," *Polity* 15 (Spring 1983), pp. 381–367.

28. Len Scott and Steve Smith, "Lessons of October: Historians, Political Scientists, Policy-makers, and the Cuban Missile Crisis," *International Affairs* 70 (October 1994), p. 677.

29. See, in particular, the exchanges at the October 19 meeting of EXCOMM. Ernest R. May and Philip D. Zelikow, eds., *The Kennedy Tapes: Inside the White House during the Cuban Missile Crisis* (Cambridge, MA: Harvard University Press, 1997), pp. 173–188. Also see Blema Steinberg, "Shame and Humiliation in the Cuban Missile Crisis: A Psychoanalytic Perspective," *Political Psychology* 12 (December 1991), pp. 653–690.

30. Stephen Dando-Collins, *The Ides: Caesar's Murder and War for Rome* (New York: John Wiley and Sons, 2010), p. 230.

Chapter 6

Why Iago Is Evil

Othello and the American Desire to Understand Corruption

Coyle Neal

The works of William Shakespeare reveal and explore the human condition in a way that has remained relevant, useful, and entertaining for the past four hundred years. In addition to learning much about humanity from Shakespeare, however, we can also learn much about specific societies by the way in which they engage his works. In this chapter, we will look at how a very specific American desire has been expressed through the cultural adaption of Shakespeare's *Othello* into Tim Blake Nelson's O. This chapter will first examine the reasonless evil of Iago in the original play. It will then look at the traditional American desire to understand the "why" behind so many things using as a baseline John Winthrop's 1630 "City on a Hill" sermon. Finally, it will look at the changes made to the villain Iago from the original in *Othello* into the character Hugo in O and how these changes are reflective of this characteristic of American political thought and culture.

Shakespeare's Iago: Evil without Cause

Iago is one of the most compelling characters in the corpus of Shakespeare's works.[1] Of all the potential avenues for exploring his actions and words, perhaps the characteristic that most draws interest is Iago's motivation.[2] Why does he do the terrible things he does? Throughout the play he gives at different times various reasons for his destruction of Othello:

- Jealousy:
  > Mere prattle without practice
  > Is all his [Cassio's] soldiership. But he, sir, had the election....
  > He, in good time, must his [Othello's] lieutenant be,
  > And I—God bless the mark! His Moorship's ancient.[3]
- Fun and Gain:
  > Thus do I ever make my fool my purse;
  > For I mine own gained knowledge should profane
  > If I would time expend with such a snipe
  > But for my *sport and profit*. [Emphasis added][4]
- Revenge:
  > It is thought abroad that twixt my sheets
  > He's done my office.[5]

  > Nothing can or shall content my soul
  > Till I am evened with him, wife for wife.[6]
- Hatred:
  > I hate the Moor.[7]

  > I do hate him as I do hell pains.[8]
- Vanity:
  > If Cassio do remain
  > He hath a daily beauty in his life
  > That makes me ugly....
  > He must die.[9]

As the play progresses, it becomes apparent that however much truth there may be in any one of these reasons at the time of their delivery, they are all at best excuses of the moment, adjusted to their given context and utterly unrevealing of Iago's true intent. No single declaration of motive rises above the others to declare itself as Iago's ultimate reason for playing the villain. It is as if he has a stockpile of intent that he draws upon whenever it best suits his goals.[10] This abundance of equally untenable excuses makes it clear that Iago is, at the end of the day, evil without reason. He is, as Coleridge called him, a "motiveless Malignity."[11] Iago grows like an aggressive cancer through Othello's world, consuming and destroying without clear purpose or motive. His evil is without cause and without goal beyond the immediate end of his destruction of everything good.[12]

This absence of motive is reinforced by Iago's final words in the play. Upon being challenged by Othello to explain himself, Iago has the opportunity to lay out his hidden agenda, to reveal to Othello and the audience just what he was working for, and to articulate the reasons for his hatred. Instead, he gives his infamous declaration of silence:

> *Othello:* Will you, I pray, demand that demi-devil
> Why he hath thus ensnared my soul and body?
> *Iago:* Demand me nothing. What you know, you know.
> From this time forth I never will speak word.[13]

And Iago remains true to his promise; he says nothing more about his actions or the reasons for his destruction of everyone around him. The audience is left with no more than the clearly insufficient reasons previously noted and his deplorable actions—actions perhaps made all the more deplorable for their seeming lack of motive. Iago did wicked things simply because he could, not because he had solid reasons for doing so.

Americans Want to Know "Why?": Winthrop's Colonial Example

Americans have a desire to understand *why* that pervades the culture. Examples of this could be drawn from virtually any aspect of society, from pop culture to criminal law.[14] We are rarely satisfied with the knowledge *that* someone has done something, we need to understand the reasoning behind it. What went through a criminal's mind before he committed his crime? Why did the philanthropist give so much of his time and money to his pet charity? Why do celebrities do the odd things they do? The larger the scale of the action in question, the deeper the desire seems to run through the American populace. The glut of books on both the popular and scholarly levels concerning the psychology of terrorists following the 1995 Oklahoma City bombing and the attacks on September 11,

2001, are recent examples of this American characteristic.[15] Yet this is no modern phenomenon in American life. From America's very beginning, Americans have been attempting to explain and understand the motive and intent behind even the grandest questions. An example drawn from the earliest colonial days will highlight this tendency.

Within three decades of Shakespeare's prime period of composition, John Winthrop preached to the immigrating Puritans a sermon titled "A Model of Christian Charity."[16] While many Americans are familiar with at least the ending—which challenges the colonists to "be as a City upon a Hill"—few people remember that the very first paragraphs in the sermon are a challenge to understand Divine intent in dividing the world into haves and have-nots:

> God Almighty, in his most holy and wise providence hath so disposed of the Condition of mankind, as in all times some must be rich some poor, some high and eminent in power and dignity; others mean and in subjection.[17]

Winthrop then proceeds to outline God's intent in so ordaining the world (including reasons such as that God is delighted "in the variety and difference of the Creatures" and "that every man might have need of [every] other").[18] Why is it that God—being all-wise and all-powerful—allows some people to be rich and some to be poor? Why are some powerful and honorable, and some weak and base? These questions have no doubt been asked at all times and in all ages, yet it is relevant that these are among the first words spoken publicly in colonial America. Winthrop's specific answers to the questions he raises are perhaps interesting, but they are irrelevant to our concern here—which is that Americans have long refused the stoicism that would simply accept the actions of people and events of history without concern or curiosity.[19] Our very founding is steeped in questions of intent and motive. Divine intent and motive to be sure, but intent and motive nonetheless.

These questions could be traced through American history in various incarnations, from the desire of the participants of the Great Awakening to understand the source of their religious fervor,[20] to the Transcendentalists' attempts to understand man's desire to commune in nature,[21] to even the attempts of the philosophical side of the New Left to understand how so affluent a society could have gone so far off course.[22] Likewise, practical political efforts have included intense examinations and attempts to answer the question "why." Why do these people want to rebel against England or free the slaves?[23] Why did this popular public figure cheat on his wife?[24] Why did we attack this country, or why did that country attack us?[25] Even when the answers are unsatisfactory the questions are always there, and to them we turn when faced with new circumstances. Motive and intent have been at the center of every major American philosophical movement and political charge. When we consider the character of Iago through this lens, he can be reinterpreted as one more reflective of this American desire.

The Americanization of Iago

Othello was reimagined for a young generation of Americans in 2001 with the release of Tim Blake Nelson's *O*.[26] In addition to rewriting the text in modern vernacular, this recent adaptation makes many changes in transferring the setting to the end of the twentieth century. For example, high school basketball—rather than war—becomes the "profession" of the main characters. Additionally, the villain, "Hugo," is the son of "Coach Duke Goulding," who favors "Odin" (the titular "O") rather than his own son; which in turn means that "Michael Cassio" has a smaller role than his counterpart in the play. There are many other stylistic and narrative changes in the updating of Shakespeare's classic (the botched attempt on Cassio's life by "Roger" as a carjacking being a particularly interesting one). And yet even with all the modernizations, perhaps the most jarring change is thematic—the elevation of a single motive to dominance in the character of Hugo. Whereas Shakespeare's play ultimately withholds any kind of final revelation of the reasons for Iago's actions, Nelson's movie repeatedly emphasizes jealousy as a single theme behind Hugo's campaign against Odin:

- After Odin chooses Mike to be his co-MVP, Hugo proclaims to Rodrigo, "I'm the MVP on this piece of s*** team and he chooses Michael."
- At the beginning of the film Hugo's father states, "I love him [Odin] like my own son." Hugo's reply at the end: "Yeah dad, who's your favorite now?"
- At the conclusion of the movie, Hugo gives a long monologue outlining his reason for his actions: "All my life I always wanted to fly. I always wanted to live like a hawk. I know you're not supposed to be jealous of anything, but to take flight, to soar above everything and everyone, now that's livin'! And a hawk is no good around normal birds. Even though all the other birds probably want to be hawks, they hate him for what they can't be: powerful, determined, dark. Odin is a hawk. He soars above us. He can fly. One of these days everyone's going to pay attention to me, because I'm gonna fly too."[27]

Notably, this last speech comes *after* Hugo's "I never will speak word" line—the very place where Shakespeare pointedly refused to give Iago a motive. Jealousy is therefore elevated to the central motivation behind Hugo's actions.[28] Although the choice of jealousy as a motive is in itself interesting and perhaps worthy of further study, it is for our purposes less significant than the fact that *any* motive was allowed to dominate, let alone be intentionally shoved to the fore. This emphasis on a motive—rather than leaving the character with his original lack of motive—in turn further highlights this characteristic of American political thought.

Conclusion

Because Shakespeare left the reasons behind Iago's evil unstated, how any given audience responds to his actions to some extent is an exploration of that audience's perceptions of evil.[29] What is revealed about the American audience, as has been emphasized here, is that Americans cannot stand evil for its own sake—we must find the motive behind it. This shift in the character of the villain and the raising of a single motive to prominence is best understood as a reflection of the political thought of the culture for which the film is intended. The idea of a villain who is evil for the sake of evil—Coleridge's "motiveless malignity"—is utterly unacceptable to an audience steeped in as long and deep a tradition of questioning motive and intent as Americans have. Just as we cannot imagine Winthrop's sermon answering the question of why there are rich and poor in the world with a shrug and a "just because," so we cannot fathom a villain who acts for no reason at all—not even Shakespeare's Iago. He *must* be given an explanation for his actions, not least for him to be palatable to a wide-ranging American audience but even to be created in the first place as a character in a mainstream American film. With this in view, the Americanization of *Othello* in the movie *O* becomes more than just an artistic adaptation (though it is of course that as well); it becomes both another entry in our long history of demanding answers to the question of "why?" and a means by which Shakespeare can be used to explore American politics and culture.

Notes

1. The best reflection on Iago I am aware of is that by Richard Raatzsch, *The Apologetics of Evil: The Case of Iago* (Princeton, NJ: Princeton University Press, 2009).

2. Perhaps the most creative study of Iago's motive is that by Rosenberg, which uses how Iago (and the other characters in the play) has been portrayed by actors. Marvin Rosenberg, *Masks of Othello: The Search for the Identity of Othello, Iago, and Desdemona by Three Centuries of Actors and Critics* (Wilmington: University of Delaware Press, 1992).

3. *Othello*, 1.1: 27–34.

4. Ibid., 1.3: 384–387.

5. Ibid., 1.3: 388–389.

6. Ibid., 2.2: 299–300.

7. Ibid., 1.3: 387.

8. Ibid., 1.1: 158.

9. Ibid., 5.1: 18–22.

10. This has led numerous commentators to suggest an intentional link by Shakespeare between Iago and Machiavelli. For an analysis of this position (along with an excellent bibliography) see Ken Jacobsen, "Iago's Art of War: The 'Machiavellian Moment' in *Othello*," *Modern Philology* 106, no. 3 (February 2009), 497–529.

11. Samuel Taylor Coleridge, *Lectures 1808–1819 on Literature II*, vol. 5 of *The Collected Works of Samuel Taylor Coleridge* (Princeton, NJ: Princeton University Press, 1987), 315.

12. As with virtually everything in Shakespeare, there is scholarly debate over this topic. Scholars have tended to pick jealousy as Iago's primary motive, though I am not convinced that the text merits such a conclusion. For further discussion of and response to this dominant scholarly position, see Bryan Reynolds and Joseph Fitzpatrick, "Venetian Ideology or Transversal Power? Iago's Motives and the Means by which Othello Falls," in *Othello: Critical Essays*, ed. Philip Kolin (New York: Routledge, 2002).

13. *Othello*, 5.2: 363.

14. As well as combinations of the two, such as the television program *Law and Order: Criminal Intent*.

15. These books may very well be legion. As good a place to start as any (and certainly no worse than some) is Bruce Bongar, ed., *Psychology of Terrorism* (Oxford: Oxford University Press, 2007).

16. Good sources for more information about John Winthrop include Francis Bremer, *John Winthrop: America's Forgotten Founder* (Oxford: Oxford University Press, 2003); and Edmund Morgan, *The Puritan Dilemma: The Story of John Winthrop* (Boston: Little, Brown, 1958).

17. John Winthrop, "A Model of Christian Charity," in *Issues in American Protestantism: A Documentary History from the Puritans to the Present*, Robert L. Ferm, ed. (Gloucester, MA: Peter Smith, 1976), 4.

18. Ibid.

19. This streak of stoicism of course appears in many times and many cultures, from the original Greek and Roman stoics to the Northern European variety expressed in the Eddas and Sagas, to even the occasional English author who would remind us that "theirs not to make reply/theirs not to reason why/theirs but to do and die." See variously Marcus Aurelius, *The Meditations* (Oxford: Oxford University Press, 2011); Ornolfur Thorsson, ed., *The Icelandic Sagas* (New York: Penguin, 2001); and Alfred Lord Tennyson, *The Charge of the Light Brigade and Other Poems* (Mineola, NY: Dover, 1992).

20. Jonathan Edwards, *Religious Affections*, vol. 2 of *The Works of Jonathan Edwards* (New Haven, CT: Yale University Press, 2009).

21. Lawrence Buell, ed., *The American Transcendentalists* (New York: Modern Library, 2006); and Philip Gura, *American Transcendentalism* (New York: Hill and Wang, 2008).

22. Irwin Unger, *The Times Were a Changin'* (New York: Three Rivers, 1998); and by the same author *The Movement: A History of the American New Left, 1959–1972* (New York: Dodd, Mead, 1974).

23. There are far too many sources to cite here for each of these. Perhaps among the most interesting for the American Revolution from the perspective of political science are the writings of Jefferson and Adams, who approach the issue from virtually opposite philosophical motives and yet reach the same conclusion. In terms of the abolition movement, the remarkable novel *Uncle Tom's Cabin* may be seen as an attempt at explaining virtually every possible perspective on slavery through the course of the novel. See John Adams, *Revolutionary Writings: 1775–1783* (New York: Library of America, 2011); Thomas Jefferson, *Jefferson: The Political Writings* (Cambridge: Cambridge University Press, 1999); and Harriet Beecher Stowe, *Uncle Tom's Cabin* (New York: Modern Library, 1996).

24. Sadly, examples here are also legion. Among the first truly national scandals was that of Henry Ward Beecher. See Debby Applegate, *The Most Famous Man in America: The Life of Henry Ward Beecher* (New York: Three Leaves, 2006).

25. We even have in our history instances of answers to such questions being fabricated (or at least embellished). See as one example Evan Thomas, *The War Lovers: Roosevelt, Lodge, Hearst, and the Rush to Empire, 1898* (New York: Little, Brown, 2011).

26. Tim Blake Nelson, *O*, DVD (United States: Lions Gate, 2001).

27. Ibid.

28. To be fair, Nelson does leave other possibilities open as motives for Hugo's actions, including hatred and vanity (to which there are a few indirect references), but the dominance of jealousy—to the point where it is openly declared to be Hugo's motive in the film's trailer—indicates that these others may have been included more to appease the Shakespeare purists than as serious reasons behind Hugo's actions.

29. A thoughtful interpretation of this idea can be found in Stanley Hyman, *Iago: Some Approaches to the Illusion of His Motivation* (New York: Scribner, 1970).

CHAPTER 7

RICHARD III, TYRANNY, AND THE MODERN FINANCIAL ELITE

Marlene K. Sokolon

If Shakespeare's Richard III lived today in a contemporary modern democracy, where might we find him? Shakespeare's Richard is the archetypical tyrant. He is willing to kill his brother, nephews, and friends to achieve his ambitions. His desires for glory and power are purely self-interested, without any regard for the common good. Contemporary interpretations connect him to the warlords and rulers of modern authoritarian states. Richard certainly does resemble these modern tyrants; however, Shakespeare also provides his audience with privileged access to Richard's mind, with all his intentions and strategies. This privileged access allows Shakespeare to explore the personality traits of a tyrant: his relentless ambition, his skillful manipulation of others, his ability to hide his own emotions, his willingness to turn on anyone to achieve his goals. It is in Shakespeare's exploration of a tyrant's personality that we may find similarities not only in contemporary authoritarian rulers but in the faces of our financial elite who led us into the subprime mortgage and other financial crises.

The portrayal of Richard III as the quintessential tyrant has a long history. Writing before Shakespeare, Sir Thomas More's "History of Richard III" describes him as "malicious, wrathful, envious, and from afore his birth ever forward ... close and secret, a deep dissembler ... often for ambition, and either for the surety or increase of his estate."[1] Adopting More's account, Shakespeare to some extent does present Richard as the character Vice, who finally is defeated by the virtuous Richmond.[2] Grandfather to Elizabeth I, Richmond brought the War of the Roses to its conclusion and founded the Tudor dynasty. From this perspective, the play contrasts Richard as a vicious tyrant with the Tudors as the true monarchs who bring peace and prosperity to England.[3] Modern interpretations of Richard tend to follow this view. Richard Loncriane's 1995 film, for example, sets the play in an alternative 1930s universe where fascist forces have overcome Britain and Richard is the consummate military dictator.[4] Such interpretations underscore the connection between the play and contemporary totalitarian regimes.[5] This means in our world, where monarchy is constitutional and political systems have checks and balances, Richard is held in check or only to be found outside western democracies. It seems we, at least, can sleep safely.

Shakespeare's play, however, questions whether democratic peace abolishes the possibility of a Richard in our world. In the only opening soliloquy Shakespeare gives to a main character, Richard reveals his inner self to the audience.[6] Since the end of the war, he tells us, the only battle "is [to] caper nimbly in a lady's chamber" (1.1.10).[7] Richard is notorious for his being "cheated of feature," with physical deformities, such as a shriveled arm, a hunchback, and the reputation of being born with teeth. Thus, he says,

> And therefore, since I cannot prove a lover
> To entertain these fair well-spoken days,
> I am determined to prove a villain,
> And hate the idle pleasures of these days. (1.1.30)

Why Richard claims he cannot be a lover is not clear. Certainly, he is not handsome, but he proves an exceedingly able seducer. In the next scene, he convinces Anne, who is the widow of the former Lancaster heir, to marry him. This seduction is astonishing since it is in public, during her father-in-law's funeral, and Richard killed both this former king and her husband.[8] Richard admits he has no interest in love and the marriage will be short (1.2.155–215). Thus, he may be only capable of seduction, not love. Alternatively, lacking erotic desire,

Richard may seduce Anne only to maintain the appearance of a lover as part of his ambition for power.[9] Either way, Richard is uninterested in the "sportive game" of romance, at least beyond the goal of seduction.

The underlying reason for his villainy is to provide entertainment on "these well-spoken days." Because he has "no delight to pass away the time … and hate[s] idle pleasures," he begins to plot. He plots against his brothers, his young nephews, the Queen's relatives, and anyone, friend or foe, who opposes him. In other words, in the security of peacetime, Richard is bored. And, to amuse himself, he determined to be a villain and "count his gains" (1.2.60). This means that rather than solving the problem of Richard's machinations, a peaceful and secure world actually fuels his devious actions. As the Old Queen Margaret says, Richard is "a troubler of the world's peace" (1.3.220). Richard, thus, is not simply ambitious for power but is someone who self-consciously chooses treachery.[10] Because our contemporary liberal democracies are comparably more peaceful than Richard's time, our peaceful environment would actually encourage those "who hate the idle pleasures of these days" to trouble such tranquility. Certainly, someone like Richard would still be attracted to political competition; however, contemporary political rivalry is subject to more checks and balances than faced by Richard.

So where would a potential Richard find an environment where he could plot with fewer legal and constitutional constraints? Since the 1980s, deregulation in the financial sector has increased self-regulation, the pace of financial activity, and the complexity of financial instruments. Richard Bookstaber, for example, argues that these changes, especially the degree of complexity, have made the market more accessible to "investment desires."[11] Disagreeing that the economic crisis was a "normal accident," Charles Perrow argues that as active agents, financial elites shaped business structures "in their own narrow self-interest."[12] With ethics rarely taught in business schools, our financial and business sectors are ripe for ambitious individuals, who are bored with the idle pleasures of our relatively peaceful democracies.[13]

Richard the Tyrant

In *Richard III*, Shakespeare explores the nature of tyranny in two different ways. First, Richard's actions are tyrannical in the classical sense. Because Richard has no claim to the throne, he usurps power by killing off the legitimate heirs. Originally in ancient Greece, *tyranny* described a monarch, good or bad, who gained power illegitimately.[14] Richard is also a tyrant in the classical philosophical sense; Aristotle calls tyranny a deviant regime because the tyrant rules in his own self-interest, without regard for community good.[15] In addition, Richard is a tyrant in our contemporary understanding of excessively oppressive and unjust rule. There is a long list of his use of force and fraud: he kills brothers, nephews, wives, and in-laws; he uses slander and false information; he turns on and eventually kills his ally Buckingham. Throughout all of Richard's machinations, never once is the good of the kingdom or of the people mentioned. In the end, his rule descends into another round of civil war.

Second, Shakespeare explores the nature of tyranny by exposing the character traits or psychology underlying Richard's actions. As mentioned earlier, this is Shakespeare's only play that opens with a main character's soliloquy. This soliloquy allows the audience privileged access to the mind of a tyrant and what drives his vicious goals. Richard's overarching character trait is pure, unrestrained, and self-interested ambition. Although *Richard III* is usually performed as a stand-alone play, it is part of a larger tetralogy that included the three parts of *Henry VI*.[16] In these plays, the young Richard is already thinking of murdering those who inherit before him.[17] In *Richard III*, Richard sets about getting the crown not because he is really interested in the crown per se; instead, he is interested in gain and conquest.[18] In one of his most unguarded moments, he reveals his joy over seducing Anne. What he celebrates is the achievement of his goal, since we know he does not intend to keep her. Famously, Richard rejoices,

> Was ever woman in this humour wooed?
> Was ever woman in this humour won?
> I'll have her, but I will not keep her long.
> What, I that killed her husband and his father,
> To take her in her heart's extremest hate,
> With curses in her mouth, tears in her eyes . . .
> And yet to win her, all the world to nothing?
> Ha! (1.2.215)

Richard's ambition is married to other personality traits that allow him to achieve his goals. Certainly, he is capable of extreme violence, especially as revealed on the battlefield and against rivals; yet, more than direct violence, Richard proves capable of reading and influencing others. Because the audience is privy to his plans, we are in the unique position to see the extent of his ability to manipulate those around him. In particular, he is adept at playing the "false friend," and many characters remain convinced of his sincerity until the bitter end. He manipulates his brothers, for example, by spreading the prophecy that King Edward will be killed by an heir whose name starts with "G"; in turn, he tells his brother George, the Duke of Clarence, that it is Edward's unpopular queen who is to blame. As for poor Clarence, he is so duped that when his executioners tell him Richard is to blame, he argues with them: "Oh no," Clarence says, "he loves me, and holds me dear / ... do not slander him, he is kind" (1.4.210–220).

Richard truly excels at this Machiavellian ability to appear to be something he is not. His greatest display of this skill is with Hastings, one of the potential obstacles to his goal. Richard manipulates the situation with the fabrication that Hastings has plotted against him. Hastings proves easy prey, because he utterly misapprehends Richard. Immediately before he is arrested, Hastings is assured that he can "read" Richard:

> I think there's never a man in Christendom
> Can lesser hide his love or hate than he;
> For by his face straight shall you know his heart. (3.4.55)

Because the audience is privy to Richard's real plans, we know just how very wrong Hastings is in this assessment. Richard rarely exposes his true emotions and is especially adept at manipulating his emotional expressions to indicate what he wants others to think he is feeling. He feigns tears, for example, with his nephew (2.2.20); he feigns cheerfulness for men like Hastings to put them at ease while he plots behind their back (3.4.50). He is able, by feigning piety and prayer, to persuade the Mayor that he has to be "convinced" to take the crown (3.7.180–220). To be sure, Richard is not perfect with this skill of not revealing his true self. When he has his falling out with Buckingham, for example, Catesby notes, "the King is angry. See he bites the lip" (4.2.25). In addition, certain characters, most notably women like his mother and the former Queen Margaret, are never fooled by his fake emotional displays. When Clarence's son tells his grandmother that Richard cried revealing his father's death, the old woman retorts, "O that deceit should steal such gentle shapes / And with a virtuous visor hide foul guile" (2.2.25). Many common Englishmen also seem to see through Richard: upon hearing that Richard will be regent, one citizen proclaims, "O full of danger is the Duke of Gloucester" (2.3.25). Significantly, when Richard is proclaimed king, the crowd stands like "dumb statues" with only "some tens of voices cry[ing], God save King Richard" (3.7.30). Yet, especially during his plotting to become king, Richard is able to manipulate his emotions and hide his true feelings from those crucial to achieving his ambitions.

Richard also manipulates others by using and controlling information. He is especially effective in using information to control reputation. For himself, he spreads rumors of piety; for others, he is the king of false information and slander. He has Clarence's death blamed on the Queen, spreads news of the King's sexual appetite and affairs, and taints his mother with accusations of adultery and his nephews with illegitimacy. Richard is also able to manipulate secret, inside knowledge, such as the prophecies and dreams that condemn Clarence. In his dealing with Hastings, Richard reveals his facility with manipulating other forms of knowledge, such as legal and historical record.[19] The best example of this is when he audaciously has printed Hastings's indictment, rushing his execution before the man is even arrested. As the astonished Scrivener tells us,

> Why who's so gross
> That cannot see this palpable device ...
> Bad is the world, and all will come to naught
> When such bad dealing must be seen in thought. (3.6.1)

Beyond his ability to hide his emotions, manipulate others, and control and use information, Richard is successful in obtaining the throne because he is willing to betray any ally or supporter. Although he betrays many former friends, including his brothers, the most prominent character he turns against is Buckingham. From the beginning, Buckingham is a willing participant in Richard's plots. As his closest confidant and spin doctor, Buckingham does most of Richard's dirty work as well as spreads Richard's reputation as a wise, virtuous, and pious man who would rather pray than be king. So close are they that Richard describes Buckingham as his "other self" (2.2.120). After Richard becomes king, however, when Buckingham hesitates to have the princes in the tower killed, Richard turns against him. "High reaching Buckingham grows circumspect," he says, "... no more shall [he] be the neighbor to my counsel" (4.2.30, 40). Richard does find a murderer willing to kill the princes, but his falling out with Buckingham is permanent. Richard refuses to grant Buckingham lands, and although Buckingham will be instrumental in Richmond's uprising, eventually he is captured and executed. Richard's relationship with Buckingham is revealing: he really has no friends or allies. In pursuing his goals, for Richard, everyone is an expendable pawn.

Shakespeare's Tyranny and the Modern Financial Elite

Shakespeare's portrayal of Richard as a tyrant offers a unique approach to understanding the character traits of our modern financial elites, from appointed government officials, CEOs of major corporations, bankers and executives, to those working in the financial sectors. To be sure, many of Richard's actions as tyrant are not comparable to the actions of contemporary financial elites. First, the type of power exercised by financial elites is both qualitatively and quantitatively different from Richard's absolute monarchy. Financial elites, for example, do not usurp political power. Second, despite the havoc created by the financial crises, the actions of financial elites fall far short of Richard's murdering of brother, nephews, enemies, and rivals. Such political violence, especially the elimination of those who challenge political authority, does exist in the contemporary world, and we only have to look to the headlines to find modern tyrannies in the continuing oppression of authoritarian regimes. Thus, it is not Richard's tangible actions that are useful for understanding our financial elites; instead, it is Shakespeare's exposure of Richard's character and the personality traits underlying these actions.

Richard's most prominent trait is his pure, self-interested, unrestrained ambition. Ambition alone is not a negative personality trait; it is ambition that drives human beings to improve themselves and the circumstances of their community and family. Richard's ambition is tyrannical because of his willingness to do anything, without any concern for others, in the pursuit of his self-interested goals. Like Richard, studies have found that the number-one trait linked to success among the most elite group of investment advisors is ambition and a concrete plan to achieve goals.[20] Of course, not all business and financial elites are driven by pure self-interest; yet, the critique of financial leaders' unrestrained pursuit of self-interest, without concern for ethics or even their own clients, has been raised many times. Perrow, for example, reveals how elites took advantage of structural conditions and embedded ideologies to serve their own interests of "wealth, privilege, and the exercise of power over others."[21] Other studies have found that the most consistent trait among market actors is their own "prestige-seeking."[22] And, long before the financial crises hit, Michael Lewis's *Liar's Poker* exposed the excessive ambition he encountered on Wall Street. He notes that

> there were no rules governing the pursuit of profit and glory, the men who worked there, including the most bloodthirsty, had a haunted look about them. The place was governed by the simple understanding that the unbridled pursuit of perceived self-interest was healthy.[23]

Importantly, it is not simply ambition that is crucial for Richard's success but his skill at manipulating others. Current studies have revealed a connection between the successful manipulation of others and leadership; even among children, the top rank in the playground pecking order has been correlated with the ability to lie and manipulate others.[24] Nicola Horlick, a chief executive in London, stresses, "There is no doubt that there are many who manipulate their way to the top ... and there are some organizations where that behavior really is the modus operandi."[25] Like Richard, the ability to read and manipulate others proves crucial to success in the business and financial sector. As Warren Buffet famously stated, "Any player unaware of the fool in the marketplace probably is the fool in the marketplace."[26]

Also like Richard, pretense is common in contemporary corporate and financial environments. Richard, for example, publicly always maintained his disinterest in the crown. "I'd rather be a pedlar" (1.3.149), he tells Rivers at the beginning of the play; and, of course, he has to be "convinced" to take the throne in act 3. Such pretense also is found among financial elites. There is plenty of evidence that conspicuous wealth is a goal of those in the financial sector. It is not just the former CEO of Tyco, Dennis Kozlowski, recently called "the poster boy of corporate greed," who is guilty of an outrageous lifestyle, which in his case included a $6,000 shower curtain.[27] Success in the financial world, however, usually requires some ability for pretense beyond greed and self-interest. Lewis emphasizes that it was actually taboo overtly to express interest in making money; he fails to secure a job, for instance, when he tells the interviewer one reason he wants to be an investment banker is to make money. "That is not a good reason," his interviewer replies. "Frankly, we try to discourage people from our business who are too interested in money."[28] Making one's ambitions for money and power known proves damaging not only for the ambitious but also for the corporation. When an executive failed to hide his ambition to become the next CEO of Marks & Spenser, his candidature destabilized the business and "in the end, it did little for his own career: he was shown the door at Baker Street and never achieved the role he sought."[29] Even though successful financial elites often feign disinterest in their carefully plotted ambitious goals, as with the common people's recognition of Richard's pretense, many of us can perceive their naked greed. Nevertheless, within the machinations of the financial world, the most successful elite, according to Lewis, is the individual similar to Richard who excels in the "ability to cloak his self-interest in the guise of high principle."[30]

Closely connected to this feigning disinterest is the importance of hiding one's true emotions from others. One of Richard's greatest skills is his ability to disguise his true self. Although Richard understands how to manipulate Clarence and Hastings, they are unaware of his true intentions. Hastings is so completely blind that he believes it is Richard who wears his emotions on his sleeve. This capacity to hide or manage emotions is also crucial to success among the financial elite. Lewis describes the personality of John Meriwether, a Solomon Brothers board member:

> He had an ability, rare among people and treasured by traders, to hide his state of mind. Most traders divulge whether they are making or losing money by the way they speak or move.... With Meriwether you could never, ever tell.... He had, I think, a profound ability to control the two emotions that

commonly destroy traders—fear and greed—and it made him as noble as a man who pursues his self-interest so fiercely can be.[31]

This ability to perceive, understand, and manage emotions, often described under the umbrella term *emotional intelligence*, has become a vital part of the way business leaders are trained to face the significant challenges of their workplace.[32] Yet, as Rebecca Alexander points out, this ability to manage one's emotions by expressing and masking emotions when used solely for personal and private gain is the "dark side of emotional intelligence."[33]

Another way Richard successfully manipulates others is to fabricate, control, and use information. In the play, he uses prophecy and dreams to manipulate Edward's opinion against Clarence. In contemporary times, such prophecy is not taken seriously, but one can still manipulate another kind of secret: inside knowledge. Although illegal, there is no shortage of cases of insider trading, which occurs when insiders—such as a company's officers or directors—take advantage of material nonpublic information about the company. Among recent scandals is the famous class-action suit against Mark Zuckerberg for his $1 billion profit from overvalued Facebook shares. In another case, the Securities and Exchange Commission seized assets of traders who profited by $13 million when they bought stock based on "non-public information" of an oil company's buy-out.[34] In addition, Richard's adeptness at manipulating information to affect reputation is still very much valid. This manipulation of reputation can be used to enhance one's own circumstances as well as ruin rivals. There are cases of corporate leaders manipulating their personal reputation (and accounting systems) to increase their level of executive compensation.[35] Information is also used to manipulate opinion against rivals. Again, there is no shortage of cases of potential fabrications used to blacken the reputation of opponents; however, in one notable Shakespearean brother-against-brother feud, the chief executive of one of the world's biggest real-estate developers was voted out by his board based on the influence of his two younger brothers.[36] In return, he sued his brothers for libel as his dismissal involved accusations of falsified medical diagnoses.

Richard's tyrannical character traits also extend to his willingness to turn on all his allies, including Buckingham—his "other self." Again, there is no shortage of stories of financial elites willing to use anyone, including employees, mentors, and friends, as pawns in their ambitious goals. One particularly illuminating story outlines how, in 1978, a Solomon Brothers partner recruited Lewis Ranieri to his mortgage department. Although history would reveal how important this department would become, upset with his "exile" from the more lucrative bond market, Ranieri decided to take over. While his boss was ill, he consolidated power until "the man whom he was quietly challenging seemed to evaporate."[37]

Many cases of former allies turning on each other only become known when they make it to court. Common cases include friends breaching contracts or stealing ideas. Mark Zuckerberg again was at the heart of such a case, which was highly fictionalized in the 2010 movie *The Social Network*. Other examples include a lawsuit against the CEO of the steel-and-mining giant ArcelorMittal, by the CEO's former friend, who claimed breach of contract after helping the company broker oil exploration licenses in Nigeria.[38] Steve Jobs apparently was infamous for taking credit for all Apple's ideas, including those of his closest friends and confidants, such as his chief industrial designer Jonathan Ive.[39]

In the play, Shakespeare does leave his audience with the happy ending of Richmond's victory over the tyrannical Richard. In his exploration of the psychological traits of Richard, the playwright also suggests that even this quintessential tyrant, who self-consciously pursues villainy, is not without a conscience. In the night before the Battle of Bosworth Field, Richard is troubled by dreams where all the individuals he murdered to gain the crown visit and curse him to "despair and die" (5.4.95–155). The same ghosts, even the enemy Yorkists, visit the saintly Tutor Richmond and bless him to "live and flourish." We know that Richard has long been disturbed by his conscience. Anne tells us that she never slept well in his bed, because she had "been waked by his timorous dreams" (4.1.80). The only time we see Richard at all unnerved is following these dreams of ghosts and despair. He wakes and admits, "O coward conscience, how dost thou afflict me ... / Cold fearful drops stand on my trembling flesh" (5.4.158). Richard recovers from his panic and returns to his favorite element of battle, where he fights ruthlessly until he is finally killed by Richmond.

Conclusion

We have no way of knowing whether modern financial elites are plagued by the same conscience as Richard was in the end. The deliberate actions of executives who chose to ignore early warnings, according to Perrow, are a contributing cause of the financial crises.[40] These crises have led to tough economic times, high rates of foreclosures, and some of the highest unemployment rates in years. Some CEOs have begun to turn down millions of dollars in bonuses; others, however, continue to accept the bonuses on top of their already high multimillion-dollar salaries. It is impossible to know whether those who turned down their bonuses did so out of a sense of guilt or simply to maintain a positive public image. Certainly many financial elites have been disgraced. The former CEO of the Royal Bank of Scotland, Fred Goodwin, was stripped of his knighthood because of the scale and severity of the impact of his actions as chief executive.[41]

Yet, it seems business as usual for many financial elites. So perhaps this is where the comparison ends between contemporary financial elites and Shakespeare's portrayal of the psychological traits of those who pursue, without restraint, their narrow self-interest. As Michael Lewis notes of his experience in the financial world, "bad guys did not suffer their comeuppance in Act V . . . they flourished."[42]

Notes

1. Thomas More, "History of Richard III," in *Richard III*, ed. John Jowett (Oxford: Oxford University Press, 2000), 386.

2. Vice was a stock character of medieval morality plays, who was noted for making mischief and tempting others. In the play, Richard is equated not only with Vice but the Devil. See Wolfgang Iser, *Staging Politics*, trans. David Henry Wilson (New York: Columbia University Press, 1993), 49–50.

3. John Jowett, "Introduction," in *Richard III*, ed. John Jowett (Oxford: Oxford University Press, 2000), 107.

4. Ibid., 107–108.

5. For example, Daniel Fischlin and Mark Fortier, *Adaptations of Shakespeare* (London: Routledge, 2000), 14.

6. Alexander Leggatt, *Shakespeare's Political Drama* (London: Routledge, 1989), 32–34.

7. All citations from William Shakespeare, *Richard III*, ed. John Jowett (Oxford: Oxford University Press, 2000).

8. Leon Harold Craig, "Beyond Love and Honor," in *Souls with Longing*, ed. Bernard J. Dobski and Dustin A. Gish (Lanham: Lexington, 2011), 209–212.

9. Ibid., 222.

10. Ibid., 207.

11. Richard Bookstaber, *A Demon of Our Own Design* (Hoboken, NJ: John Wiley and Sons, 2008).

12. Charles Perrow, "The Meltdown Was Not an Accident," in *Markets on Trial*, ed. Michael Lounsbury and Paul M. Hirsch (Bingley, UK: Emerald Group, 2010), 328.

13. G. R. Bassiry, "Ethics, Education, and Corporate Leadership," *Journal of Business Ethics* 9, no. 10 (1990).

14. Many ancient tyrants, such as the Athenian Pisistratus, were praised for their fair and moderate rule. See Herodotus, *The Histories*, trans. Robert Strassler (Toronto: Anchor, 2009), 1.59.

15. Aristotle, "The Politics" (Chicago: University of Chicago Press, 1984), 1270a.

16. Iser, *Staging Politics*, 45–46.

17. William Shakespeare, *Henry VI, Part III*, ed. Randall Martin (Oxford: Oxford University Press, 2008), 3.2.150–184.

18. Leggatt, for example, notes that Richard never actually says he wants the crown. Leggatt, *Shakespeare's Political Drama*, 35.

19. Graham Holderness, *Shakespeare: The Histories* (Hampshire, UK: Macmillan, 2000), 91–96.

20. Steven Boswell and Kevin Nichols, "Four Traits of Elite New Advisors," *Registered Rep Exclusive Insight* (May 10, 2012), 3.

21. Perrow, "The Meltdown Was Not an Accident," 314.

22. Jean Pierre Hassoun, "Emotions on the Trading Floor," in *The Sociology of the Financial Markets*, ed. Karin Knorr Cetina and Alex Preda (Oxford: Oxford University Press, 2005), 117.

23. Michael Lewis, *Liar's Poker* (New York: W. W. Norton, 1989), 87.

24. Caroline Keating and Karen Heltman, "Dominance and Deception in Children and Adults," *Personality and Psychology Bulletin* 20, no. 3 (1994).

25. As quoted in Rebecca Alexander, "Dark Side of Emotional Intelligence," *Management Today* (April 1, 2011), 47.

26. As quoted in Lewis, *Liar's Poker*, 44.

27. Kaja Whitehouse, "Ex-Tyco CEO Dennis Kozlowski Agrees to Forfeit Some of the Looted Money," *New York Post*, August 10, 2012.

28. Lewis, *Liar's Poker*, 35.

29. Patience Wheatcroft, "Destructive Aspiration," *Management Today* (January 1, 2005).

30. Lewis, *Liar's Poker*, 280.

31. Ibid., 15–16.

32. Silvia Iuscu, Catalin Neagu, and Laura Neagu, "Emotional Intelligence, Essential Component to Leadership," *Global Conference on Business & Finance Proceedings* 7, no. 2 (2012).

33. Alexander, "Dark Side of Emotional Intelligence."

34. Aibing Guo, "SEC Freezes Another $6 Million in Nexen Insider Trading Case," *Bloomsburg Businessweek*, August 7, 2012.

35. Bert Cannella, Sydney Finkelstein, and Donald C. Hambrick, *Strategic Leadership: Theory and Research on Executives, Top Management Teams, and Boards* (Oxford: Oxford University Press, 2008).

36. Jonathan Cheng, "Decision in Family Feud Leaves CEO Vulnerable," *Wall Street Journal—Eastern Edition*, May 29, 2008, B3.

37. Lewis, *Liar's Poker*, 115–117.

38. Valerie Flynn, "Court Case Throws Light on Mittal Brothers' Rivalry," *Metal Bulletin*, July 18, 2011.

39. Walter Isaacson, *Steve Jobs* (New York: Simon and Schuster, 2011).

40. Perrow, "The Meltdown Was Not an Accident," 314.

41. Patrick Wintour, "A Reputation Shredded," *The Guardian*, January 31, 2012.

42. Lewis, *Liar's Poker*, 86.

Chapter 8

Cymbeline and the Origins of Modern Liberty

David Ramsey

No one seems to know quite what to make of Shakespeare's late play *Cymbeline*. As one scholar has noted, the play seems to require that the reader "accept an element of the esoteric" when turning to the task of its interpretation.[1] At once a British play and a Roman play, it combines elements of history and romance, tragedy and comedy. The play resists simple classification. To the extent that scholars and critics have engaged the play in recent years, their focus has been almost entirely extra-textual, treating either the sources of the play or its place within the context of the Shakespearean canon.[2] To read such scholarship, one might be inclined to concur with Johnson's dismissal of the play as "unresisting imbecility" full of "faults too evident for detection, and too gross for aggravation."[3] And yet the play concludes with what may very well be the most carefully crafted, comprehensive, and theatrically satisfying of Shakespeare's finales, a virtuoso display demonstrating the capacity of a mature artist to bring about unity and concord from what must otherwise appear to be a chaotic convergence of multiple plotlines presented as a series of disorganized, meandering episodes.

Act 5, scene 5 of *Cymbeline* has been referred to by one critic as Shakespeare's great "twenty-four fold denouement."[4] Every prominent character on stage is made to experience in some way that recognition and restoration that in other comedies is often confined to only a few characters, or one. By extending the scope of the experiences of revelation and restoration so as to encompass the entire stage, Shakespeare produces in characters and engaged audience alike an unparalleled degree of wonder. One leaves the play, or sets down the text, feeling as though a veil has been lifted. Every major character in the scene is shown to have been deceived in his understanding or belief or opinion of at least one other character, and all are restored and left with a deeper appreciation of one another. Although some important scholarship on the play has emerged in recent years, the chief problem or question of *Cymbeline* has received little attention from scholars. The question arising from the action of the play appears to be a simple one—"What does England owe to Rome?"[5]—but in the process of teasing out Shakespeare's answer to this question, the reader is drawn to consider anew the theologico-political question that, arguably, continues to animate political development in the West, and perhaps now the world over. This chapter examines Shakespeare's artful resolution of this tension through his novel reworking of a traditional plotline in *Cymbeline*.

The question of England's debt to Rome arises within the play on two distinct levels. In the more evident sense, the play as a whole can be read as a working out or thinking through of the problems that arise when Britain's sovereign is presented with the question of what tribute his kingdom will pay to Rome. One could imagine *Cymbeline* recast as a history or tragedy, treating primarily the problems of statesmanship involved in addressing this question.[6] But to read the play as merely a deficient or misshapen history would be to ignore the many ways in which it works within the conventions of the romance. Such a reading would also encounter difficulties explaining the many scenes devoted to the development of the wager plot that arises between the king's daughter, Imogen; her banished husband, Posthumus Leonatus; and the Italian he meets during his banishment, Iachimo. It is to this wager plot that we now turn.

The Wager

Most commentators[7] cite Giovanni Boccaccio's *Decameron* II.9 as Shakespeare's chief source for the wager plot in *Cymbeline*. While there are a number of parallels between the two stories—most notably Shakespeare's imitation of the romantic cast Boccaccio gives to the story—both seem to owe a great debt to a third, common source, Livy's treatment of the rape of Lucretia in *Ab Urbe*

Condita. Lucretia was the subject of one of Shakespeare's early narrative poems, *Lucrece*, a work that, if nothing else, makes clear that he had already devoted a great deal of thought to the psychological dynamics of the young tyrant and erotic, and the paragon of republican Roman virtue, by the time he would have begun work on the mature Roman plays. Indeed, after thoughtful comparison, it becomes difficult not to concede that what Shakespeare undertook in *Cymbeline* was the recasting of the founding myth of the Roman Republic, appropriating and refashioning Roman themes for his own founding myth about the origins of English republicanism. If this is indeed the case, Shakespeare would not be the first to have done so.[8]

Students of Roman history will recall Livy's account of the events leading up to the expulsion of the Tarquins, the end of the Roman monarchy, and the creation of the republic by Lucius Junius Brutus, the forbear of Marcus Junius Brutus, whom Shakespeare memorialized for the English-speaking peoples as deliverer of that "unkindest cut of all" to Julius Caesar in the attempt to preserve the republic through the assassination of the aspiring emperor. For Livy, the birth of freedom in Rome begins with the story of the rape of the virtuous Lucretia, wife of Collatinus, at the hands of Sextus Tarquinius, son to Lucius Tarquinius Superbus. While the Roman forces were encamped at Ardea, the officers fell to talking about their wives, each extolling the virtue of his spouse.[9] Among those present was Lucius Tarquinius Collatinus, son of the king's nephew, who persuaded these officers to leave off talking about their wives and seek out knowledge of their respective merits by riding back to Rome. Upon their arrival, all the wives but one were discovered to be engaged in some form or other of luxurious relaxation; only Lucretia, the wife of Collatinus, was discovered at home. Collatinus invites the officers to dine in his home and, upon seeing her, the young Tarquin is seized with a desire to debauch Lucretia by force, provoked alike by her chastity and beauty. He returns a few nights later, bringing only a single attendant, and presents himself as a guest at the home of Collatinus. Waiting until the house falls silent and all in it are sure to be asleep, he steals into Lucretia's room and, sword drawn, with his left hand on her breast, awakens her, warning her that if she makes a sound he will kill her. He then offers her a choice—either she can submit to him, or she can die. Finding her unafraid of death, he appeals to her sense of honor, promising her that if she does not submit, he will kill both Lucretia and his own slave, placing both bodies together so that he could claim to have slain them upon discovery of her shameful adultery with a commoner. If she submits, however, he will tell no one and her honor will remain intact. Faced with the choice, Lucretia submits, then sends word the next day to her father and husband, telling both to bring a friend and come home quickly. Lucretius brings Publius Valerius, and Collatinus, Lucius Junius Brutus. Upon their arrival, Lucretia confesses to the crime, promising that her body only has been violated—her heart remains guiltless. She names Sextus Tarquinius as the villain, asks these four men to avenge her, and, having received their pledges to do so, stabs herself in the heart with the knife she had kept concealed. While Lucretius and Collatinus bewail her death, Brutus takes up the bloody knife and swears before the men to overthrow the Tarquins and never again suffer them, or any other men, to be king in Rome. Dumbfounded, the three follow Brutus into the market, carrying Lucretia's lifeless body to stand as a silent testament to the despotism of Tarquin rule. And, as Livy tells the tale, "every man had his own complaint to make of the prince's crime and violence." Thus, bearing the body, the knife, and the tale, Brutus rallied the Roman people to banish the Tarquins and institute republican rule through the office of the divided rule of an elective consulate. Brutus was able to persuade the Romans to assert and jealously protect their liberty, and to swear oaths never again to yield to a king, by making use of the powerful imagery of the corpse and the bloody knife. Lucretia's chaste virtue was contrasted with the tyrannical assertiveness of the prince, over whom even marriage vows and the sacred law of hospitality held no sway. The tyrant's nature was made manifest as unchecked appetite, erotic longing unbounded by any of the constraints of honor or nobility.[10] In erecting a counterforce within the regime that would oppose this unbounded willfulness, Brutus helped to define and create a space wherein the citizens of Rome could exercise their liberty.

The significance of this liberty would be called into question by Augustine in his *City of God against the Pagans*, where his deconstruction of the Roman order begins with a reconsideration of the justice of Livy's founding myth. If Lucretia did not will the rape, then the sin is that of Sextus Tarquinius. Why, then, did she bear the heavier penalty? Why is it Lucretia who dies, and why at her own hand? How is it that the murder of the innocent has come to be praised as virtue?[11] Augustine goes on to argue that Lucretia was forced to suicide because of her great shame. Supposing she was indeed guiltless and had suffered the rape without consent, she was aware that there was no course open to her, short of voluntary suicide, to exhibit to men her conscience. To the example of Lucretia, image of Roman honor, Augustine offers the comparison of those Christian women who, having suffered the indignities and violence of rape at the hands of the invading barbarians when Alaric and his Goths sacked the city in 410, chose not to "avenge upon themselves the guilt of others" but rather to "enjoy the glory of chastity," knowing that in the sight of God, if not of men, their purity is known, and they need not answer the wrong of their rape with the further sin of prideful suicide.[12]

Prior to Boccaccio, Machiavelli, or Shakespeare, Augustine found it necessary to address and reformulate the founding myth of Rome in order to make more clear the supremacy of the city of God to even the greatest of earthly cities. Augustine introduces into Roman psychology a markedly different perspective. Against the political liberty ensured to the Roman citizen by the institutions of the republic's mixed regime and the military virtue upon which it rests, he places the spiritual liberty of the Christian citizen of the city of God, and the inspired virtues of faith, hope, and love directed to the realization of peace. Developing the implications of the Incarnation, Augustine elevates the cosmic significance of the individual, and consequently the prominence of the interior life of each individual. A full account of the cosmos or the whole is now shown to require more than just a sufficient understanding of the causes that can be known through the appearances of things. It must also incorporate what a later thinker would call "knowledge of the heart,"[13] the primary instance of which we find recorded in Augustine's *Confessions*, a record of one soul's quest for knowledge and understanding in itself through pursuit of a deeper understanding of God. In both his words and his deeds, Augustine introduces a new challenge to classical political philosophy in general, and to Rome in particular. After Augustine it will no longer be assumed that the gods serve the city. Nor will it be assumed that man is indeed merely a rational, political animal, suited for life in the city. For Augustine, rather, the truth about human nature is that mankind can never be fully at home in this world. The individual is called to something more than political participation. He seeks incorporation within a larger whole. All subsequent reformulations of the rape of Lucretia would, in one way or another, derive their form from the conversation initiated by Augustine's critique of Livy's tale.

It is in the light of these preliminary statements that we turn now to *Cymbeline*. Political enquiry begins with the question of what mode of association leads to human happiness or flourishing, but the play begins with two gentlemen of Cymbeline's court discussing why it is that "you do not meet a man but frowns."[14] One Posthumus Leonatus—the most noble of men in Britain, according to the first gentleman—has wed Imogen, daughter to the king. This wedding has frustrated the plans of Cymbeline, later shown to be dominated by the will of the Queen, who had intended that Imogen wed her stepbrother Cloten, the Queen's son from another marriage. Imogen has been imprisoned and Posthumus banished. But the problems extend even deeper. Cloten is known to be a miserable creature, "too bad for bad report," while Posthumus "is a creature such / As, to seek through the regions of the earth / For one his like, there would be something failing / In him that should compare."[15] Shakespeare's story begins with the praise of his Collatinus, not his Lucretia. Imogen's merit is that she discerns Posthumus's virtue despite her father's dim opinion of him, and his humble birth. Posthumus is an orphan, the son of one Sicilius, who fought beside the father and great uncle of Cymbeline and died of grief when his two older sons were killed in Rome's civil wars. Like Posthumus, Imogen has two older brothers whose loss is mourned by her father. These princes—Guiderius and Arviragus—were stolen away from their nursery at a very young age twenty years before the action of the play begins. Perhaps it is to make up for this loss, and also out of sympathy for the grieving Sicilius, that Cymbeline chose to take Posthumus in and raise him at court. The play does not indicate how long Posthumus remained in the king's favor, nor how he came to lose it. Neither does the play mention the events surrounding the death of Imogen's mother or the way in which he came to remarry. There is much in the play that is left out or passed over in silence, and so, for all its intricacy of plotting, there is also a great deal upon which we are invited to speculate. The play invites a particular sort of thinking, and it leads us to acknowledge the great gaps in our knowledge that may prevent a perfect reconciliation of the part and the whole.

Before departing, Posthumus exchanges tokens with Imogen—his a ring, hers a bracelet. Each swears to remain faithful in love to the other. Posthumus is to travel to Rome, where he will reside with one Philario, a friend of his father. He leaves behind his servant Pisanio to attend Imogen. The subsequent scenes in Rome, in the house of Philario, are thoroughly cosmopolitan. Unlike the setting of the wager scene in Livy, these Romans preside over an empire already established, and each noble holds court in his own home. Present here are a Frenchman, a Dutchman, a Spaniard, and the Italians Philario and Iachimo. Just as in the first scene of the play, Posthumus's entry is preceded by a discussion of his merit, but here we find that neither Iachimo nor the Frenchman are impressed by his character. Nevertheless, Philario entreats his guests to treat Posthumus as they would a noble friend. The conversation turns to the praise of women, and Posthumus takes up the praise of Imogen, to which Iachimo objects. How can Posthumus know that she is more beautiful and virtuous than Italian women he has not yet seen? Catching sight of the ring bestowed on Posthumus by Imogen before his departure, Iachimo finds a metaphor for his argument: "If she went before others I have seen, as that diamond of yours outlusters many I have beheld, I could not but believe she excelled many; but I have not seen the most precious diamond that is, nor you the lady."[16] Posthumus maintains that there is a clear distinction between the token of his beloved and the beloved herself, that the woman herself is a gift of the gods, and therefore rates her higher than any token. To the suggestion that her virtue and love may be stolen as easily as the ring, Posthumus maintains his distinction: love is not a ring, but an outward manifestation of an inner reality. A ring may indeed be stolen, but not the love of Imogen, no matter how sweet the words of the courtier. To this Iachimo proposes to wager half the value of his estate against Posthumus's ring that he need only two meetings with Imogen in order to win her. Posthumus proposes to change the terms—gold for gold, but not the ring—but when Iachimo sneers that this reluctance smacks of some religion in him, Posthumus agrees to give him the ring as surety until the wager is resolved. Iachimo asks also to be given a letter of commendation, so as to be assured access to the princess in Britain, and to this, too, Posthumus agrees.

Upon his arrival in Britain, Iachimo gains access to the princess with Posthumus's letter of commendation and twice tries to deceive her. The first attempt comes with false reports of Posthumus's dissipation upon arriving in Rome, but Imogen is disinclined to believe the tale, and as a result Iachimo's plan to exploit her grief founders. But rather than retreat after this failed first attempt on her virtue, Iachimo explains that he has been sent by Posthumus to try Imogen's virtue—and she has confirmed his trust. Having failed to create in Imogen's mind the image of a Posthumus given over to dissipation, Iachimo now turns to excessive praise of his virtue. When this second tactic succeeds, he secures her permission to store a trunk packed with treasure for the emperor in her bedchamber. Iachimo's persistence and creativity appear to outmatch not only the reputed virtue of Posthumus but even the rare gifts of Imogen, his bride.

Having won access to her bedchamber through the false praise of Posthumus and the stratagem of the trunk, Iachimo waits until she has fallen asleep before emerging. But unlike Livy's young Tarquin, Iachimo is not driven by a desire to debauch the maiden by force. Instead, he surveys the décor of the room, observes the mole beneath her left breast, and steals the bracelet given to her by Posthumus. There is no rape in Shakespeare's telling. The story is made to turn on the husband's belief that the rape happened, rather than the fact of an actual rape. Faith and deception become the prominent themes here, not tyranny and honor. Believing he has gathered enough evidence to control Posthumus's perception of the appearances, Iachimo returns to the trunk, and then to Rome.

Shakespeare's chief addition to the tale of Boccaccio at this point is the way in which he uses Iachimo's knowledge of the mole to legitimate what Posthumus has already begun to fear upon seeing the (stolen) bracelet. This is particularly puzzling given his ability to distinguish between the appearances (the token of the beloved—i.e., the ring or bracelet) and the thing itself (the love of the beloved) when they last spoke. Why is Posthumus so quick to mistrust the love Imogen bears him when he has already admitted that such tokens may easily be stolen? Though revelation of the mole beneath her breast confirms in the minds of others present the truth of Iachimo's claims of conquest, Posthumus needs no more persuading after seeing the bracelet. He gives the ring to Iachimo immediately after seeing it a second time, and departs the scene in a rage shortly thereafter, to deliver the most misogynistic soliloquy ("Is there no way for men to be, but women must be half-workers?"[17]) we have from Shakespeare.

The grieving Posthumus writes letters to Pisanio and Imogen, telling the latter that he will meet her at Milford Haven, and telling the former to accompany her on the journey and kill her en route. Pisanio spares Imogen and devises the plan by which she is to adopt the look and manner of a young man, and seek to enter into the service of Lucius, whom Pisanio deems to be both honorable and most holy.[18] From this point on, the play is purely the invention of Shakespeare. And it is precisely at this point that things begin to get strange. Upon returning to court, Pisanio enters into the service of Cloten, who discovers that Posthumus was to return to Britain in order to meet Imogen at Milford Haven. He sets out to find the husband of the woman his mother wanted him to marry, dressed in the suit of clothes Posthumus wore when he departed from Britain, so that he can avenge a cruel comment Imogen made in the course of repulsing his advances.[19] Meanwhile, Imogen meets three strangers in the forest—an old man (Morgan/Belarius) and two younger men (Polydore/Guiderius and Cadwal/Arviragus). We know from a soliloquy delivered by Belarius that these are the missing sons of Cymbeline, stolen by the king's servant (Belarius) while they were boys. The siblings take to the young "boy" (for she is now dressed in preparation to enter into the service of Lucius under the assumed name of Fidele) immediately, and she to them, with all three observing their surprise at the sudden, deep, and natural affection he has for the stranger. They invite Fidele back to their cave, where she drinks a potion given to her by Pisanio (who had himself received it from the Queen) that puts her into a deep sleep resembling death. While the princes in exile are hunting, Guiderius encounters Cloten, still dressed in Posthumus's clothes. They exchange insults, then draw swords, and when Guiderius returns to the stage he bears Cloten's severed head in his hands. They arrange the body, cloaked in flowers, and lay it next to the sleeping Imogen/Fidele, whom they believe also dead. When Imogen at last awakes, it is in the dark, next to the headless body of a man wearing the clothes of the husband who has tried to have her killed. She swoons, perceiving herself to have been betrayed by Pisanio and Cloten. Lucius, the Roman general sent by Caesar to collect Cymbeline's delinquent tribute, finds her and, impressed by her clear devotion to her dead master, takes Fidele into his care.

Upon receiving confirmation in the form of a bloody handkerchief from Pisanio that he has indeed killed Imogen, Posthumus resolves to take up the British banner once more despite having traveled to the island with the Italian gentry for precisely the opposite purpose. His anger seems to have exhausted itself, and he now expresses a desire to die in order to atone for the death of his beloved. The language at this point is significant, and so I quote at length:

> So I'll fight
> Against the part I come with; so I'll die
> For thee, O Imogen, even for whom my life

Is every breath a death; and thus, unknown,
Pitied nor hated, to the face of peril
Myself I'll dedicate. Let me make men know
More valour in me than my habits show.
Gods, put the strength o' the Leonati in me!
To shame the guise o' the world, I will begin
The fashion, less without and more within.[20]

The soliloquy shows us that Posthumus has recognized the nature of his error, mistaking the token for the thing itself, and resolved not to repeat it again. For the remainder of the play he will endure in rapid succession the reversals of fortune and sudden, startling revelations of the hero in a romance. His journey for self-knowledge can be said to begin with the resolution found in the final couplet here, marking the inward turn characteristic of the Christian citizen Augustine anticipated. Posthumus's most noble actions in the play come when he begins to forsake all worldly cares and focus on his death.

Shakespeare gives us three accounts of the British victory over Rome. The first two are delivered by Posthumus on the field of battle in response to the queries of a British lord beating a retreat. In his first account, Posthumus forgives the cowardice of the fleeing noble, as "all was lost, but that the heavens fought."[21] But as he proceeds to tell the tale of how Belarius and the kidnapped princes took their stand in a narrow lane and rallied the spirits of the broken British lines, his spiritedness returns briefly, and he begins to mock the cowardice of the noble, leading him to recall once more the resolve of his soliloquy in act 5, scene 1 to shame the guise o' the world by wearing less without, more within. Now that he has helped the British to victory, he will surrender to the first British soldiers he finds, and he remembers his resolve to die for Imogen's sake. Two British captains enter the scene, praising Jupiter for the unlikely victory, and it is from them that we learn that a fourth man had been present with the three identified by Posthumus, this one dressed in a "silly habit." Posthumus's newfound humility extends so far as to deny himself the credit he might deserve for the British victory. When asked who he is, his answer is something between a lie and a confession, for he answers, simply, "a Roman," upon which he is taken into custody, to be delivered to the king.

Act 5, scene 4 finds Posthumus alone and in chains, musing on the paradoxical nature of human freedom. "Most welcome, bondage, for thou art a way, I think, to liberty."[22] His soliloquy takes the form of a prayer of repentance, asking of the gods "for Imogen's dear life take mine."[23] He sleeps, and things once again take a bizarre turn. As solemn music begins to play, Sicilius, the dead father of Posthumus, appears on stage, accompanied by his dead wife and two dead sons.

Each in turn speaks in archaic verse, appealing to Jupiter for restoration of their son lest "we appeal and from thy justice fly."[24] At this provocation the great Jupiter appears onstage, "descending in thunder and lightning," and, hurling a thunderbolt, the shades fall to their knees. Jupiter reassures the shades of his superintendence over "mortal accidents," explaining "whom best I love I cross; to make my gift, / the more delayed, delighted. Be content. / Your low-laid son our godhead will uplift."[25] Though the play is set during the time of the nativity, in more ways than one it anticipates the crucifixion and the resurrection, and never more clearly than here, in Jupiter's speech, where he tells Posthumus and the shades of his family what he is like. But not only does Jupiter tell Posthumus about himself, and promise him a restoration, the god also leaves behind a tablet on which is engraved the prophecy of these things. Posthumus's reaction upon reading the tablet, this artifact of a revelatory dream, is that "'Tis still a dream, or else such stuff as madmen / tongue, and brain not; either both, or nothing, / or senseless speaking, or a speaking such / as sense cannot untie. Be what it is, / the action of my life is like it, which / I'll keep, if but for sympathy."[26] In this way Posthumus, summoned before the king for what he assumes must be his death as a Roman, becomes an unlikely instrument of Jupiter, delivering his prophecy into the midst of the conflict between the Romans and the British, and touching off the single greatest recognition scene in all of Shakespeare.

Beyond Tragedy, Comedy, and History

It has become conventional to speak of Shakespeare's late plays—*Pericles, Cymbeline, A Winter's Tale*, and *The Tempest*—as romances, setting them off from all the plays that came before as something new and experimental. Shakespearean scholars today tend to agree that the young Shakespeare, winning fame for his first tetralogy of English histories (detailing the vicissitudes of the War of the Roses), turned next to comedy, then to tragedy, interspersed with the histories of the second tetralogy (examining the origins of the conflict treated in the first tetralogy), before concluding with his turn to romance. Harry Jaffa has written that Shakespeare seems to have been the greatest, perhaps even the only, practitioner of the whole art called for by Socrates in the closing lines of the Platonic dialogue *Symposium*, that of the poet able to compose both comedy and tragedy.[27] According to the argument recounted there, the poetry of neither comedian nor tragedian will be whole until he learns to compose that of the other.[28] Wilson Carey McWilliams reminds us that the distinction between comedy and tragedy can be understood as just another presentation of the metaphysician's distinction between the part and the whole: "Comedy turns on the exposure of human incompleteness—our 'halfness,' Emerson called it—unmasking the human pretension to be a whole, to claim to have final answers to the great mysteries."[29] It falls to the tragedian to dramatize the equally human aspiration to be a whole unto oneself. Tragedy speaks to our desire to rid ourselves of the demands of political life, or any other natural limitation, even that of death; comedy reminds us that human life is contingent upon these limits, and its work is to celebrate the goodness to be discovered in a life shown to be dependent on such particularity, such as the distinctly human unities of love and friendship. Tragedy reveals the error in the hero's attempt to become a wholly independent and complete being ("I am myself alone"); comedy shows us how individuals understanding themselves as in some sense incomplete can be made to fit into a sort of whole. Placing all consideration of the Platonic argument involving the differences between the activity of the poet or maker[30] (which necessarily consists in the shaping of likenesses) and that of the philosopher (whose thinking is about the beings themselves) to one side, we may yet see how, in one sense, the task of the complete poet is revealed to be not altogether unlike that of the philosopher: both are driven to reflect on the problem of reconciling or doing justice to the demands of both the part and the whole. For those who find Jaffa's thesis persuasive, the later plays may present something new in the old debate between the poets and the philosophers. If this is the case, then on these grounds alone *Cymbeline* merits further attention from the students of political philosophy.

But further consideration reveals another reason why political theorists might reconsider the merits of *Cymbeline*. At the center of this play is Jupiter's speech revealing to Posthumus the nature of the godhead in the statement that his love manifests itself to men as a cross. The shape of the cross is itself a paradox, pointing as it does in two directions, and achieving a unity at a single point through this opposition. This doubleness, this paradox, this unrelenting complexity, is found throughout *Cymbeline*. Indeed, the play itself is located precisely at the crossroads between Shakespeare's Rome and Shakespeare's England. Jaffa suggests that the Roman and English plays serve as "the axis upon which Shakespeare's account of the political things turns," and draws attention to "that strange and complex 'comedy' *Cymbeline*," which "may be seen as a 'British-Roman play,' and hence as the link between the two great series, Roman and British."[31] But Jaffa's recognition of the curious place of *Cymbeline* is underdeveloped. While one may agree with Jaffa's roughly stated thesis that the Roman and English plays constitute some sort of axis, I would go further to suggest that Shakespeare's account of political things rests upon an adequate understanding of the problem treated in *Cymbeline*. Through its treatment of the question of what Britain owes to Rome, the play points us to Shakespeare's understanding of the theologico-political question that continues to inform any serious treatment of the political things. According to

Jaffa, Shakespeare's understanding of the political things turns about an axis that concludes with the fact of England's break with Rome.[32] But if we see *Cymbeline* as somehow drawing together and uniting the two parts of that axis, then Shakespeare's understanding of the political things is cast in a new light. The problem of man comes into focus at a discrete moment in history, and the theologico-political problem becomes just another manifestation of the cross, which, once noticed, becomes apparent throughout the play. As the final words and deeds of Cymbeline suggest, England, it turns out, need not break with Rome. The transformation of Posthumus Leonatus that occurs within the play can be seen as a Shakespearean synecdoche for the historical development of the Roman Empire. Like Plato before him, Shakespeare apprehends a connection between the city and the soul, and realizes that like souls, nations, too, can be turned, or reborn. Rome can and will be transformed from within. Aware of the origins of Roman liberty, he works within the founding myth of the Roman Republic to create a likeness of what he sees about him in seventeenth-century England. Rome will be born anew on English shores,[33] and human freedom will achieve a more personal significance reflected in the inward turn of Posthumus Leonatus.

Jaffa's formulation of the Shakespearean whole—comedy, tragedy, and history—neglects the most important transformation within Shakespeare's writings—the transition to romance in the late plays. Now, there are likely some who are not yet persuaded by Jaffa's attempts to put Shakespeare into conversation with Plato. And yet, even for these skeptics, it should still be clear from a reading of the romances vis-à-vis the remainder of the Shakespearean canon that, having thought through the problems of each poetic form, and discovered through his writing the merits of each, the mature Shakespeare turned in his old age to a tragicomic form, beginning perhaps with his revisions to the text of *King Lear*,[34] and developing this form in the later plays. Traditional elements of the romance are an episodic structure consisting of a variety of scenes and contexts forcing the characters to play many roles while experiencing the vicissitudes of fortune, and ultimately centering on the theme of a lost or wandering hero in search of identity or recognition.[35] The romantic hero wants to know, but also to *be known*. The meandering and episodic structure of the romance allows the reader or audience to watch characters unfold over time, across a variety of different scenarios.[36] These scenarios may require the hero to assume the appearance of another, adopt an assumed name, and perhaps even do violent or peculiar things that "aren't like him." But the romantic hero, like Augustine's Christian, is above all a seeker and a wayfarer in this world, and the inadequacy of his own self-knowledge is always before him.

The pattern of the romantic tale is particularly appealing to audiences emerging from a period of social disorder or dissolution.[37] The virtues of the seeker are those of the lost and lonesome individual seeking to find his place within a tumultuous universe that can at times seem chaotic. He longs to discover order and harmony, and this longing often leads the romantic hero to become a seeker of signs. His narrative will often incorporate more than its share of events that inspire wonder, and he *will* wonder at them. *Cymbeline* is a play full of signs and wonders, none of them greater than its twenty-four-fold denouement. It suggests the consummation of a multitude of romantic narratives, only one of which have we seen in any detail. The romance affords the playwright the freedom to show man passing through the comic and tragic moments of life and proceeding onward, in search of a greater unity. It allows him the opportunity to study that aspect of the human soul that transcends the political, and longs for ultimate self-knowledge, longs to know that each person is somehow significant in light of eternity.

Conclusion

Shakespeare wrote no Passion play. The closest he came to doing so is his *Cymbeline*, which presents us with the journey and transformation of a single human soul in the person of Posthumus Leonatus, neither a Roman nor a Briton but a seeker who is restored to his parents and his wife only after seeking his own death in recognition of his folly. Resolving to "wear less without and more within,"[38] Posthumus reminds us from the stage of the paradox, the cross, of human freedom, which he discovers only when he is placed in chains and anticipating his own death. Told by his jailer that he is to be sent to the king, Posthumus speaks a double truth when he says that "Thou bring'st good news; I am called to be made free."[39] By reimagining the action of Livy's wager story, Shakespeare's *Cymbeline* turns our attention from the reckless lust of the aspiring tyrant and the stoic nobility of the ravished wife to the search of the flawed husband, whose pain at the recognition of his own error, mistaking the images for the things themselves, opens him to the possibility of that search—a search that ends in restoration, recognition, and a discovery of uniquely human freedom. In the process of unveiling the progress of that search, the play invites audiences and readers alike to take up the question in earnest once more, *quid sit deus?*

Notes

1. Robin Moffet, "*Cymbeline* and the Nativity," *Shakespeare Quarterly* 13 (1962): 207–218. See p. 215.

2.　John E. Alvis, "*Cymbeline* in Context: The Regime Issue," and in *Shakespeare's Last Plays*, ed. Steven W. Smith and Travis Curtwright (Lanham, MD: Lexington, 2002); Willy Maley, "Postcolonial Shakespeare: British Identity Formation and *Cymbeline*," and Alison Thorne, "'To write and read / Be henceforth treacherous': *Cymbeline* and the Problem of Interpretation," in *Shakespeare's Late Plays: New Readings* (Edinburgh: Edinburgh University Press, 1999); MacDonald P. Jackson, "A Lover's Complaint, Cymbeline, and the Shakespearean Canon: Interpreting Shared Vocabulary," *Modern Language Review* 103 (2008): 621. There is some evidence, however, of a very recent renewed interest in addressing the peculiarities of the play. See Grace Tiffany, "Shakespeare's Miracle Plays," *English Studies* 93 (2012): 1; and Maurice Hunt, "A New Taxonomy of Shakespeare's Pagan Plays," *Religion and Literature* 43 (2011): 29.

3.　Bertrand H. Bronson and Jean M. O'Meara, eds., *Selections from Johnson on Shakespeare* (New Haven, CT: Yale University Press, 1986), 307.

4.　Frank Kermode, *Shakespeare, Spenser, Donne* (London: Routledge, 1971), 237.

5.　I note in passing that this is also a question that appears with great urgency in what is now assumed by many to be Shakespeare's final play, *Henry VIII* or *All Is True*. Some future work might examine the unities of these two plays when read side by side, Shakespeare's first and last words, as it were, on the English monarchy and the theologico-political question.

6.　Cf. Robin Moffet, "*Cymbeline* and the Nativity," *Shakespeare Quarterly* 13 (1962): 207–218; and Howard B. White, *Copp'd Hills towards Heaven: Shakespeare and the Classical Polity* (The Hague: Martinus Nijhoff, 1970).

7.　Cf. Geoffrey Bullough, ed., *Narrative and Dramatic Sources of Shakespeare*, vol. VIII (New York: Columbia University Press, 1975); William Witherle Lawrence, "The Wager in Cymbeline," *PMLA* 35 (1920): 391–431; Kenneth Muir, *The Sources of Shakespeare's Plays* (New Haven, CT: Yale University Press, 1978). The recent essays of Alvis (2002) and Arbery (2002) are exceptions to this rule, and they suggest the need for a more careful consideration of the way in which Shakespeare has presented his understanding of the theologico-political problem in the play. Cf. Alvis, note 2 *supra*; and Glenn Arbery, "The Displaced Nativity in Cymbeline," in *Shakespeare's Last Plays*, ed. Steven W. Smith and Travis Curtwright (Lanham, MD: Lexington, 2002).

8.　Harvey Mansfield shows how, quite unlike the romantic mode adopted by Boccaccio and Shakespeare, Machiavelli's retelling of the rape takes the form of an elaborate conspiracy. "The Cuckold in *Mandragola*," in Vickie B. Sullivan, ed., *The Comedy and Tragedy of Machiavelli: Essays on the Literary Works* (New Haven, CT: Yale University Press, 2000). Shakespeare's treatment of the rape of Lucretia differs from those of both Livy and Machiavelli. To my knowledge, no one has devoted serious attention to the comparison of *Mandragola* and *Cymbeline*.

9.　What follows is a summary of the account given by Livy in the closing lines of Book I.

10.　For a compelling exposition of Shakespeare's understanding of the balances and imbalances of thumotic and erotic souls under the Roman Republic and Roman

Empire, see Paul A. Cantor, *Shakespeare's Rome: Republic and Empire* (Ithaca, NY: Cornell University Press), esp. pp. 155–208.

11. Augustine, *City of God against the Pagans*, trans. Marcus Dodds (New York: Modern Library, 1993), I.19, p. 25.

12. Ibid.

13. "The heart has its reasons of which reason knows nothing.... It is the heart which perceives God and not the reason. That is what faith is: God perceived by the heart, and not by reason." Pascal, *Pensees*, trans. A. J. Krailsheimer (New York: Penguin, 1995), 127: 423, 424. Cf. *Cymbeline*, IV.ii, 22: "Love's reason's without reason."

14. Shakespeare, *Cymbeline*, I.i.1.

15. Ibid., 16–22.

16. Ibid., I.iv, 68–72.

17. Ibid., II.v.

18. Ibid., III.iv, 170–178.

19. "With that suit upon my back will I ravish her; first kill him, and in her eyes," ibid., III.v, 136–138. It is Cloten who most resembles the tyrannical Tarquin in the play, but all his violent impulses are made comic by his complete failure to achieve any of his designs. It is the deceiver, not the aspiring tyrant, who is presented as the true villain of Shakespeare's reformed *Lucretia*, and even he will be forgiven in the final scene. It should not escape notice that Cloten and his mother are the only characters to die in the play.

20. Ibid., V.i, 24–33.

21. Ibid., V.iii, 3–4.

22. Ibid., V.iv, 3–4.

23. Ibid., V.iv, 22.

24. Ibid., V.iv, 90. I have found no adequate explanation of the theology of this scene, or this cryptic comment. Do the dead threaten Jupiter? To whose authority would they appeal? The scene is pregnant with anticipation of the Incarnation, as even the words of Jupiter imply.

25. Ibid., V.iv, 100–104.

26. Ibid., V.iv, 145–150.

27. Harry V. Jaffa, "The Unity of Tragedy, Comedy, and History: An Interpretation of the Shakespearean Universe," in *Shakespeare as Political Thinker*, ed. John E. Alvis and Thomas G. West (1981; 2nd ed., Wilmington, DE: ISI, 2000), 29–58, esp. 29–31.

28. Plato, *Symposium*, 223d.

29. Wilson Carey McWilliams, "Poetry, Politics, and the Comic Spirit," *PS: Political Science and Politics* 28 (1995): 197–200. See p. 198.

30. John White, "Imitation," in Joe Sachs's translation of *Republic* (Newburyport, MA: Focus, 2007).

31. Jaffa, "The Unity of Tragedy, Comedy, and History," 43.

32. Ibid.

33. Recall the augury Lucius receives before his battle with Cymbeline: "I saw Jove's bird, the Roman eagle, winged / from the spongy south to this part of the west,

/ there vanished in the sunbeams" (Shakespeare, *Cymbeline*, IV.ii, 348–350), and that this augury receives a new and more fitting interpretation in the closing lines of the play (V.v, 470–475).

34. We possess two significantly different versions of the play, the quarto of 1608, thought now to be a draft printed before the play was performed, and the play printed in the First Folio of 1623, thought to be a performing version of the play. See Stephen Orgel's introduction to the side-by-side comparison of the texts in *The Complete Pelican Shakespeare* (New York: Penguin, 2002), 1480–1485. For evidence of the comic elements blended into the tragic subject material of the play, an intimation of the balance that would be discovered in the romances, consider the bittersweet scenes of reunion and recognition in act 4 with the reunion in *King Lear* of Gloucester and Edgar, and Gloucester and Lear in scene 5 and that of Lear and Cordelia in the following scene. The two texts give us some insight into how and when Shakespeare began to introduce elements of the comic art into his great tragedy. Both Lear and Cymbeline were ancient British kings Shakespeare discovered in Holinshed. Their reigns were devoted to preserving the British monarchy under the Roman Empire and predated the events treated in Shakespeare's history plays.

35. My understanding of the romance owes a great deal to John Dean's *Restless Wanderers: Shakespeare and the Pattern of Romance* (Salzburg: Institut fur Anglistik und Amerikanistik, 1979).

36. Ibid., 11, 13.

37. Thus the pertinence of the Augustinian theology to a Rome that had just been sacked by the Goths, and Augustine's frequent recourse to Vergil's *Aeneid*, which, like the *Odyssey*, presents the reader with tales of adventure and restless wandering in search of a home in the aftermath of a great war. Consider also the preference of the brigata in Boccaccio's *Decameron* for romance tales involving the vicissitudes of Fortune, given the setting of the narrative in the aftermath of the plague of 1348, Shakespeare's turn to romance in the years following the English civil wars, and, perhaps, the popularity of George R. R. Martin's *A Song of Ice and Fire* today.

38. Shakespeare, *Cymbeline*, V.i, 33.

39. Ibid., V.iv, 93.

Chapter 9

Shakespeare's *Henry V* and Responsibility for War

John M. Parrish

Shakespeare's *Henry V* gives us perhaps the playwright's most complete portrait of political leadership.[1] In the course of the play, we see King Henry do practically everything a leader must do to be successful in public life: decide, threaten, inspire, negotiate, pass judgment, make war, even woo and seduce (in French, no less). Yet if Henry is Shakespeare's most comprehensive study in political leadership, he is by no means the most straightforward. Shakespeare's interpreters have long been divided over the question of how the playwright means us to take the king. As Norman Rabkin noted in an influential essay, one school of thought epitomizes Henry as the ideal ruler, whose bold and inspiring leadership leads England to victory over nearly impossible odds; the other school reads the play as subtly disclosing beneath the king's outwardly honorable façade a calculating Machiavel.[2] Rabkin proposes a third possibility: that Shakespeare means us to view Henry as both at the same time—that he is, in Rabkin's memorable phrase, a kind of "rabbit/duck," resembling the optical illusion that shifts back and forth between two alternative interpretations without ever definitively affirming or denying either perspective. This last reading, though not wholly satisfying, nevertheless puts its finger directly on the central difficulty of evaluating the character of Shakespeare's most complete political leader, and consequently also of evaluating the task of political leadership itself.

What has not been discussed so frequently in this context, however, is the close entanglement of these questions regarding how to interpret Henry's character with the play's central focus of action: England's war with France. This seems a rather significant loss to the conversation, in two respects. First, if *Henry V* is Shakespeare's most complete portrayal of leadership, it is equally his most extensive meditation on the nature of war, even among a body of work in which war features rather prominently. This is hardly coincidence: war is the proper setting for evaluating leadership because it is perhaps its most treacherous testing ground, where the stakes of success or failure are highest. Second and even more important, however, the play is (once one is primed to look for it) fairly riddled with insistent questions and doubts regarding where the responsibility for the war and its consequences properly rests. As we will see, these occur not just in the opening scenes, in which Henry and his council weigh the decision to make war with France, but quietly haunt much of the remainder of the play's action as well. The concerns come to a head, rather remarkably, in the famous campfire scene, where the disguised monarch converses with what we might call a randomly sampled focus group of his infantrymen (notably the strongly opinionated Michael Williams) and finds himself unexpectedly ensnared in a philosophical dialogue on the extent of the king's responsibility for the wars he undertakes and for the conduct of his soldiers in those wars. This dialogue becomes the catalyst for the play's moment of crisis, when Henry, left alone with his conscience and his responsibilities, considers in soliloquy the burdens of political leadership and his own inherited guilt, and the effect of each on the fateful battle to come the following morning.

The ethics of war, particularly "wars of choice" and the responsibility that political leaders hold with regard to such wars, has reemerged as one of the most pressing theoretical and practical questions confronting contemporary democracies.[3] In this chapter, I offer a reading of *Henry V* that focuses sharply on this theme as a sustained concern of Shakespeare's play and his characterization of King Henry. I argue that Henry is neither a paragon nor a Machiavel, nor even a rabbit/duck, but instead a distinct individual leader, driven by the ruthless requirements of his public role, but subconsciously preoccupied with equal insistence by the promptings of his conscience; someone shifting constantly, and unsuccessfully, to try to satisfy those promptings amid the actions he feels compelled to take in his public role. In this light, we can see more clearly

Shakespeare's own account of the morally complex nature of political leadership, and also about the problematic ethics of war and the heavy responsibilities it necessarily lays upon those who lead.

The Displacement of Responsibility: Acts 1–3

The question of the king's responsibility for the war between England and France is a principal focus of *Henry V* from its very beginning. It first arises in a serious way in act 1, scene 2, in which Henry invites the Archbishop of Canterbury to discourse in front of the king's council about the merits of Henry's claim to the throne of France. From the scene immediately preceding, we know that much of the Archbishop's presentation is merely for show: the Archbishop has already communicated privately to Henry his rationale for Henry's claim to the French throne.[4] Throughout this key scene, Henry repeatedly directs the question of responsibility for the war away from himself toward two alternate agencies: first, the Archbishop and the Catholic Church, for vouching for the war's moral legitimacy; and second, the Dauphin of France, for his taunting and provocative reply to Henry's diplomacy.

It is Henry himself who first introduces the problem of moral responsibility for the war for our consideration, as he invites the Archbishop to address the question of the *casus belli* and the church's role in vouchsafing that the proposed war is justified: "God forbid," he says, that the Archbishop "should fashion, wrest, or bow your reading, / Or nicely charge your understanding soul, / With opening titles miscreate, whose right / Suits not in native colours with the truth" (I.ii.13–17, p. 85).[5] Henry goes on to stress the scope and severity of the consequences that will fall upon ordinary soldiers, and the root of those consequences in the Archbishop's present recommendation,

> For God doth know how many now in health
> Shall drop their blood in approbation
> Of what your reverence shall incite us to....
> For never two such kingdoms did contend
> Without much fall of blood, whose guiltless drops
> Are every one a woe, a sore complaint
> 'Gainst him whose wrongs gives edge unto the swords
> That makes such waste in brief mortality. (I.ii.24–28, p. 86)

Yet here Henry also gives us his first hint that he is not fully satisfied that responsibility for war can be displaced onto the Archbishop's recommendation.

He notes warningly how the Archbishop's vouching for the war has the potential to implicate the king in responsibility for what will follow: "Therefore take heed how you impawn our person, / How you awake our sleeping sword of war. / We charge you in the name of God take heed" (I.ii.21–23, p. 85). At the same time, however, this cognizance of his own inevitable responsibility for any choice to undertake war is balanced by a suggestion that the royal implication can in a sense be laundered—or more precisely cleansed through baptism—by the clergy's action in endorsing the proposed conflict as just:

> Under this conjuration speak, my lord,
> For we will hear, note, and believe in heart,
> That what you speak is in your conscience washed
> As pure as sin with baptism. (I.ii.29–32, p. 86)

Thus, after a long and laughably complex exploration of the legal ins and outs of Henry's title to France, capped by the Archbishop's unintentionally ironic remark that the claim is "as clear as is the summer's sun," Henry brings the point straight back around to the question of moral responsibility shared between the king and his priestly counsel. "May I with right and conscience make this claim?" Henry asks the priest. "The sin upon my head, dread sovereign," he replies, at last supplying the precise sentiment Henry has been trolling for all along (I.ii.86, 96–97, p. 88).

Not entirely satisfied that this maneuver has displaced the responsibility from his own shoulders adequately, however, Henry seizes upon another opportunity to assign blame for the forthcoming war, this time to the Dauphin of France, and particularly to his gift of tennis balls as a mock tribute in settlement of Henry's claim. Once again, Henry's response closely connects the question of responsibility for the war's beginning with a vivid sense of war's human costs.

> Tell the pleasant prince this mock of his
> Hath turned his balls to gun-stones, and his soul
> Shall stand sore charged for the wasteful vengeance
> That shall fly with them; for many a thousand widows
> Shall this his mock mock out of their dear husbands,
> Mock mothers from their sons, mock castles down,
> And some are yet ungotten and unborn
> That shall have cause to curse the Dauphin's scorn.... (I.ii.281–288,
> pp. 96–97)

One would think that between the unctuousness of the Archbishop and the callowness of the Dauphin, Henry would have already assembled enough of a cast of alternative suspects to give himself at least a plausible alibi. It is therefore a measure of his compulsiveness in deflecting responsibility that he goes on in the same passage to invoke God himself as the ultimate holder of responsibility for the choice of war and victory. "All this lies within the will of God, / To whom I do appeal ... / To venge me as I may, and to put forth / My rightful hand in a well-hallowed cause" (I.ii.289–290, 292–293, pp. 96–97). We therefore observe in this first scene how central the problem of responsibility for the war has been marked to be, both in the mind of the playwright and in the conscience of his central character.

This tendency to redirect responsibility for morally questionable acts, we soon learn, is a persistent habit of mind with Henry V, not to say a compulsion. Throughout the play, Henry recurs with almost obsessive regularity to frame each act of proposed violence in a way that displaces moral responsibility from his own shoulders to those of others around him.[6] When the Duke of Exeter delivers Henry's demands to the French king, for instance, England assigns all responsibility for future violence to the French adversary if he refuses Henry's rightful demands:

> and on your head
> Turning the widow's tears, the orphan's cries,
> The dead men's blood, the privéd maiden's groans,
> For Husbands, fathers, and betrothéd lovers
> That shall be swallowed in this controversy. (II.iv.106–110, p. 121)

In the course of making his demands at Harfleur, the English king does not miss the opportunity to recall the Dauphin's mocking gift of the tennis balls and allude again to the suffering this mockery threatens to bring upon France (II.iv.121–127, pp. 121–122). But he goes on to describe in some of the most graphic language in all of Shakespeare the brutal horrors that will befall the citizens in the pillage that will inevitably follow, and in doing so explicitly displaces responsibility for the unspeakable carnage to follow from himself to the obstinate residents of the besieged city. "What is't to me, when you yourselves are cause ...?" he asks, before imploring the citizens to instead "Take pity of your town and of your people / Whiles yet my soldiers are in my command ..." (III.iv.19, 28–29, p. 134).[7]

We find a somewhat looser but still relevant parallel to this dynamic in the thwarted betrayal of Cambridge, Scroop, and Gray in act 2, scene 2. Notwithstanding Henry's clear justification for punishing these aristocratic conspirators, the king nevertheless twice seeks to displace responsibility for their execution from his own shoulders in several interesting ways. His first displacement of responsibility devolves upon the conspirators themselves. Having employed the same trick that the prophet Nathan used with King David[8] of inviting his nobles to judge mercilessly in a (fictional) parallel case, the king subsequently reveals that the conspirator-nobles have in reality been pronouncing judgment on their own actions. "The mercy that was quick in us but late," Henry states, "By your own counsel is suppressed and killed" (II.ii.76–77, p. 109). Not satisfied with this initial displacement of responsibility onto the guilty parties before him, however, Henry invokes the impersonal and impartial justice of the law as further bearing responsibility for the judgment that falls on his erstwhile friends, notwithstanding his clear royal prerogative to pardon as monarch. "Touching our person seek we no revenge," Henry states, "But we our kingdom's safety must so tender, / Whose ruin you have sought, that to her laws / We do deliver you" (II.ii.169–172, p. 112). Henry's view here partly echoes Seneca's argument in his classic treatise "On Mercy" that it is more appropriate for a monarch to show mercy for an offense against himself (or herself) personally than an offense that affects other parties.[9] Yet Henry adroitly adapts the close ideological association between the king's private person and the status of the realm in order to represent the assassination attempt against himself as a *general* offense that the king could not in good conscience pardon for fear of its effects on the public safety.[10]

Henry similarly appeals to the need for the impartiality of the law to explain his lack of mercifulness upon discovering that his former friend and drinking companion Bardolph has been charged with unauthorized looting.[11] "We would have all such offenders so cut off," Henry states before Bardolph is hanged (III. vii.92, p. 146). The response is rather cold, but it is consistent with Henry's pattern of placing responsibility for the choice elsewhere: in this case, on the need for consistent application of the law and the implied argument that showing mercy in such a case would necessarily constitute a dangerous form of partiality that would undermine the public safety. This argument, especially as applied to the widely accepted royal power to show clemency, ran directly contrary to the spirit of Seneca's influential argument that the ruler was exalted in showing mercy precisely because of its discretionary character.[12] Henry's thinking on this point does, however, correspond rather neatly to another influential argument on the same subject: Machiavelli's analysis of mercy in chapter 17 of *The Prince*. There Machiavelli had held that a prince

> so as to keep his subjects united and faithful, should not care about the infamy of cruelty, because with very few examples he will be more merciful than those who for the sake of too much mercy allow disorders to continue, from which come killings or robberies; for these customarily hurt a whole community, but the executions that come from the prince hurt one particular person.[13]

In this case, the one particular person hurt (hanged, actually) happens to be Henry's former friend and reveler, Bardolph; but in a sense the choice to ignore his particular relationship with Bardolph merely constitutes the completion of the forswearing of personal identity for royal identity he had begun in the final scene of *Henry IV, Part 2.* Viewing that same choice in this context lets us notice the choice's Machiavellian roots, yet now refracted through his own evasive personality—in striking contrast to the assertive individual agency Machiavelli associates with the virtuoso prince. What precisely we are to make of Henry's evocation of the Machiavellian prince while simultaneously shrinking from its full implications remains to be puzzled out in the scenes of act 4.

The Williams Episode: Act 4, Scene I (Lines 1–166)

The question of responsibility for war at last takes center stage in act 4, scene 1, wherein we witness Henry's midnight sojourn in disguise through his camp on the eve of the battle of Agincourt.[14] Shakespeare's audience would have understood this situation to be an especially appropriate setting for considering the question of responsibility for war, because of the close linkage in the early modern mind between the courage exhibited by soldiers in battle and the rightness of the cause for which they fought.[15] Among men confronting their fears and mortality before a doubtful battle, the question of the justice of their cause would consequently have been one of the most pressing matters on their minds, because it directly affected the likelihood that God would favor their undertaking. Yet despite this fittingness of setting and situation, there is really no precedent in any other Elizabethan drama for what Shakespeare presents us with in this scene. Three realistically portrayed ordinary soldiers, with the vivid English names "John Bates," "Alexander Court," and "Michael Williams," debate like philosophers the justice of the king's cause and the moral implications thereof, and unbeknownst to them they do so in the very presence of the king they are judging.[16] Nor is there a precedent for it in any of the sources for the play; this scene is entirely an invention of Shakespeare's.[17]

The scene begins, in a note that artfully foreshadows its eventual destination, with Henry's rather wistful remark on the king's essential humanity. The king, the disguised Henry states, is no different from any of "us" common soldiers: he "is but a man as I am…. His ceremonies laid by, in his nakedness he appears but a man …" (IV.i.97, 99–100, p. 161). To some extent, the scene itself is evidence that this claim is not without an element of truth; the very fact that Henry is able to discourse with his soldiers around the campfire is proof that in the absence of the "ceremony" surrounding his royal state, the king does indeed "appear but a man." But the purported commonality between the king and his subjects quickly changes in significance when the subject of discussion turns to the war they are fighting and the question of the king's moral responsibility for it.[18] Henry accidentally invites this dangerous line of argument through his yearning for commonality with his men, by observing, in what must express the sentiments he hopes his own soldiers will share, that "Methinks I could not die anywhere so contented as in the king's company, his cause being just and his quarrel honorable" (IV.i.116–118, p. 162). Michael Williams responds to this introduction of the question of the war's justice by observing, "That's more than we know"—certainly true for a common soldier in the army, but given the ambiguity of what has transpired in act 1, scene 2, equally true of us, the much better informed audience (IV.i.119, p. 162).

Williams's compatriot John Bates seeks to come to the king's defense but in the process also inadvertently raises the moral stakes by claiming that common soldiers need not inquire into the justice of the cause they fight in. "We know enough," he claims instead, "if we know we are the king's subjects. If his cause be wrong our obedience to the king wipes the crime of it out of us," a view generally supported by the just war theory tradition (IV.i.120–122, p. 162).[19] This, however, as Williams is quick to point out, transposes moral responsibility wholesale from the soldiery to the king himself:

> But if the cause be not good the king himself hath a heavy reckoning to make, when all those legs and arms and heads chopped off in a battle shall join together at the latter day and cry all "We died at such a place," some swearing, some crying for a surgeon, some upon their wives left poor behind them, some upon the debts they owe, some upon their children rawly left. I am afeard there are few die well that die in a battle, for how can they chari-tably dispose of anything when blood is their argument? Now if these men do not die well it will be a black matter for the king that led them to it, who to disobey were against all proportion of subjection. (IV.i.123–133, p. 163)

Henry's response begins unpromisingly, drawing on a set of fairly specious analogies with other principal-agent relationships. The king's responsibility for his soldiers, he suggests, is comparable to a merchant father whose son is lost at sea while transporting his father's goods, or a master whose servant is way-laid and killed on an errand.[20] In both cases Henry focuses on the principal's responsibility for the *spiritual* state of the agent: the father should not have "the imputation of [the son's] wickedness" imposed upon him, nor should the master's business be viewed as "the author of the servant's damnation" (IV.i.134–140). Henry goes on to defend the principal's (and his own) moral blamelessness with reference to the issue of moral intention. "The king," he argues, "is not bound to answer the particular endings of his soldiers, the father of his son, nor the master of his servant, for they purpose not their death when they purpose their services" (IV.i.141–143). Because the agent's death is not the effect aimed at, but rather only an accidental by-product of the primary (mercantile or military) purpose, the principal bears responsibility only for the intended effect, not for its unfortunate consequence.

In raising this line of defense, Shakespeare conspicuously puts into Henry's mouth an argument familiar from just war theory: the doctrine of "double effect."[21] According to this doctrine (constructed from elements of the theologies of Augustine and Thomas Aquinas) harmful actions that would otherwise be wrong in themselves can be justified if the wrong is a side effect (or "double effect") of the actor's intention, rather than its true aim. As educated listeners would have known, however, the argument's original purpose had been to justify the unavoidable deaths of innocent casualties of *civilians* in war, in the face of just war theory's principle of noncombatant immunity.[22] The deaths at stake in Williams's original question, however, were *not* noncombatants, but soldiers, a fact that strongly undermines Henry's analogy. Not only do the merchant father and the master "purpose not" the deaths of their agents, they also do not foresee them and might well act differently if they did—whereas the monarch knows full well that many of those he sends to fight will die as a direct result. Thus even if the double-effect argument itself is taken to be valid in general (a contested point among moral philosophers), Henry undoubtedly makes the case far too easy for himself by employing imperfect analogies that tend to suggest far more inadvertence on the ruler's part than could possibly apply to most wars—especially one arrived at through such a dubious process as the one portrayed in act 1, scene 2.

Rather than connect this line of argument to the larger concerns raised by Michael Williams about the king's responsibility for the initial decision to undertake the war, however, Henry instead uses Williams's passing invocation of the "latter day" judgment to pivot to more favorable ground, arguing that the king cannot be held responsible for the moral purity of his soldiers' private souls.[23] He explicitly separates this matter from the question of *ius ad bellum* (while rather conspicuously avoiding engaging its merits) by noting that "there is no king, be his cause never so spotless, if it come to the arbitrament of swords can try it out with all unspotted soldiers" (IV.i.144–146, p. 163). Some robbers, some seducers, even some murderers will necessarily be among those the king must recruit to field an effective army, and they will bring their prior sins with them to the battlefield. Indeed, the war itself is often God's intended means for properly punishing their sin. Though these offenders may have evaded domestic justice, Henry argues, "they have no wings to fly from God": war is in this sense God's "beadle" and God's "vengeance," as well as an encouragement to repentance for those soldiers who rightly respond by preparing their consciences in the face of impending death (IV.i.146–154, 160–166, p. 164). It is on this basis that Henry concludes that if such soldiers "die unprovided, no more is the king guilty of their damnation than he was before guilty of those impieties for the which they are now visited" (IV.i.156–159, p. 164). Or as he pithily sums the matter up, "Every subject's duty is the king's, but every subject's soul is his own" (IV.i.159–160).

The King's Soliloquy: Act 4, Scene 1 (Lines 167–279)

Despite its logical shortcomings, Henry's argument appears at first glance to satisfy Williams, who replies that "'Tis certain, every man that dies ill, the ill upon his own head; the king is not to answer it" (IV.i.167–168).[24] A closer look at his response, though, discloses that it is rather shrewdly limited in scope: he accepts Henry's argument about the moral responsibility of individual soldiers for their private sins while at the same time declining to return to the original issue he had raised regarding the king's moral responsibility for undertaking a war of questionable justification.[25] Yet a few moments later, when the soldiers depart and Henry is left alone with his own thoughts in soliloquy, he reveals that for himself the arguments he has made are far from conclusive reasons. "Upon the king!" he begins, and proceeds to paraphrase the full force of Williams's argument as it stood *before* "Henry Le Roi"'s ostensible refutation of it: "'Let us our lives, our souls, our debts, our careful wives, our children and our sins, lay on the king'"—then switching to verse: "We must bear all. / O hard condition, twin-born with greatness, / Subject to the breath of every fool" (IV.i.203–207, p. 166).[26]

From this point of departure, Henry returns to ground very familiar to audiences of Shakespeare's histories: namely, a soliloquy meditating on the burdens of kingship. Here Henry moves swiftly from the specific question of royal responsibility for war to a broader consideration of the special cares of monarchy and the inadequacy of the "ceremony" that accompanies kingship to compensate for those cares.

> What infinite heart's ease must kings neglect
> That private men enjoy?
> And what have kings that privates have not too,
> Save ceremony, save general ceremony? (IV.i.209–212, p. 166)

Throughout Shakespeare's plays, from *Titus Andronicus* to *Richard II* to *Hamlet*, the invocation of "ceremony" tends to invoke the idea of shallow ritualistic displays empty of true significance.[27] In this passage, Henry's interrogation of the idea of ceremony—"Art thou ought else but place, degree, and form, / Creating awe and fear in other men?"—seems not only to derogate ceremony but to define it with reference to "place, degree, and form." Those features are usually associated with the essentially hierarchical and conservative conception of social order often attributed to Shakespeare (based, for example, on Ulysses's ode to "degree" in *Troilus and Cressida*), but about which Henry's comparison here raises significant doubts as to whether this conservative picture accurately captures the playwright's social philosophy.[28]

Henry therefore concludes that the ceremony and spectacle that distinguishes the king's life from those of his subjects in fact offers the monarch himself no genuine benefits, only costs (IV.i.213–222, p. 166). He characterizes this "thrice-gorgeous" ceremony as not only an "idol"[29] but positively toxic, giving rise to "poisoned" flattery (IV.i.213, 223–224, 239, pp. 166–167). Instead, this "proud dream" is in reality the source of the king's greatest miseries. This point is further driven home by the soliloquy's return to the image of the soundly sleeping "wretched slave" (IV.i.241, p. 167). Unlike the king, the lowly slave is able to achieve the restfulness of oblivion, "with a body filled and vacant mind"; the slave "never sees horrid night, the child of hell," but rather sleeps each night "in Elysium," and over the course of his life "follows so the ever-running year / With profitable labor to his grave" (IV.i.242–250, pp. 167–168). The imagery of the slave used here closely parallels Henry IV's image of the ship-boy's slumber in *Henry IV, Part 2* (III.i.18–31, pp. 115–116),[30] as well as Henry V's own pre-kingship meditation on the sleepless cares of the ruler in *Henry IV, Part 1* (IV.ii.151–158, p. 158).[31] In the Agincourt soliloquy, however, Shakespeare develops the divergence between the king's fate and the slave's much more fully. Yet Shakespeare's echoing of those earlier treatments is undoubtedly deliberate, as signified by the conclusion Henry draws from the image:

> And but for ceremony such a wretch,
> Winding up days with toil and nights with sleep,
> Had the forehand and vantage of a king.
> The slave, a member of the country's peace,
> Enjoys it, but in gross brain little wots
> What watch the king keeps to maintain the peace,
> Whose hours the peasant best advantages. (IV.i.251–257, p. 168)

Thus, as in *Henry IV*, the soliloquy views the slave as surpassing the king in happiness because he lacks responsibility, and specifically because the slave can uncomplicatedly be a mere "member of the country's peace" whereas the king is charged with the "watch" that is necessary "to maintain the peace."[32] The irony, of course, as signaled by what immediately follows, is that the king's own actions, far from maintaining the peace, have in fact brought his band of subjects to the most desperate straits of war, together with all its cares. One imagines that in the remaining hours of the night, neither Williams, Bates, nor Court will be getting much more sleep than their king. The king, meanwhile, having laid aside his "ceremony" by means of his nocturnal disguise, in fact finds (contrary to his own argument) that his sense of responsibility is increased, not diminished, by its absence, forced as he is to confront directly the fear and mortality of his men and his direct causal role in bringing on the peril they now face.

Interrupted by the arrival of Sir Thomas Erpingham announcing that the king's absence has been noticed by his nobles, Henry promises to return quickly and meet them at his tent. Alone again for one final moment before the battle, Henry's thoughts turn revealingly from the uncertain future to the troubled past. Prompted by the fears he has encountered among Williams and his fellows at the campfire, the king first implores a warlike conception of the almighty ("O God of battles") to "steel my soldiers' hearts" and to "possess them not with fear" (IV.i.263–266, pp. 168–169). But confronted in the process with the thought of God his own sovereign and judge, Henry's thoughts are drawn to questions of sin and guilt—though rather characteristically, not his own.

> Not today, O Lord,
> Oh, not today, think not upon the fault
> My father made in compassing the crown. (IV.i.266–268, p. 169)

This crisis of conscience concerning Henry's succession is the playwright's own hand at work, having no precedent in his sources; and yet we may infer it was indeed central to Shakespeare's design, both because it appears in both the Quarto and the Folio versions of the scene and also because it so aptly rounds out at this critical dramatic moment the main themes of the second tetralogy as a whole.[33] As proof of his sincerity, Henry lists the extensive steps he has already taken to distance himself from responsibility for his father's act of usurpation: he has reburied Richard II's body, built two chantries and paid five hundred paupers to pray for Richard's soul, and has himself in the presence of Richard's body wept "more contrite tears / Than from it issued forcéd drops of blood" (IV.i.269–276, p. 169).

Yet despite all these actions deploring his father's misdeeds, Henry continues to doubt their efficacy in addressing his own share of guilt in the matter:

> More will I do,
> Though all that I can do is nothing worth

Since that my penitence comes after all
Imploring pardon. (IV.i.276–279, p. 169)

Shakespeare would later[34] echo this soliloquy in the famous prayer scene in *Hamlet*, act 3, when the murderous Claudius similarly doubts the effect of his prayer of penance for the murder of his brother. Claudius questions whether he can be forgiven while he remains "possessed / Of those effects for which I did the murder," asking, "May one be pardoned and retain th'offence?" (III. iii.51–56, p. 184).[35] Henry's situation is different from Claudius's in at least one important respect: the offense he repents is not his own deed, but rather the sin of his father Bolingbroke visited upon his son. Notably, however, Henry's prayer also appeals for forgiveness to a different agency than Claudius's does, reflecting an underlying difference in the basis on which their hope (or despair) of salvation rests. Claudius asks "may one be pardoned?" indicating his doubt that even God can forgive a sinner unwilling to atone for the sin by forfeiting its worldly profits; Henry instead opines that "all *that I can do* is nothing worth," leaving open (in a rather presciently Protestant spirit) the possibility that God may be able to effect a redemption to which Henry's own deeds can contribute nothing.[36]

Henry's prayer thus creates a climactic moment of dramatic as well as spiritual crisis weaving together the primary problem of the second tetralogy— Bolingbroke's usurpation and its consequences for England—with the distinctive issue driving the play at hand—the war with France and its consequences for the king and his men. Crucially, Henry's prayer openly connects his backward-looking concern (repentance) with his forward-looking petition (survival and improbable victory), asking God's forgiveness of past wrongs as the necessary precondition of present salvation. The astonishing sequel, the triumph at Agincourt, in a sense constitutes God's response, showing not only his mercy to the contrite king but also his blessing to the favored Henry.[37] And here Shakespeare leaves us with one final and more positively construed instance of Henry's transference of responsibility, now in a more reverent key. Just as Henry had sought throughout the play to assign responsibility for the war to everyone up to and including God, so now in the aftermath of Agincourt Henry shows his recognition (whether sincerely felt or shrewdly feigned) of the divine hand at work by unstintingly giving all the credit to God, requiring his soldiers to sing *Non nobis* and *Te Deum* and forbidding his army to boast of the victory because its glory belongs to God alone (IV.viii.98–115, pp. 196–197). For a king who had confessed as recently as that morning the trait that is perhaps the truest motive for the war we are ever offered—that "if it be a sin to covet honour, / I am the most offending soul alive"—such a tribute is no mean feat, and may reflect a willingness on Henry's part to transfer responsibility, not for the war but for its redemptive outcome (at least for the English) where Shakespeare's audience would have agreed it properly belongs, to God himself (IV.iii.28–29, p. 174).

Conclusion

Where does the moral responsibility for war properly lie? The insistent if subtle message of *Henry V*, our greatest dramatist's greatest play about war, is that such responsibility ultimately resides, inevitably, with the monarch himself (or, in 1599 England, herself). The responsibility a king assumes when he brings fire and destruction to another nation's villages or leads his own loyal company of men to the brink of pitiless slaughter is awesome indeed, and Henry's repeated attempts throughout the play to displace responsibility for the war and its consequences in the end only serve to underscore that no advisor, no priest, no enemy, no conspirator, no criminal, not even God himself can take that responsibility away. Henry's persistent efforts to deflect it—through legal technicalities, theatrical diplomatic maneuvers, and sophistical applications of moral philosophy alike—cannot suffice, as Henry finally recognizes (at least in part), to prevent ultimate responsibility for the conflict from returning to his own doorstep. Wars of choice are chosen, and choices have consequences, both moral and otherwise.

No sixteenth-century playwright, no matter how brilliant, can speak to us directly about the problem of responsibility for war as it confronts the representative democracies of contemporary nation-states; and one feels reasonably confident that the idea of attempting to do so never crossed the mind of William Shakespeare. What Shakespeare can, however, tell us with authority even today is the essential truth he perceived about the kinds of choices that lead to war, and the resulting choices one makes when fighting a war. What he can tell us is the essential truth he saw about the character of a man, vivid and compelling if also elusive, who systematically chooses to put his role as a political leader ahead of his own human particularity, and reaps both the glory and the misgivings that accompany that choice. He can offer us the hope that while the responsibility held by leaders is unavoidable, it need not cost them their humanity, that their timely penitence can in the end lead to absolution. And he can remind us that while war's responsibility may often rest with a single person, wars are always ultimately about much more than a single person. War's costs are borne by the thousands who fight and die on its front lines and the thousands more who suffer in its wake. And for this reason, whether leaders (or countries) choose to share credit for their triumphs among those "happy few" who fight on their behalf, or offer it instead in pious tribute to God alone, it is, as Henry learns, fitting always to say of the glories of war: *Non nobis.*

Notes

1. All citations to *Henry V* are given parenthetically. Shakespeare, William (2005), *Henry V* (The New Cambridge Shakespeare, updated edition), ed. Andrew Gurr, Cambridge: Cambridge University Press.

2. Rabkin, Norman (1981), "Either/Or: Responding to *Henry V*," in Rabkin, *Shakespeare and the Problem of Meaning*, Chicago: University of Chicago Press. For examples of the ideal monarch school of interpretation, see Dover Wilson, John (1943), *The Fortunes of Falstaff*, Cambridge: Cambridge University Press; and Reese, M. M. (1961), *The Cease of Majesty*, London: Edward Arnold. For examples of the Machiavellian school of interpretation, see Van Doren, Mark (1939), *Shakespeare*, New York: Henry Holt; Goddard, H. C. (1951), *The Meaning of Shakespeare*, Chicago: University of Chicago Press; Battenhouse, Roy (1962), "*Henry V* as Heroic Comedy," in R. Holsey, ed., *Essays on Shakespeare*, Columbia: University of Missouri Press; and Greenblatt, Stephen (1988), *Shakespearean Negotiations: The Circulation of Social Energy in Renaissance England*, Berkeley: University of California Press. On the problem more generally, see also Wentersdorf, Karl P. (1976), "The Conspiracy of Silence in *Henry V*," *Shakespeare Quarterly* 27: 264–287; and Smith, Gordon Ross (1976), "Shakespeare's *Henry V*: Another Part of the Critical Forest," *Journal of the History of Ideas* 37: 3–26.

3. On these questions, out of a very broad range of studies see Ramsey, Paul (1968), *The Just War: Force and Political Responsibility*, New York: Charles Scribner's Sons; Nagel, Thomas (1972), "War and Massacre," *Philosophy and Public Affairs* 1: 123–143; Levinson, S. (1973), "Responsibility for the Crimes of War," *Philosophy and Public Affairs* 2: 244–273; Walzer, Michael (1973), "Political Action: The Problem of Dirty Hands," *Philosophy and Public Affairs* 2: 160–180; Walzer, Michael (1977), *Just and Unjust Wars: A Moral Argument with Historical Illustrations*, 3rd ed., New York: Basic; Dubik, J. (1982), "Human Rights, Command Responsibility, and Walzer's Just War Theory," *Philosophy and Public Affairs* 11: 354–371; May, Larry, and S. Hoffman, eds. (1991), *Collective Responsibility: Five Decades of Debate in Theoretical and Applied Ethics*, Savage, MD: Rowman and Littlefield; Miller, David (2001), "Distributing Responsibilities," *Journal of Political Philosophy* 9: 453–471; Abdel-Nour, Farid (2003), "National Responsibility," *Political Theory* 31: 693–719; Crawford, Neta C. (2007), "Individual and Collective Moral Responsibility for Systematic Military Atrocity," *Journal of Political Philosophy* 15: 187–212; Parrish, John M. (2009), "Collective Responsibility and the State," *International Theory* 1: 119–154; Stilz, Anna (2011), "Collective Responsibility and the State," *Journal of Political Philosophy* 19: 190–208; and Young, Iris Marion (2011), *Responsibility for Justice*, Oxford: Oxford University Press.

4. Indeed, there may even be a suggestion that Henry's proposal to increase the financial burdens upon the English Church constitutes a veiled threat designed to encourage clerical support for the war. See also Alvis, John E. (2000), "Spectacle Supplanting Ceremony: Shakespeare's Henry Monmouth," in John E. Alvis and Thomas G. West, eds., *Shakespeare as a Political Thinker*, Wilmington, DE: ISI, pp. 125–126.

5. On the highly questionable character of the argument the archbishop puts forward from the perspective of just war theory, see especially Gurr, Andrew (1977), "*Henry V* and the Bees' Commonwealth," *Shakespeare Survey*, vol. 30, ed. Kenneth Muir, Cambridge: Cambridge University Press; and Pugliatti, Paola (2010), *Shakespeare and the Just War Tradition*, Burlington, VT: Ashgate.

6. Many studies have noted this tendency of Henry's in a more general sense, including Smith (1976), pp. 16–17; Meron, Theodor (1998), *Bloody Constraint: War and Chivalry in Shakespeare*, Oxford: Oxford University Press, pp. 156–161; Foakes, R. A. (2003), *Shakespeare and Violence*, Cambridge: Cambridge University Press, p. 104; Rebholz, Ronald A. (2003), *Shakespeare's Philosophy of History Revealed in a Detailed Examination of Henry V and Examined in Other History Plays*, Lewiston, NY: Edwin Mellen Press, pp. 46–47; Cantor, Paul A. (2006), "Shakespeare's *Henry V*: From the Medieval to the Modern World," in John A. Murley and Sean D. Dutton, eds., *Perspectives on Politics in Shakespeare*, Lanham, MD: Lexington, pp. 22–23; and Pugliatti (2010), pp. 217–218.

7. On the gross disparity between Henry's threats here and the requirements of the just war tradition, see Pugliatti (2010), pp. 218–221.

8. 2 Samuel 12.

9. Seneca, Lucius Annaeus (1995), "On Mercy," in Seneca, *Moral and Political Essays*, ed. John M. Cooper and J. F. Procopé, Cambridge: Cambridge University Press, I.20–24, pp. 152–155.

10. On the development of this emerging ideology see further Kantorowicz, Ernst H. (1957), *The King's Two Bodies: A Study in Medieval Political Theology*, Princeton, NJ: Princeton University Press; and Skinner, Quentin (1989), "The State," in Terence Ball, James Farr, and Russell L. Hanson, eds., *Political Innovation and Conceptual Change*, Cambridge: Cambridge University Press.

11. Barton, Anne (1975), "The King Disguised: Shakespeare's *Henry V* and the Comical History," University Park: Pennsylvania State University Press, pp. 100–106, draws a connection between Henry's insistence on the impartial application of law to his friend Bardolph and the impersonality of the monarch's person implied by the theory of the king's two bodies (see further Kantorowicz [1957]).

12. See further Tuckness, Alex, and John M. Parrish, *The Decline of Mercy in Public Life* (forthcoming, Cambridge University Press, 2014), ch. 2.

13. Machiavelli, Niccolo (1998), *The Prince*, trans. and ed. Harvey C. Mansfield, 2nd ed., Chicago: University of Chicago Press, ch. 17, pp. 65–66.

14. On the peculiarity of this disguised sojourn as a matter of contemporary military life, see Taunton, Nina (2001), *1590s Drama and Militarism: Portrayals of War in Marlowe, Chapman, and Shakespeare's Henry V*, Burlington, VT: Ashgate, pp. 159–183. On its subtly ironic relationship to similar scenes in "comical-histories" of the time, see Barton (1975).

15. Jorgensen, Paul A. (1956), *Shakespeare's Military World*, Berkeley: University of California Press, ch. 4, pp. 160–161.

16. See ibid., pp. 161–162.

17. See further Hadfield, Andrew (2004), *Shakespeare and Renaissance Politics*, London: Arden Shakespeare, ch. 1, p. 61.

18. On the political implications of the soldiers' critique of their sovereign in the context of late Tudor England, see Herman, Peter C. (1995), "'O, 'Tis a Gallant King': Shakespeare's *Henry V* and the Crisis of the 1590s," in Dale Hoak, ed., *Tudor Political Culture*, Cambridge: Cambridge University Press.

19. See Russell, Frederick H. (1975), *The Just War in the Middle Ages*, Cambridge: Cambridge University Press, ch. 1, pp. 21–23.

20. Vickers, Brian (1979), *The Artistry of Shakespeare's Prose*, New York: Methuen, pp. 163–165, notes that the cool and rational tone of Henry's prose lines here contrasts with Williams's more emotional appeal in the passage immediately preceding.

21. On the history of the concept, see Mangan, Joseph T., S. J. (1949), "An Historical Analysis of the Principle of Double Effect," *Theological Studies* 10: 41–61; and Pugliatti (2010). On its application to the Williams episode, see Pugliatti (2010), pp. 23–25, 217–218. For contemporary perspectives, see Walzer (1977); Woodward, P. A., ed. (2001), *The Doctrine of Double Effect: Philosophers Debate a Controversial Moral Principle*, Notre Dame, IN: University of Notre Dame Press; and Scanlon, T. M. (2008), *Moral Dimensions: Permissibility, Meaning, Blame*, Cambridge, MA: Belknap Press of Harvard University Press.

22. See further Walzer (1977), ch. 9.

23. Meron, Theodor (1993), *Henry's Wars and Shakespeare's Laws: Perspectives on the Law of War in the Later Middle Ages*, Oxford: Clarendon, ch. 5, explores the connections between the questions of royal responsibility for war raised here and just war theory, both in its 16th–17th century forms and in its later development.

24. In another context, one might have suspected Williams's acquiescence to this not-altogether-convincing series of arguments to indicate he had recognized the identity of his royal interlocutor (perhaps intended to be signaled, as sometimes is the case in Shakespeare's plays, through acting and staging choices rather than overtly through dialogue). Yet this interpretation is clearly ruled out by the subsequent quarrel between Williams and "Harry" leading to the exchange of gloves at lines 180–196.

25. Jorgensen (1956), ch. 4, pp. 166–167; Barton (1975), p. 100; and Gurr (1977), p. 66, separately notice this evasion as well.

26. Hadfield (2004), ch. 1, p. 64, reads this as Henry accepting, in the privacy of soliloquy, the full moral responsibility for the war that Williams had attributed to him. I read the passage as more conflicted and evasive on the point.

27. This was consistent with the dominant contemporary usage at the time and significantly was frequently linked to the criticism of religious ritual and superstition that constituted a mainstay of Protestant critiques of Catholicism. See further Smith (1976), at pp. 19–20; Kastan, David Scott (1986), "Proud Majesty Made a Subject: Shakespeare and the Spectacle of Rule," *Shakespeare Quarterly* 37: 459–475; and Alvis (2000).

28. Shakespeare, William (2003b), *Troilus and Cressida* (The New Cambridge Shakespeare), ed. Anthony B. Dawson, Cambridge: Cambridge University Press, act 1, scene 3.

29. "Idol" is also presumably intended also to invoke "idle" by means of paronomasia: in a theatrical context, of course, the two words would be aurally indistinguishable.

30. Shakespeare, William (1989), *The Second Part of King Henry IV* (The New Cambridge Shakespeare), ed. Giorgio Melchiori, Cambridge: Cambridge University Press.

31. Shakespeare, William (1997), *The First Part of King Henry IV* (The New Cambridge Shakespeare), ed. Herbert Weil, Cambridge: Cambridge University Press.

32. On the connection between the two speeches, see Williamson, Marilyn L. (1969), "The Episode with Williams in *Henry V*," *Studies in English Literature, 1500–1900*, 9: 275–282, pp. 278–279. As Alvis (2000) notes (pp. 108–109), the idea that *tyrants* were unable to sleep easily was a familiar trope going back to antiquity; the fact that both Bolingbroke and his son see it as applicable to *all* kings adds to our picture of Shakespeare's complex evaluation of these two rulers.

33. Smith (1976), p. 21. The Quarto omits the "ceremony" soliloquy entirely, instead moving directly to the "O God of battles" speech, which it seems to present not as a private soliloquy but rather as a public prayer spoken in the presence of the king's noble attendants. See Shakespeare (2005), p. 165 fn. 202, p. 168 fn. 263.

34. Or possibly contemporaneously—*Hamlet* probably followed *Henry V* in composition, but may possibly have been worked on at the same time.

35. Shakespeare, William (2003a), *Hamlet, Prince of Denmark* (The New Cambridge Shakespeare), ed. Philip Edwards, Cambridge: Cambridge University Press.

36. Rebholz (2003), pp. 51–52, reads this moment as Henry approaching the brink of (unforgivable) spiritual despair, whereas my reading sees the prayer as contrite to the point of genuine doubtfulness but nevertheless accompanied by a degree of authentic spiritual hope.

37. Alvis (2000) interprets Henry's humility about the Agincourt victory as largely for show, masking a continued competition between Henry and his God for the true glory of Henry's achievements. Foakes (2003), pp. 104–105, by contrast, shares my reading of it as a moment of genuine humility (or at least, as much humility as an ego like Henry's can fairly be expected to muster).

Chapter 10

Troilus and Cressida

The Value of Reputations and the Corruption of Society

Lilly J. Goren

During the first week of March 2012, there was a tempest in the United States over remarks made by talk-show radio personality Rush Limbaugh about a thirty-year-old law student, Sandra Fluke, who had testified to a congressional panel about the need for religious universities to cover the cost of contraceptive health care for women within their insurance plans. Ms. Fluke related the events of her roommate in law school, who ultimately had to have an ovary removed because of a medical condition that could have been prevented with the use of birth control pills. The pills cost $3,000 a year and were beyond what Ms. Fluke's roommate could afford. Limbaugh went on a three-day rant on his radio show—impugning the reputation of Ms. Fluke, calling her a "slut" and a "prostitute" and demanding that, in order to have her birth control pills paid for by the American tax-payers, in exchange Ms. Fluke should make videos of herself having sex and make them available for the viewing public. This contretemps went on for quite some time, and in the process there was a galvanizing of demands that advertisers pull their ads from Limbaugh's radio show. Many advertisers did so.[1] But one of the lingering questions, especially throughout the unprecedented boycott by the show's advertisers, was why the conglomerate that owns the show, Clear Channel, had not fired or suspended Limbaugh for going beyond the bounds of what is even acceptable for him to say. Alyssa Rosenberg, a writer and popular culture analyst at the ThinkProgress.com website brought up this point as she concluded a column on the topic, explaining that Sandra Fluke's reputation has been priced by the advertising market for the Limbaugh Show: "given the profits Limbaugh rakes in, Clear Channel established the price of a woman's reputation."[2] Rosenberg concluded that the radio show's owners had done a valuation of Fluke's reputation in comparison to the profits from the Limbaugh show and had decided that Limbaugh's show was "worth more." The long-term profits from a fairly popular radio show with one of the best-known conservatives in the country is certainly a different commodity than the "reputation" of a thirty-year-old law school student. But this comparative valuation is not new, and it continues to contribute to our cultural understanding of the place of women within society, and the reified societal confines of gender and sexuality.

Five years before this particular Limbaugh incident, there was a parallel incident involving talk-show radio host Don Imus. In April 2007, Imus, on his radio program, referred to the Rutgers University women's basketball team, the majority of whom were African American, as "nappy-headed hos." The team had been on an unexpected winning streak, and Imus made this comment while discussing the team. The response to these comments was quite extensive and ultimately led to Imus's dismissal from his radio show at CBS. The combination of both racially and sexually derogatory commentary galvanized criticism of Imus, in this instance, setting the value of the Rutgers women's team higher than the long-term income from Imus. The network dismissed Imus after he was initially suspended for two weeks without pay.[3] Limbaugh, in 2012, was neither suspended nor fired from his syndicated radio show.

Women as Property

William Blackstone explained, two hundred years after Shakespeare, that women, when they enter into a marriage, change their "standing": "By marriage, the very being or legal existence of a woman is suspended, or at least incorporated or consolidated into that of the husband, under whose wing, protection, or cover she performs everything."[4] Thus, the mature woman in Anglo-American society ceases to exist as an individual, legally and culturally, and is "incorporated" into marriage, or into being part of her husband. While Blackstone's argument—with regard to the subsuming of women within marriage—became the foundation for many of the issues that modern feminism rose up to combat and change, Blackstone was codifying the general western perspective with regard to women, who moved from their father's house to their husband's house, where they again became part of the broader consolidation of property.

This connection between women, their relative value to men—be they fathers or husbands—and often their appearance, is as ancient as most human interactions. These same tales dominate the Old Testament; for example, Jacob gave fourteen years of his life so that he could finally marry his beloved, and beautiful, Rachel, after having been deceived at his first marriage to Leah. Many of the ancient traditions had some form of the "bride price," which, though not setting a value on a human being, did embody the exchange of money from the groom for a woman who would become his wife. And while the ancient biblical stories pay homage to a variety of beautiful women, it is Helen of Troy who is probably most renowned for her unmatched beauty, for it is her "face that launched a thousand ships," according to Shakespeare's contemporary, Christopher Marlowe, in his work *Doctor Faustus*.[5] Though Marlowe also binds together Helen's beauty with the war that followed from it, acknowledging the burning of Troy within the same sentence he writes, "Was this the face that launched a thousand ships / And burnt the topless towers of Ilium?"[6] Beauty can be a very valuable commodity, but it is a commodity that one is born with or without (though it can certainly be enhanced through a variety of means) and does not indicate skill, capacity, intelligence, strength, learning, or many of the other qualities that often can be translated into some form of remunerative reward. And women, as the so-called fairer sex, have most often been valued based on how they look—only recently has a woman's worth been estimated based on capacities other than appearance or biological capabilities to produce children/heirs.

Beauty and Value

In *Troilus and Cressida*, Shakespeare presses on this societal convention, with regard to the commodification of women based on their appearance and beauty and what that value might mean to a society, especially a society battling over a particular woman. Though Shakespeare does not confine his analysis only to women in the play, he does more overtly present that analysis with regard to the predominant female characters. These are some of Shakespeare's less famous female characters—though Helen was rather famous in her own right, in an iconic way. The playwright characterizes both Helen and Cressida as beautiful, and he uses *Troilus and Cressida* to examine the value placed on beauty. Shakespeare also shows that this valuation of female beauty seems to lead to or contribute to the corruption of honor or the constrained evaluation of the place of honor within societies that may themselves be corrupt.

Shakespeare presents these parallel evaluations through an interesting comparison—mostly setting Helen and Cressida in contrast to each other, not personally, but in the discussions and actions surrounding each woman. Delving into Shakespeare's presentation of these two women in *Troilus and Cressida* is as relevant today as it might have been when he wrote the play, because the theme that he focuses on with regard to the female characters is this question of value and the price, literally, of one's reputation. In fact, Shakespeare is exploring the "beauty myth" long before the term was coined; the play examines "emotional distance, politics, finance, and sexual repression [within the context of male] institutions and institutional power."[7] The women, alas, have little input with regard to their value, but the play swirls around the two battling camps, the Greeks and the Trojans, and the price each side is willing to "pay" in blood and honor for Helen and for Cressida. The play also considers, in a less overt manner, the reputations of the men, especially Achilles, but Shakespeare ultimately explores the value and reputation of all of the famous Greeks and Trojans.

Helen and Cressida

Cressida is more fully "drawn" as a character, though she also absorbs others' estimation of her worth, value, and quality compared to Helen, who is more static in presentation and whose "price" is also more stable—she is better known, especially to modern audiences. Cressida was fairly well known during Shakespeare's time, because of the number of medieval texts that had centered upon her.[8] These renderings of Cressida were not all that favorable—highlighting her inconstancy, her reputation for promiscuity, and her willingness to barter with sex. This picture of Cressida was quite well known to the Elizabethan audiences but is less well known to modern audiences.

Cressida is said to be smart and shrewd, though not valued for those qualities. Instead, the women of the play are seen as objects to be valued based on their beauty, which itself is a commodity, and their input is easily dismissed without consideration. The contestation within the play centers on the value of the female, and, intertwined with that value, the "cost of keeping" beauty,[9] and how this cost is connected to the sexual appeal of women. All of this is set in competition with the role of honor among men and how that honor shapes or misshapes the society. Ultimately the honor of two warring societies is placed in competition with the price ("What's aught, but as 'tis valued") of female beauty and sexuality.

Given the better known and, to a degree, more valued women within the Shakespeare oeuvre (Juliet, Cleopatra, Cordelia, Portia, Gertrude, Ophelia, Desdemona, even Lady Macbeth)—many of whom are also known for their beauty as well as their other capacities—the women of *Troilus and Cressida* are distinct in their contrast; they are very specifically constructed, by the discussions around them, as objects—valued, but not of any intrinsic worth, since their price keeps fluctuating.

Helen's Value

The initial scene, in act 2, that introduces the Trojan house is a discussion of whether to return Helen or to keep her, since the Greeks have made an offer that the war will be concluded without enmity if she is returned to Greece. Hector—essentially the leader of the House of Troy—argues that she should be returned. Troilus immediately counters with an argument not about peace or security (Hector's first approach to this offer, and the essential basis for the cease-fire) but of weighing "the worth and honour of a king / so great as our dread father on a scale / of common ounces" (II.ii.26–28). Troilus then pivots to respond to his brother Helenus's argument, which Helenus had based on reason. Troilus disparages reason as well as peace and security. Hector finally states his point directly to Troilus: "Brother, she is not worth what she doth cost / The holding" (II.ii.51–52). But this prompts Troilus to make the case with regard to attaching a value as one sees fit—not based on an intrinsic worth—to such an object: "What's aught but as 'tis valued?" Hector responds that "value" "holds his estimate and dignity / As well wherein 'tis precious of itself / As in the prizer" (II.ii.54–56). Hector argues that the value applied to something must come from the item itself, not merely what the "prizer" applies to the item as a value—there is an intrinsic value, separate from an applied value. And this, of course, is the case with regard to the value of women, most especially, in this discussion, Helen. In modern terms, this is an argument about the "market" in beauty and worth when it comes to Helen, the war, and the honor of the House of Troy.

Troilus moves from the abstract notion of valuing items to the value of Helen, which he describes as valuable to the entire House of Troy, because the family urged Paris to seek revenge on the Greeks:

And for an old aunt whom the Greeks held captive
He brought a Grecian queen, whose youth and freshness
Wrinkles Apollo's, and makes stale the morning.
Why keep we her? The Grecians keep our aunt.
Is she worth the keeping? Why, she is a pearl

Whose price hath launched above a thousand ships
And turned crowned kings to merchants....
If you'll confess he [Paris] brought home noble prize—
As you must needs, for you all clapped your hands
And cried "Inestimable!"—why do you now
The issue of your proper wisdoms rate
And do a deed that never Fortune did,
Begger the estimation which you prized
Richer than sea and land? O theft most base,
That we have stol'n what we do fear to keep! (II.ii.77–93)

There is much to be made of Troilus's speech here—where he is both trying to hold his family responsible for the initial move to claim the veracity of taking Helen from her husband and bringing her to Troy *and* urging them to keep her value somewhat more constant than he thinks that they are so doing. He is turning the argument around on his family, especially on Hector, arguing that they are weak and lacking honor if they are afraid to keep Helen, impugning their character and virtue since then the "theft" of Helen becomes common and completely dishonorable when it was previously considered at least a tit-for-tat situation with the Greeks. Helen is a pearl, not because she is described in the way a pearl may be described and from which it derives is value, but because she has become a token of bartering; her "price" launched the Greek armada and turned "crowned kings to merchants" looking to strike a deal. Her value will go from "inestimable" to simple theft according to Troilus, if they refuse to keep her. Thus the value of this pearl is not connected to her specifically, but to the estimation that the Trojans (and the Greeks) make of her in relation to what they are willing to do to keep her. If the Trojans choose to return Helen, as per the Greek offer, then her worth will be much diminished. So too will be the Trojan honor, because the cause upon which they were fighting will be seen as sullied, corrupt, and niggardly. These qualities will then be transferred to the Trojans themselves for having staked their honor on this worthless item and thrown their martial prowess behind defending something of such little value.

Paris, who has "the honey still" in his possessing of Helen, enters the argument and posits that it would be treasonous and disgraceful to Helen if they should return her to Greece:

What treason were it to the ransacked queen,
Disgrace to your great worth, and shame to me,
Now to deliver her possession up
On terms of base compulsion! (II.ii.150–154)

This argument moves between the honor of the Trojans, enlisting the disgrace of Troy's great worth and Paris's own shame to buttress the treason Paris sees in returning Helen to the Greeks.

In the midst of this discussion Cassandra interjects that Troy will be destroyed unless Helen is returned: "A Helen and a woe! / Cry, cry! Troy burns, or else let Helen go" (II.ii.111–112). Troilus quickly dismisses her shouts as madness, though Hector suggests that they should listen to her admonishments. Priam and Hector both dismiss Paris's argument because of his personal connection to Helen and the Trojan claim to her, but Hector takes on Troilus's and Paris's arguments. According to Shakespeare scholar Jan Kott,

> Helen had been abducted with Priam's permission and that of the Trojan leaders. Helen's cause has become Troy's cause. Helen has become the symbol of love and beauty. Helen will become a whore only when the Trojans return her to Menelaus and admit themselves that she is a whore, not worth dying for. How much is a jewel worth? A trader weighs it on the scales. But a jewel can be worth something else; worth the price of passion it aroused; the price it has in the eyes of the person who wears it; the price given it.[10]

This discussion is about how much value can be ascribed to Helen's reputation and ultimately how to keep that reputation intact. Should she be returned, her value and reputation would decrease, as would the reputation of the Trojans. This is Troilus's argument. Through most of the discussion, Hector opposes Troilus's argument.

Hector notes that keeping Helen is in opposition to the moral laws of nature and of nations because she is Menelaus's wife. He explains that continuing to keep her "extenuates not wrong, / But makes it much more heavy" (II.ii.186–187). While conceding that holding Helen is wrong, Hector notes that it would not be honorable to return her to her husband, as he says,

> I propend to you
> In resolution to keep Helen still;
> For 'tis a cause that hath no mean dependence
> Upon our joint and several dignities. (II.ii.190–194)

Troilus is overjoyed by Hector's concession that they shall keep Helen, as he goes on to make the case that their honor and martial greatness is likely to stem from Helen, though he also explains that he would like to see no more Trojan blood spilled defending her: "I would not wish a drop of Trojan blood / Spent more in her defense. But, worthy Hector, / She is a theme of honour and renown, / A spur to valiant and magnanimous deeds, / Whose present courage may beat down our foes / And fame in time to come canonize us" (II. ii.198–202). Helen's worth is determined by what kinds of actions may be done in her name—she is a "theme of honour and renown" and she is valuable, in an abstract, almost talismanic way.

Achilles and the Problem of Reputation for the Greeks

The discussion in act 2 introduces the audience to the Trojan family and presents, rather directly, the predominant evaluation of the current situation with regard to the Trojan War with the Greeks. The Greek perspective preceded the Trojan debate with an extremely long-winded disquisition in act 1, scene 3. Shakespeare purposefully makes this discussion tedious, again teasing at the well-known reputations of all those famous Greek generals. When read or performed, this scene is exceptionally tiresome, full of flowery words with little substance. Ulysses—one of the most loquacious orators among the Greeks, and certainly a rather prickly character as presented in *Troilus and Cressida*—explains that the reason why the Greeks haven't yet conquered the Trojans is because there is little respect among the troops for the leadership. The theme of honor and respect is sewn into the problem, as the Greeks see it, with their languishing on the Trojan field for the play's seven years.

> The general's disdained
> By him one step below, he by the next,
> That next by him beneath, so every step,
> Exampled by the first pace that is sick
> Of his superior, grows to an envious fever
> Of pale and bloodless emulation....
> Troy in our weakness lives, not in her strength. (I.iii.129–137)

And the person behind this undermining of order is Achilles, who "Having his ear full of his airy fame, / Grows dainty of his worth and in his tent / Lies mocking our designs" (I.iii. 144–146). There are battles of egos within the Greek camp—Achilles, the most ferocious of warriors, can't be bothered to fight—and the rest of the Greek generals seem incapable of persuading Achilles to return to the battlefield. This prominent example is proving even more troublesome because the disrespect demonstrated by Achilles—and Patroclus and Thersites—is filtering down throughout the ranks. The fraying of order within a military force is generally a sign of significant weakness, but it often highlights a deeper problem:

that the cause upon which the war is based is neither persuasive nor compelling. Retrieving Helen from the Trojans and "restoring" her to her husband is not part of the discussion among the Greeks. The discussion is about reputation and the order that follows from the proper respect accorded to those of particular reputations. If that respect is withheld, or if the reputations are undermined, the expected results are scrambled. This is the situation that the Greek generals define as their problem in the midst of the war. For the men in this conversation, there is a keen value placed on reputation, though it is more about an individual's worth and the value that he or she supplies or provides to society than beauty.

Cressida's Worth

Cressida is a much more obscure character in our historical memory, and her story is more complicated than Helen's. Cressida's betrayal of Troilus, late in the play, is generally difficult to accept because we have come to know both Cressida's heart, through a number of soliloquies, and her as a person. In comparison to Troilus, Cressida is a more interesting and fully developed character. In many respects, Troilus is closer to Romeo—he is in love, rash, and not often persuaded by rational arguments. Troilus is also caught in the dilemma that binds the actions of the play: is his commitment to his family and thus Troy's side of the war more important to him than his attested love of/for Cressida?[11] Cressida would rather not be a commodity in this ancient economy, but alas, she has little choice when told she is being "traded" and no one takes up her cause.

Her reputation is also a complex matter, because there is little to indicate its value until she becomes a traded commodity. Cressida's worth is certainly not at the level of Helen's, even according to Troilus, who quickly complies with the deal struck between the Trojans and the Greeks to exchange Cressida for a Trojan soldier captured by the Greeks. This trade indicates a kind of abstract value attached to Cressida by the Greeks, but when she arrives at the Greek camp and kisses are demanded and "stolen" from her by almost all of the Greek commanders, the value of her reputation declines rather precipitously. A recent analysis of the play suggests that Cressida's reputation is, in fact, blank until it is little valued:

> There is no single, reliable choral observer within the play who can orient our responses.... In a sense, Cressida is the text. Without responding to how she presented herself, without allowing her any autonomy, men impose on her their own evaluation; just as Cressida answers to people's expectations, so does the play.[12]

Unlike Juliet—who is oddly separated from the activities that swirl in *Romeo and Juliet*, almost always learning about events outside the walls of her home by others who tell her about them—Cressida is actually present and interactive, but her value is imposed upon her by the men on either side of the war. She has little or no capacity to determine her own worth, noting that

> Women are angels, wooing;
> Things won are done; joy's soul lies in the doing.
> That she beloved knows naught that knows not this:
> Men prize the thing ungained more than it is.
> That she was never yet that ever knew
> Love got so sweet as when desire did sue.
> Therefore this maxim out of love I teach:
> "Achievement is command; ungained, beseech." (I.ii.277–284)

Cressida is quite aware of the reality that the value of a woman is easily changed, and that women have little control over these fluctuations. Her clarity in regard to this commodification of women has perplexed many a critic of the play and of Cressida.[13] She was well aware of the maxim "women are angels, wooing" and that once women are achieved they are then commanded by those who have "achieved" them. But it is also clear from her words, especially her soliloquies, that Cressida is in love with Troilus and is torn between her understanding of the world of men and women and the precarious value that women have within it, and her desire to pursue that which she loves: Troilus.

Cressida is willing to give into her heart to Troilus. From the outset Cressida presents her love for Troilus to the audience. Troilus also acknowledges his love for Cressida, from the first scene of the play, but the oddity of his presentation is that he presents a conflicted image: he comes off the battlefield and unarms because he is not master of his heart (I.i.1–5). Troilus, before he describes Helen as a pearl to be valued, discusses Cressida in similar but more sensual terms:

> [Cressida's] bed is India; there she lies, a pearl.
> Between our Ilium, and where she resides,
> Let it be called the wild and wand'ring flood,
> Ourself the merchant, and this sailing Pandar
> Our doubtful hope, our convoy and our bark. (I.i.96–100)

Troilus has couched his pursuit of Cressida in terms that define commodity trading—either of the flesh or of other commodities. Cressida is a pearl, lying upon her bed. Troilus is the merchant who must do business with Pandarus in order to "purchase" Cressida. Even as he pursues Cressida, Troilus sees her more as a kind of property than as a human being.[14] At the end of the play, Cressida's "final appearance ... is as a letter [to Troilus]—a complete reduction of woman to text,"[15] with her reputation and value being ascribed by Troilus and Ulysses.

Troilus and Cressida are brought together by Pandarus only to awake the next morning to find that Cressida has been traded to the Greeks. Troilus, who argued so valiantly to keep Helen, responds to this news with four words: "Is it concluded so?" (IV.ii.68). Troilus does not say or do any of the things that he says and does on behalf of Helen, who is a prize, but is Paris's prize. And Cressida, who has given in to love, even as she doubted her ability to maintain her sense of value in so doing, is overtly turned into a tradable Trojan commodity.

Cressida's arrival in the Greek camp lays bare this commodification as Cressida is made to play a game, designed by Ulysses, to elicit kisses from the various Greek generals, as he says, "'Twere better she were kissed in general" (IV.v.22). Before Cressida has said a word in this scene, Agamemnon, Nestor, Achilles, Menelaus, and Patroclus have all kissed Cressida. She is a possession of the Greeks, they may do with her what they choose, they "own" her. And, as presaged by the discussion of Helen's value upon her return to the Greeks, Cressida's value has been much degraded when she is traded to the Greeks, especially when she is received in a sexually threatening manner, without an ally and with only her wits to defend herself.

Ulysses's immediate response to Cressida is to first situate her in a sexually aggressive "game" and then to draw conclusions with regard to her degraded reputation because she interacted with him rather than passively giving in to him and to others. It becomes clear that because Ulysses can't "prescribe" her behavior, his opinion of her immediately declines.[16] In Cressida's engagement with the men in an effort to "give as good as she gets" Ulysses and Nestor conclude that she is a "daughter of the game" (IV.v.64). Cressida is compromised by her demonstration of wittiness and intelligent sparring. Demonstrations of this kind of engagement, which includes flirtation, immediately undermine Cressida's reputation and value. This is often part of the "double bind" for women—engaging intelligently apparently antagonizes men, but not engaging means that women remain passive observers and observed but not participants in the world around them. Cressida and Sandra Fluke were both devalued because they chose to try to participate in determining their worth and role in the world around them.

Concluding Thoughts

Much is made within *Troilus and Cressida* of the role of beauty, how female beauty generally has an adverse effect upon society by leading both to its physical corruption through sexually transmitted diseases (the play is almost overburdened with such references and conflations) and the corruption of the foundations of both the Greek and Trojan society, namely, honor and martial glory. This trajectory is particularly apt in considering not only the characters within *Troilus and Cressida* but also in extrapolating modern teachings from this particular play. The Limbaugh-Fluke incident and others like it would suggest that modern cultures are still operating, at least in segments, to measure women's reputations as a commodity and set a value on their honor, whether one is clearly evaluating the substance of that honor or disparaging it in context of the fact that women, like men, are sexual beings.[17] Cressida acknowledges her love for Troilus and, like him, acts on it. The societies that surround her seem to be less than clear and consistent with regard to marriage and its permanence, and the play itself focuses on the often transactional nature of sex in war zones and the fleeting value of both women and their beauty. *Troilus and Cressida* is particularly interesting in the way in which the women or the value placed on them is the source of blame for the corrupt nature of both societies presented within the play.

Modern feminism has been wrestling with the role of female beauty within society and how this impacts both the way men evaluate women and the way that women think about themselves. As Naomi Wolf explains, "'Beauty' is a currency system like the gold standard. Like any economy, it is determined by politics, and in the modern age in the West it is the last, best belief system that keeps male dominance intact."[18] This is exactly what Shakespeare is spotlighting. Shakespeare could have written the play about Paris and Helen. He essentially writes a play along those lines in *Anthony and Cleopatra*, focusing on mature adults, married to other people, in love with each other, and in significant positions of power and rule. Instead, in taking on the Homeric tale of the Trojan War, Shakespeare focuses on the relationship between two of the more obscure characters in Homer's story. It is a play named for lovers—only two other plays are so named, *Romeo and Juliet* and *Anthony and Cleopatra*[19]—but it begins with a Prologue armed for battle. This Prologue is immediately followed by Troilus's entrance, where he, in opposition to the Prologue, unarms. Troilus's first five lines present some of the play's conflict, as he determines that he needs to unarm because he is not master of his heart—he can no longer "war without the walls of Troy" because there is such "cruel battle" within him (I.i.1–5). This is the contested history of *Troilus and Cressida*: it is about the war between the Trojans and the Greeks, which is the setting for the play, and it is also about these two lovers, Troilus and Cressida, who find their affections for one another tested because of the war surrounding them.

The play neither starts nor ends neatly, concentrating on the relationship between honor and battle, and individual reputations and the reputations of entire societies and nations. Shakespeare presents neither side as particularly virtuous and honorable. He has humanized many of the larger-than-life heroes of western literature, undercutting their reputations, highlighting various failings, and showing a lack of respect among the soldiers for their commanders.

Shakespeare also took on the medieval traditions and tales and undermined them as well. He presents Cressida as vulnerable and insecure—especially in the Greek camp, but not nearly the sexually corrupt and debased character that she had been drawn in so many of these stories. Troilus is undercut in much the same ways that Shakespeare undercuts Ulysses and Achilles. His virtue is flimsy, and his commitment to Cressida is fleeting. In a sense, the play brings together characters who were quite well known to the audiences—with clear reputations that Shakespeare undoes in this play. He literally undermines the reputations of western cultures' preeminent heroes.

What are we to make of this "undoing" in so many different ways, of reputation, of position, of virtue? Consider the various valuations of reputation as outlined within this chapter: Helen, in the Trojan discussion, is literally the world's first "trophy wife"—and she is quite the trophy. Achilles, after dithering and undermining authority, finally takes to the battlefield only after his dear friend and lover Patroclus is killed, and he scores Hector's death when Hector is unarmed.[20] Finally there is Cressida, who, in many ways, presents a modern conundrum: a woman willing to follow her heart and her desires only to find herself undermined by the demands of her society as she is traded like any other commodity in the context of a war. All three examples indicate the compromised value of a human being, especially in context of warring societies where honor is highly esteemed but where the underlying value of that honor is transactional, fluid, and degraded.

Conclusion

Because honor itself is so fluid in both societies, connecting a woman's reputation to her honor does her an immediate disservice; there is neither a static nor an objective barometer of what that might mean in any particular situation or by any particular group. The debate among the Trojans in act 2 is not about Helen's honor, it is about her value—a value projected upon her by both the Trojans and the Greeks to give their fight a value, to imbue it with honor given the value of the prize being contested. Unlike the argument made by Henry in his St. Crispin's Day speech in *Henry V*, which focuses on the honor of the deed itself, the people doing the deed, and the rightfulness of the fight, the discussion among the Trojans is about Helen's value and how the honor of the House of Troy is defined by that value. Ultimately, *Troilus and Cressida* questions the value of reputation and the costs to society in projecting variable estimations of a person's worth merely by an external evaluation. This doesn't prevent people from projecting these variable estimations of a person's worth, as the Limbaugh-Fluke incident indicates. The Greeks and the Trojans are both undone by this drive toward commodification, especially the commodification of women within the society. And the most problematic dimension of the weighing of reputations is the corruption of a woman's reputation through a demonstration of her wits and intelligence. This remains a perpetual problem, even in modern society, especially when combined with the acknowledgment of female sexuality.

Notes

1. Forty different national and local advertisers pulled advertising from the show. See "Rush Limbaugh: Over 40 Advertisers Flee, Host Says 'Everything's Cool,'" at abcnews.com, March 7, 2012, http://abcnews.go.com/blogs/politics/2012/03/rush-limbaugh-over-40-advertisers-flee-host-says-everythings-cool/.

2. Alyssa Rosenberg,"Why Hasn't Clear Channel Punished Rush Limbaugh?" March 5, 2012, *Think Progress,* http://thinkprogress.org/alyssa/2012/03/05/437597/rush-limbaugh-clear-channel/.

3. David Bauder, "Don Imus Loses Job in Stunning Fall," *USA Today,* April 12, 2007, http://usatoday30.usatoday.com/life/television/2007-04-12-739667894_x.htm.

4. William Blackstone, *Commentaries on the Laws of England,* vol. 1 (1765), pp. 442–445.

5. Christopher Marlowe, *The Tragical History of Doctor Faustus,* scene XIII, line 88.

6. Ibid., lines 88–89.

7. Naomi Wolf, *The Beauty Myth: How Images of Beauty Are Used against Women* (New York: Harper Perennial, 2002), p. 13.

8. See particularly Chaucer's *Troilus and Criseyde,* Lydgate's *Troybook,* Henryson's *Testament of Cresseid,* William Caxton, etc.

9. Hector notes to Troilus, before Hector changes his mind, that Helen "is not worth what she doth cost/the keeping" (T&C, II.ii.51–52).

10. Jan Kott, *Shakespeare Our Contemporary,* (New York: W. W. Norton, 1974), pp. 77–78.

11. Paris is in a similar bind in regard to Helen until he and Troilus are able to persuade the family that Helen and the House of Troy are entwined.

12. Claire M. Tyree, "The Text of Cressida and Every Ticklish Reader: Troilus and Cressida, the Greek Camp Scene," *Shakespeare Survey* 41, p. 5.

13. Tyree goes through many of these critiques in her essay "The Text of Cressida and Every Ticklish Reader" as she highlights various conflicted readings of Cressida.

14. Shakespeare scholar G. Wilson Knight suggests that Troilus's love for Cressida

is "presented throughout as a thing essentially noble and pure." Cressida is not said to have such a rarified love for Troilus according to Knight, *The Wheel of Fire: Interpretations of Shakespearean Tragedy with Three New Essays* (New York: Meridian, 1960), pp. 47–72.

15. Carol Cook, "Unbodied Figures of Desire," *Theatre Journal*, Vol. 38, No. 1, Dramatic Narration, Theatrical Disruption (March 1986), p. 52.

16. As Wolf explains, "The beauty myth is always actually prescribing behavior and not appearance," *The Beauty Myth*, p. 14.

17. And because women are sexual beings, and may not want to become pregnant at points, they will also pursue contraception in order to prevent unwanted pregnancies and in an effort to control their lives, their careers, and ultimately their value and worth.

18. Wolf, *The Beauty Myth*, p. 12.

19. I have often considered Troilus and Cressida the young adult match, since Romeo and Juliet were teenagers and Anthony and Cleopatra were mature and certainly along in years, and they also had realms to rule and families of their own. Of the three plays named for lovers, only the teenagers, Romeo and Juliet, actually get married to each other. Of course, Troilus and Cressida are the only lovers who are still alive at the play's end.

20. Compare Achilles's killing of Hector in act 5, scene 8, where he orders his Myrmidons to do it, as Hector has taken off his armor after the day of battle, to Hamlet's decision not to kill his uncle, Claudius, when he finds him in prayer (*Hamlet*, act 3, scene 3). Both are revenge killings/attempted killings, but Achilles's choice to slay an unarmed Hector suggests both compromised virtue and inappropriate actions on the battlefield. Hamlet chooses not to murder his uncle while he prays because he concludes that doing so would dispatch his uncle's soul to heaven, not to hell, where Hamlet thinks it belongs.

Chapter 11

Deception and Persuasion in *Measure for Measure*

Carol McNamara

Does Shakespeare's *Measure for Measure,* a sixteenth-century play portraying the political events reestablishing political order in the Dukedom of Vienna, have anything significant to tell the twenty-first century about the nature of effective political leadership? Shakespeare introduces Vienna's Duke Vincentio in act 1 as a reluctant governor who loves the people (I.1.67) but who does "not relish well their loud applause" (I.1.70). In fact, he confesses to suspicion of any human being who seeks out the public realm, who chooses "to stage" himself to the people and who revels in their admiration. Such a man cannot be "of safe discretion," according to the Duke's judgment. In contrast to the politically ambitious, who "haunt assemblies" with the intention of ostentatiously displaying their "witless bravery," the Duke reminds Friar Thomas, in a private conversation early in the play, that he has always preferred a quiet life, "the life remov'd" (I.3.8). The Duke is clearly contemptuous and mistrustful of the personal desire for power and glory of a human being who likes politics and public approbation too much. Yet, the Duke also acknowledges to the Friar that his contempt for politics per se has led him to neglect the pressing necessities of political life, which has allowed the political order in Vienna to fray (I.3.18–55). At the beginning of *Measure for Measure*, the Duke takes the advice of Niccolo Machiavelli when he advises princes to become well-acquainted with the nature of the people in order to govern them effectively.[1] The "fantastical" Duke may have secretive means available to him that a contemporary democratic leader cannot employ, but he contends with the same challenges posed by extreme ideological parties on the political spectrum that a prudential twenty-first-century political leader must also tackle.

In the early scenes of *Measure for Measure*, Shakespeare's Duke reflects upon the tension inherent in the effort to institute judicious leadership. A leader is one who aims at achieving a common political good within a society. An important qualification for leadership is knowledge of the people. To acquire this knowledge a leader must go out among the people to understand their way of life, their virtues and vices. And yet, there is a profound difference between a true leader who comprehends what will bring about justice and the common good in a state, and one who merely reflects the transitory desires of the people for the sake of accumulating personal power and glory. It is neither safe nor wise to be so dependent on the opinion of the people that one becomes their flatterer, rather than their leader. The Duke, who is a careful student of politics, understands this tension; he seeks not merely to purchase the fleeting regard of the people but to inspire their confidence in his stable and prudent leadership. To do so, he knows he must proceed in a way that establishes his authority with the people without incurring their hatred or contempt.[2] In *Measure for Measure*, Shakespeare demonstrates the requirements of political leadership through the Duke's clandestine plan to reestablish in Vienna a political order of a moderate and lasting nature.

This chapter will first consider the traditional explanations of Shakespeare's political teaching in *Measure for Measure*. There is much value in understanding Shakespeare's use of literary sources. Nevertheless, there is a compelling case to make that he uses those sources in *Measure for Measure* as a means to understand and portray through Duke Vincentio's thoughts and actions the nature of effective political governance.

Critics and the Troubling Nature of *Measure for Measure*

Shakespearean critics frequently classify *Measure for Measure* as a "problem" play. *Measure for Measure* ends well, without any actual executions, tied up nicely in the fifth act with several suitable—or at least necessary—marriages, but critics only reluctantly classify it as a comedy. The morally questionable nature of the Duke's methods—deception, trickery, his willingness to bend the law, to encourage apparently sinful deeds, and to use the cloak of the clergy to disguise his devious methods—creates in the hearts and minds of the critics a profound discomfort with *Measure for Measure*. The critics clearly raise valid objections: are all political tactics justifiable in the pursuit even of the public good? Are the Duke's tactics truly morally dubious? Are they justified by political necessity? Does he stay within the limits of the law in his effort to right his political ship? Or does the Duke cross the moral line?

Measure for Measure begins with the abrupt and mysterious departure of the Duke from Vienna, leaving Angelo, a severe, even puritanical character, as his first deputy, with Escalus, a trusted and judicious counselor, as the second. From here unfolds the traditional tale on which Shakespeare builds his own story of political and moral corruption. The Duke's investment of authority in the hands of a deputy is consistent with the literary sources scholars have identified.[3] The basic outline of the story involves "three traditional plot components.... The first, concerning the actions of Angelo, Claudio, and Isabella, ... may be described as the story of the corrupt magistrate; the second, relating to the role of the Duke and Lucio, as the legend of the Disguised Ruler; and the third, which concerns the part played by Mariana, as the tale of the Substituted Bedmate."[4] All three of these literary devices provide a foundation for Shakespeare's story, but it is Shakespeare's innovations, chiefly involving the actions of the Duke, that trouble the critics. In the first case, Isabella is not a beautiful wife, seeking to save the life of her condemned husband, propositioned by the lecherous, corrupt magistrate, but instead a sister. Quite literally, Isabella is almost a nun. Lucio must fetch her from the convent of St. Clare, where she has recently sought refuge from the libertinism of Vienna, so that she might plead for the life of her brother, Claudio. Angelo, is, in turn, attracted to Isabella for her beauty and her virtue. In the second case, the Duke takes on a disguise in order to move freely among his people, learning their secrets and vices, to right wrongs and introduce effectual political reform. Here, critics are troubled by the Duke's disguise as a Friar, becoming the voice of the church for those in distress, but willing to bend the truth, as he does to Isabella when he allows her to believe, in act 5, that Angelo has executed Claudio. The critics are also troubled by the Duke's willingness to use the authority of his religious disguise to suborn sin, in particular, when he persuades Isabella and Mariana to participate in the bed trick, by which Angelo is duped into sleeping with Mariana, his betrothed by a pre-contract, instead of Isabella. In addition to these "problems," critics are uneasy with "the forced marriages, blanket pardons, and the duke's proposal to Isabella," which receives no response before the play concludes.[5] But what if these innovations to the traditional plot devices are not merely Shakespeare's shaky efforts to right a wobbly plot but instead, they form an essential part of his effort to portray the leadership of a prince who must operate in the imperfect political realm?

The Duke's Adversaries

A thorough consideration of act 1, scenes 1, 2, and 3, makes clear that the Duke has a strategic plan: first, to put to rest resistance to his leadership from factions in Vienna, represented on one side by religious extremists and moral purists, like Angelo, and, on the other, by libertines, like Lucio; and, second, to reestablish his own political and moral authority, somewhere in the center between the two extremes.

First, the Duke seeks to expose and tame his opposition, represented chiefly by Angelo, who demonstrates by his actions as the Duke's agent that he believes moral standards in Vienna require a stricter enforcement than the Duke has been willing to uphold. The Duke immediately instills us with the confidence that Escalus, an ancient lord and trusted advisor in Vincentio's court, has the worth and understanding of the nature of Vienna's people and its institutions to be a sound custodian of justice (I.1.3–13). In contrast to his obvious trust in Escalus is the Duke's apparent mistrust of Angelo. Instead of reassuring the audience of Angelo's integrity, as he does with Escalus, the Duke asks Escalus how he believes Angelo will comport himself as the duke's surrogate: "What figure of us, think you, he will bear?" (I.1.16). It is surprising that the Duke, who will momentarily invest in Angelo all the "terror" and "power" of his office, seems unsure how Angelo will act on his behalf, but the question implants in us a misgiving about Angelo from the start.

Nevertheless, the Duke's initial public interaction with Angelo suggests that he supports him fully. He explains to Escalus that he has selected Angelo "with special soul" as his deputy (I.1.17). The Duke praises Angelo's virtues and encourages him to make them shine like a torch as a guiding light for the Viennese people, over whom he will exercise the power of "mortality and mercy in Vienna" in the Duke's absence (I.1.44). The Duke, thus, emboldens Angelo to use his own virtue as a guide "to enforce or qualify the laws / As to your own soul seems good" (I.1.65–66). This impression of Angelo is reinforced through his exchanges with Escalus and Isabella concerning the case of Claudio, accused and condemned to death by Angelo for fornication, and it conforms to the Duke's public presentation of Angelo's strict moral character. Angelo sets about imposing the laws of Vienna as they are written as soon as the Duke departs. He demands that the law set a clear, high, and enforceable standard for moral behavior to which everyone must conform. He stresses his belief that the laws of Vienna have become more like a "scarecrow," which provides a fierce appearance but without preventing the birds from raiding the fields for their dinner, just as the unenforced laws are only window dressing without implementation (II.1.1–4). Escalus understands the necessity of enforcing the law, but he is also aware that the law universally enforced may be unjustly applied in any particular case, like that of Claudio, whose marriage to Juliet, lacking only the final consecration of the sacramental union, would be recognized by the English common law.[6] Escalus's effort to moderate Angelo's religious zeal proves futile. He can only express his regret that Angelo is severe to the point of taking a man's life for a very human frailty that could easily be rectified by marriage. He reflects that "Some rise by sin, and some by virtue fall" (II.1.37). Some gain a position of authority through sinful, dishonest, or corrupt actions, while others often fall when they refuse to compromise their moral principles. Escalus does not seem to have the Duke's knowledge of Angelo's corruption, but he does understand that the rigid imposition of the law alone is not the simple answer to the administration of justice and good government.

Angelo, similarly, rejects Isabella's plea for mercy on Claudio's behalf. Isabella reminds Angelo that appropriate mercy is the sign of a judicious leader, but Angelo remains rigid in his insistence that the law must be applied without regard for family ties or particular circumstances (II.2.105–107). When Isabella argues that Angelo's sudden enforcement of a long-dormant law without public notice against her brother is arbitrary and unjust, Angelo is steadfast in his determination to make an example of Claudio to save others from committing the same "future evils" (II.2.122). Angelo's argument is that the strict imposition of the law is the only means to a moral order. Isabella, and, as we will see, the Duke, disagree. Isabella's suggestion, much like that of Escalus earlier (I.2.8–16), that Angelo is as likely as Claudio to fall victim to the same natural inclination to succumb to his desires, is the moderating argument that, though unsuccessful with Angelo, wins the day.

Despite Angelo's apparent moral consistency, the Duke's opinion of Angelo is dark indeed. He announces somewhat opaquely that he has observed Angelo's nature and it has revealed his story to him, a story that, in fact, exposes Angelo's moral hypocrisy (I.1.30–32). The evidence for this conclusion is that the Duke has prior knowledge that Angelo had broken off his pre-contract to marry a young woman, Mariana, when her dowry was lost at sea and she was left penniless. Despite his public show of morality, Angelo is a dishonorable scoundrel. The Duke tells Friar Thomas of his plan to make a test of Angelo's moral precision to see "If power change purpose, what our seemers be" (I.4.57–58). The Duke clearly expects Angelo to reveal his hypocrisy through his actions, as he does in his proposal to exchange Claudio's life for Isabella's virginity.

Shakespeare next introduces his audience to the Duke's opposition on the other side of the civic equation. Lucio is a seductive and irreverent character who represents the liberation of the passions the Duke's loose administration of the city's laws has permitted.[7] Lucio's inclinations are, however, both noble and base. He is willing to go out of his way for friendship but is also capable of a potentially dangerous lawlessness.[8]

For friendship, Lucio takes courageous risks. When Claudio asks for his help in fetching Isabella from the convent, Lucio not only retrieves her but also schools her on how to employ her persuasive talents most effectively with Angelo. Isabella's first inclination is to doubt her persuasive ability and to submit to what she considers, regrettably, to be a "just but severe law." Lucio's coaching instructs Isabella how to make an argument for the necessity of moderation in the allocation of justice. With Claudio and Isabella, Lucio demonstrates a spirited and generous nature.

Lucio also serves as a spokesman for the naturalness of the passions in *Measure for Measure* when he tells the Duke, disguised as the friar, that lechery will only be extirpated when "eating and drinking be put down" as well (III.2.98–99). Following his passions freely without external or self-restraint, however, has left a mark on Lucio's character. Barbara Tovey argues that "Lucio is a greater threat to the duke's Vienna than any other character in the play" because he is "a highly intelligent person who is nevertheless devoid of morality."[9] Lucio lives quite freely in Vienna without taking personal responsibility for the consequences of his actions. The Duke has left the people free, but Lucio's libertinism contributes to his difficulties in Vienna because the coarser characters in town with whom Lucio associates have taken this liberty as permission to live outside of the law. While the Duke's plan is chiefly focused on preventing the ascension of religious severity, he must also concern himself with the reimposition of the rule of law.

The Duke's Political Strategy

It is not long after the Duke's departure in act 1, scene 1, that we learn from a surreptitious exchange between the Duke and Friar Thomas that the Duke has not left Vienna but, instead, intends to remain in the city, disguised in the habit of a friar. His purpose is to observe how Angelo exercises his power and to what effect, by visiting "both prince and people" (I.3.45). The similarity between the Duke and Henry V is striking. Henry visits the nobles and the common men among his troops on the eve of the Battle of Agincourt to discover their state of mind and to test it against his own without the encumbrance of his crown on their interactions (4.1). It is often difficult for a leader to learn the straightforward truth from political subordinates, knowledge of which a prudent leader must be aware. The Duke's disguise has a similar investigative purpose.

Friar Thomas astutely challenges the Duke's plan to disguise himself as a friar. He wonders whether the Duke seeks "secret harbor" for the purpose of a clandestine romantic rendezvous. The Duke's warning not to believe "the dribbling dart of love / Can pierce a complete bosom" suggests that he has not taken the time for matters of the heart (I.3.3). He has dedicated himself to becoming "a scholar, a statesman, and a soldier," according to his own account (III.2.147) and supported by Escalus's judgment that he was "One that, above all other strifes, contended especially to know himself" (III.2.233). The Duke seeks to disguise himself not to indulge his secret passions but instead to address the pressing political challenges facing Vienna.

We are left with a pressing question, which Friar Thomas himself poses: why has the Duke allowed the "strict statutes and most biting laws" of Vienna to lie dormant for fourteen years, especially when the power "to unloose this tied-up justice" was always available to the Duke, and with "more dreadful" effect than Lord Angelo could impose (I.2.20, 32–34)? The Duke suggests that he has been like a fond father who brandishes his whip in the hope that he will never be compelled to use it against his children. Furthermore, the Duke explains to Friar Thomas that the imposition of such laws by him would have appeared too severe. Instead, the Duke has imposed the office on Angelo and, dressed as a friar, intends to watch how Angelo proceeds with the reinvigoration of the religious laws the Duke, who has not instructed him to do so, expects him to undertake.

We are still left, however, to sort out, first, why the Duke has been reluctant to impose the full force of the laws on the people of Vienna; and, second, why the Duke has chosen this time to confront the city's defects. Several plausible explanations for the Duke's inaction exist. Tovey attributes the Duke's failure to enforce the harsh laws to his philosophic nature. She argues that Duke Vincentio chooses to dedicate himself chiefly to the pursuit of knowledge through study and contemplation, which causes him to neglect the political duties necessary to effective governance. Tovey supports her argument by pointing to the Duke's disinclination to engage in political theater (I.1.67) and to his preference for "the live remov'd" (I.3.8). Tovey argues further that political rule requires a spirited character who will impose harsh penalties when necessary, a characteristic that Vincentio seems to lack (I.3.36–50).[10]

Certainly, Tovey has a point when she identifies the Duke as a serious man who concerns himself chiefly, as Escalus asserts, with the acquisition of self-knowledge (III.2.234). It is important to recall, however, that the Duke, disguised as a friar, describes himself to Lucio as a "statesman, and a soldier," as well as a scholar. The Duke's philosophic nature may account for his distaste for the empty pageant and demonstrations of ambition characteristic of political life, but he understands himself as the leader of Vienna, in court and on the battlefield. Consequently, we must look further to understand the nature and timing of his actions in *Measure for Measure*.

In fact, the Duke's focus on Angelo provides evidence that he is indeed politically astute. The Duke explains to Friar Thomas that because he has left the people at liberty for so long, "'Twould be my tyranny to strike and gall them / For what I bid them do" (I.3.38–40). The Duke chooses his words carefully. He claims responsibility for leaving the people too much at liberty, but he also suggests that it was his intention that they live freely. The Duke is disinclined to rule tyrannically. Instead, he has left Lord Angelo, "a man of stricture and firm abstinence, / My absolute power and place here in Vienna" (I.3.13). Our initial impression is that the Duke has left Angelo to be his temporary henchman, to impose order on Vienna through whatever means necessary. The circumstances are reminiscent of Machiavelli's account of how Cesare Borgia gave Messer Ramiro d'Orco, "a cruel and ready man," "the fullest power" to reduce the Romagna, recently acquired by Borgia, to "peace and unity." Like Angelo, Ramiro quickly became hated among the people due to his "excessive authority." Machiavelli informs us of Borgia's procedure. In order "to purge the spirits of the people and to gain them entirely to himself, he wished to show that if any cruelty had been committed, this had not come from him but from the harsh nature of his minister."[11] Cesare Borgia employs Ramiro to impose order and then sacrifices him to purge the angry spirits of a conquered people in order to establish the appearance of justice. Does the Duke use Angelo as Borgia uses Ramiro? Significantly, Angelo does not meet his end in the town square with his body "in two pieces, with a piece of wood and a bloody knife beside him," but the Duke does manipulate Angelo in his political plan.[12]

Angelo appears deferential, but immediately following the Duke's assumed departure, Angelo reimposes a rigid rule upon Vienna, just as the Duke anticipated, but exactly contrary to the Duke's own (what we might call today) small government or classical liberal inclinations. Claudio accuses Angelo of awaking "all the enrolled penalties / Which have, like unscoured armor, hung by th' wall / So long that nineteen zodiacs have gone around, / And none of them worn; and for a name / Now puts the drowsy and neglected act / Freshly on me" (I.2.164–169). Claudio has a point. Angelo is clearly anxious to use this opportunity to restore an ancient understanding of the laws that the Duke has deliberately allowed to fall into disuse. When Escalus inquires of the Duke disguised as a foreign friar what news he has from abroad, the Duke reflects that there is nothing really new. Perhaps his meaning here is that human nature is constant. He observes that there is

> None but there is so great a fever on goodness that the dissolution of it must cure it. Novelty is only in request, and it is as dangerous to be aged in any kind of course as it is virtuous to be constant in any undertaking. (III.2.216–220)

The traditional understanding of this speech is that the Duke believes "goodness" is sick with a fever, and that only "death can cure the disease."[13] But it is also plausible the Duke's meaning is that there is in Vienna both a feverish attachment to goodness and virtue, of the kind exhibited by Angelo, and a destructive fascination with novelty—the sort represented by Lucio, who lives to satisfy his momentary desires, without civic or personal responsibility—both of which are detrimental to a judicious civil order.

The Duke is clearly concerned with these two extremes represented by Angelo and Lucio. The Duke's explanation to Friar Thomas that he intends to use his friar's disguise to watch Angelo's implementation of the laws is true, but it is incomplete. The Duke anticipates that Angelo will yield to temptation and reveal his true nature. At the conclusion of act 3, the Duke reflects privately on his strategy to expose Angelo's duplicity. A man like Angelo "should be as holy as severe," but instead he has failed to live up to his own standards. The result is that he sentences himself because his "cruel striking / Kills for faults of his own liking!" (III.2.250, 255, 260–261). The Duke tells us of his plan to employ "Craft against vice" to expose Angelo's corruption and compel him to honor his contract with Mariana (III.2.270). With this soliloquy, we understand that the chief vice festering in Vienna is among the religious extremists. Angelo is unyielding in his determination to execute Claudio for their shared vice of fornication, rather than take the obviously humane and moderate path of marrying him to Juliet, to whom he is betrothed in private agreement (I.2.142–146). The Duke's so-called bed trick, while irregular and sneaky, is not quite equivalent to Borgia's impressive execution of Ramiro. In fact, the Duke actually rescues Angelo from his own depravity.

Lucio too is saved from debauchery through his involvement with the Duke, which, ironically, derives from his good intention to save Claudio from a severe and unjust penalty. But it is Lucio's lack of self-restraint that leads him to reveal too much to the Duke in disguise as the friar of his irresponsible behavior, particularly in the case of the impregnated wench. Lucio is a cad, but he is also an important partner and foil for the Duke. Whereas the Duke is by nature a self-sufficient and studious man, impatient with human weakness, Lucio possesses an intuitive understanding of human nature, especially the desires that move individuals to act. This intuitive understanding makes Lucio a natural leader of human beings. As a result, the Duke relies on Lucio during the play. In fact, Lucio is strangely drawn to the disguised Duke. He shares with the "friar" his secrets and fears, including that he was once brought before the Duke "for getting a wench with child," an act to which he would not admit publicly because it would result in his forced marriage. And he informs the Duke as friar that he will stay with him, that he will stick with him like "a kind of burr" (IV.4.170–177). It is a puzzle why the morally loose Lucio is drawn to the disguised Duke. Maybe he confesses his sins because the Duke is disguised as a friar. But he expresses a confidence in the Duke's leadership. He tells the grieving Isabella that "if the fantastical duke of dark corners had been at home," Claudio would have lived. He is also eager to talk about the Duke and portray him as a companion. The humorous effect results from Lucio's effort to portray himself to the Duke as an intimate acquaintance, which is, of course, bound to fail. Nevertheless, Lucio proves useful to the Duke. He shows a moderate practicality in the way that he acts quickly and effectively to address Claudio's perilous circumstances. He sagely calms the young nerves of Isabella and directs her toward a rhetorical triumph with Angelo. In the end, however, Lucio receives the same punishment as Angelo: marriage. The Duke uses the information Lucio has shared with him to enforce marriage with the prostitute he was imprudent enough to impregnate. Angelo and Lucio both must marry to restore accountability and demonstrate the necessity of a common standard according to which everyone must live in a well-ordered city. As David Lowenthal argues, "Marriage seems to be the mean between the life of the brothels and the life of the nunnery."[14] It is even a standard to which the Duke, who had appeared disinterested in matters of the heart, willingly subjects himself, when he proposes marriage to Isabella (V.1.531–536). While this proposal strikes the critics as oppressive, because Isabella can hardly refuse it, the Duke subjects himself to the same rules he has imposed on others, the very definition of the rule of law.

The Duke's Political Endgame

Measure for Measure may be a problem play for some critics, but it is a problem play only for the politically squeamish. The Duke does, in fact, express distaste for the public elements of political life, staging himself for the people, competing in the assembly for advantage and recognition, but he also demonstrates, in the end, his acknowledgment that he must participate in the public realm. He is neither neglectful nor naïve about political life. Instead, after careful observation of the political landscape, he orchestrates a plan to combat the extremes to which political life is prone and to bring the political spectrum back to the moderate center. The Duke is much like a contemporary American political leader, caught between the extremes of liberalism and conservatism, who is able to strike a prudent balance. He knows there is no one political or theoretical solution that answers all the political challenges of his day or any other, but that all the solutions are dependent on time, place, and circumstances.

The Duke is well aware that people are disinclined to listen to arguments about their faults. So, instead, he persuades the people of Vienna by leading them to see for themselves the flaws of the alternative extremes in political life by revealing the defects of these positions in a public trial in act 5. He is able to discredit the draconian and unjust religious laws that had hung over Vienna for many years and to institute political and legal reform. Machiavelli tells us that the greatest princes introduce "new modes and orders," new methods of operation and new laws and institutions.[15] The Duke has apparently allowed, even encouraged, the liberation of desire from rigid control by the city's ancient religiously inspired laws.

Conclusion

The timing of *Measure for Measure* is not accidental. It is set at the precise moment the Duke judges the city is ready for a correction, for his new modes and orders. In the end, the Duke's victory over his severe religious opposition and the vice that has infected the people's liberty appears to be complete. He teaches the people and the participants in the political drama to reject the uninhibited and destructive rule of the passions and the imposition of moral severity that results in cruelty rather than justice and to accept the necessity of subjecting themselves to the rule of good laws and a moderate or measured political order.

Notes

1. Machiavelli, Niccolo, *The Prince*, Harvey Mansfield translation (Chicago: University of Chicago Press, 1998), 4.

2. Shakespeare does not call the Duke a "Machiavel," but his use of deception and disguise to assert his political authority without incurring the hatred of the people is reminiscent of Machiavelli's advice to the Prince in chapter 17 of *The Prince*, on the subject of "Cruelty and Mercy, and Whether It Is Better to Be Loved than Feared, or the Contrary," 67. We do not know the extent of Shakespeare's knowledge of Machiavelli's text, but we do know that he utilized the term "Machiavel" three times in his plays,

Henry VI, Part I (III.2.193), *Henry VI*, Part III (V.4.74–75), and *The Merry Wives of Windsor* (III.1), suggesting familiarity with the understanding of the Machiavellian as a subtle and likely subversive man.

3. Scholars have identified several sources for the basic story on which Shakespeare bases the plot of *Measure for Measure*. See J. W. Lever's "Introduction" to *The Arden Edition of William Shakespeare's Measure for Measure*, section III, "Sources" (London: Thompson Learning, 2001), p. xxxv.

4. Ibid., pp. xxxv–xxxvi.

5. Craig A. Bernthal, "Staging Justice: James I and the Trial Scenes of Measure for Measure," *Studies in English Literature, 1500–1900*, Vol. 32, No. 2, Elizabethan and Jacobean Drama (Spring 1992), p. 256.

6. Lever, "Introduction," *Measure for Measure*, pp. lxv–lxvi.

7. Shakespeare describes Lucio as a "fantastique" in his list of actors. See David Lowenthal (*Shakespeare and the Good Life* [Lanham, MD: Rowman and Littlefield, 1997], p. 254) and Barbara Tovey for a fuller explanation of Lucio's nature. Tovey's essay is "Wisdom and Law: Thoughts on the Political Philosophy of *Measure for Measure*," in *Shakespeare's Political Pageant: Essays in Politics and Literature*, edited by Joseph Alulis and Vickie Sullivan (Lanham, MD: Rowman and Littlefield, 1996), p. 65.

8. Lowenthal, *Shakespeare and the Good Life*, pp. 255–256.

9. Tovey, "Wisdom and Law," p. 65.

10. Ibid., pp. 62–63.

11. Machiavelli, *The Prince*, pp. 29–30.

12. Ibid., p. 30.

13. The interpretation is common to the Folger Shakespeare Library edition of *Measure for Measure*, edited by Barbara A. Mowat and Paul Werstine (New York: Washington Square, 1997), 125, and the Arden Shakespeare, edited by J. W. Lever (London: Thomson Learning, 2001), note for lines 216–217, 92.

14. Lowenthal, *Shakespeare and the Good Life*, p. 252.

15. Machiavelli, *The Prince*, p. 23.

CHAPTER 12

ABSURDITY AND AMATEUR HOUR
IN THE AMERICAN POLITICAL FOREST
A MIDSUMMER NIGHT'S DREAM AND THE NIGHTMARE
OF POLARIZATION

Kevan M. Yenerall

What can Shakespeare teach us about the state of twenty-first-century American politics? *A Midsummer Night's Dream*, filled with lovers, fairies, and amateur actors producing a play for sophisticates, provides insight into the way we select our leaders. In particular, our most recent quadrennial exercise in nationwide partisan politicking, the 2012 presidential primaries—with the likes of Rick Perry, Herman Cain, and Michele Bachmann auditioning for the role of Republican standard-bearer—suggests that while there is great humor to be gained from absurdity, the price of political polarization and niche and network media that often serve as a conduit for their primary performances, have tremendous costs for our political discourse and governance. While Shakespeare's notoriously unaware actor Nick Bottom notes that "to say the truth, reason and love keep little company together," it may well be that when it comes to the presidential selection stage, truth and reason keep little company together.

Yet, applying Shakespeare's enduring classic to our times, we can also find ways to laugh at, *and place in proper context*, the political process that reveals human foibles, pandering, ideological hubris, policy incoherence, and perhaps, significant systemic imperfections. The three aforementioned political actors of this play—ultimately, unsuited for their roles and poorly trained in the basic skills necessary for the big stage—did not win over enough voters in the audience and exited the theater before curtain call, but did succeed in providing fodder for late-night satirists and comedians. And, while it was most certainly not their intention, like Shakespeare's whimsical tale, the amateur political actors in the 2012 primaries also succeeded in pointing out a few of the eccentricities, absurdities, and imperfections of our political elites, everyday folks, and our times. Like *A Midsummer Night's Dream*, focusing on political mechanicals aids in our quest to find the humor and absurdity in the conditions and processes of our fractured politics. And in the end, that may be the healthiest outcome possible for this partisan political play performed by amateurs in the contemporary electoral forest.

Not Ready for Prime Time: The Mechanicals (Candidates) Take the Stage (Republican Primaries)

Seeking a path to comprehending some of the more absurd or comical aspects of our recent primary season? Might there be a piece of literature, a few fictional characters from the past to guide our assessment? Certainly students of politics have ample traditional news sources to make some sense of our fractured, polarized politics. Nate Silver's fivethirtyeight.com, Politico, Slate, Salon, and so on, are but a small sampling that stand alongside traditional lions like the *New York Times, National Journal, PBS's Newshour,* the *Atlantic,* and the *Washington Post.* However, when stopping to consider the entrance and exit of the likes of Gov. Rick Perry, Herman Cain, and Rep. Michele Bachmann, some Shakespeare would come in handy. That's right—*A Midsummer Night's Dream* as a prism through which to reconsider some of the also-rans of the 2012 Republican presidential primaries.

There are many glorious moving parts to the Shakespeare classic, which centers on the love interests, exploits, and foibles of elites; their interaction with a group of fairies in the forest; and the production of a play during this midsummer night by a bunch of unintentionally hilarious, incompetent "mechanicals"—or average Joes. And, of course, there is the delightfully uber-mischievous fairy, Puck (Robin Goodfellow), who stands out by casting some of the most notorious and devious spells on unwitting human beings and fairies, especially one aimed at the biggest, clueless ham of the amateur acting troupe, Nick Bottom, who at one point has his head transformed into that of an ass. The mechanicals fancy themselves professional, competent writers, directors, and actors, but as their play-within-the-play illustrates, quality actors they are not. If there were "B" movie actors on the Athens stage, these might qualify as the C- or D-level!

For the sake of this application of Shakespeare to the American political stage—namely, the 2012 Republican primaries—the main characters of relevance are the *mechanicals*—the everyday workingmen who view themselves as thespians and try ever so hard to execute a play: Nick Bottom (weaver), Peter Quince (carpenter), Francis Flute (bellows-mender), Robin Starveling (tailor), Tom Snout (tinker), and Snug (joiner).[1] Taken together, their cluelessness on the theatrical stage could be seen to mirror the ramshackle, unrefined, and sometimes preposterous performances of particular presidential candidates in 2012, as they were ill-equipped to execute their mission and exhibited maladroit behavior with regularity. In short: the 2012 amateur political actors in the Republican primaries were no more adept at their political play than the likes of Bottom, Quince, Flute, Starveling, Snout, and Snug performing for and with Shakespeare's lovers and fairies in the forest.

In the fall of 1975, *Saturday Night Live* famously took late-night network television by storm with the counterculture comedy troupe labeled the "Not Ready for Prime Time Players." This moniker was tongue-in-cheek, as producer-writer Lorne Michaels had assembled the talents of John Belushi, Chevy Chase, Dan Aykroyd, Gilda Radner, and Jane Curtin, among others. Yet one can make the case that the loudest mechanicals on the primary stage in 2012, putting on a play for media, partisans, and activists assembled, were the *truly authentic* Not Ready for Prime Time Players.

The Political Process: Puck and the Primaries Cast a Spell

> This year's primary cycle was aberrant in another way: it featured so many debates, promoted by so many networks, with a cast of so many flamboyant characters, in such a rapidly changing variety of promising and disappointing roles.[2]

The presidential primaries can have an intoxicating, perplexing, otherworldly effect on candidates. It can cast a spell, if you will, eliciting comments and actions otherwise known in simple English as ... foolish. As working craftsman-turned-actor Nick Bottom's head becomes a donkey's head courtesy of a spell from Shakespeare's fairy Puck, we have seen the 2012 primaries turn some candidates into clueless actors. And yet, the political culture of the Republican Party has historically worked against an unsettled field of amateur actors on the stage. So-called Establishment candidates—those who have run before, have significant national campaign experience, or come from prominent positions and families tend to be the go-to people when the primary process gets serious.

Noting that former Arkansas governor turned Fox News talk show host Mike Huckabee had actually won more delegates than the assumed pseudo-establishment second-time candidate, Gov. Mitt Romney, to the 2008 Republican National Convention, and that the Republican Party's establishment's preferred candidates for 2012—perhaps most notably, the likes of Indiana Gov. Mitch Daniels, had decided against running—Republican "fund-raisers and Washington validators resisted making commitments, hoping to enlist a candidate they knew and trusted."[3] Hence, the likes of Texas governor Rick Perry, businessman Herman Cain, and Minnesota congresswoman Michele Bachmann, at various points in the summer and early fall of 2011, rose in the polls, filling, if temporarily, the void. As the *New York Times'* Matt Bai observed in a cover story in the fall of 2011 as the debates were well under way and the actual voting was right around the proverbial corner, "For the first time in what feels like forever (though it's more like 1968), Republicans are going into this election without a consensus choice or a guy who had clearly earned his shot."[4] In the face of early chaos in the unsettled field, several political actors stepped to the stage, eager to perform for the masses and elites, learning their lines, determined to succeed, and entering downstage right. Far right.

Not all members of the conservative Republican intelligentsia or Establishment found fault with the seemingly open and freewheeling nature of Republicans' pre- and early primary season, however. The *Weekly Standard's* William Kristol, for example, with one foot firmly in Establishment party politics and past White House governance and another as opinion entrepreneur through his conservative magazine, stated, "I get annoyed with all the establishment types who speak as if they're supposed to be controlling everything, who sound annoyed when things happen when they don't expect. I mean, welcome to the world."[5] In the face of a wide-open nomination battle, one state executive seemed poised to stop Mitt Romney, and he had enormous statewide success in his home state of Texas. To the stage: Gov. Rick Perry.

The Mechanicals: Welcome to the World, Rick Perry, Herman Cain, and Michele Bachmann

Rick Perry: Governor of Texas . . . Stumbling Out of the Gate

Calling himself a conservative of "conviction" and not of "convenience"—a sly broadside against the one-time moderate Republican governor of Massachusetts, Mitt Romney—the popular three-term chief executive of Texas, Rick Perry, catapulted to the top of national polls in late summer 2011. Though Perry entered the primaries later than his rivals, he had the support of a number of governors and activists. He had won favor with the base of his party for his policy of low taxes, embrace of evangelical Christianity, and a solid Texas economy. By calling Federal Reserve Chairman Ben Bernanke's quantitative easing policy "treasonous" in Iowa, and suggesting the Fed chairman might be roughed up in Texas for "printing money," he further cemented his stature as a straight-talking populist conservative.[6] He famously ran with a gun in a proud conceal-carry state, had military experience (he flew C-130s in the Air Force) unlike all other rivals save for Rep. Ron Paul (TX), and served longer than any Republican governor in Texas history.[7] Speaking to Perry's conservative acumen, executive experience, and money, one experienced Republican politician told the *Atlantic*'s James Fallows in May 2012, "In any normal, year, Perry would have sewn this up by February."[8]

Yet like an awkward mechanical on a midsummer night, Perry "Bottomed" out quickly, fading nearly as quickly as he rose to the top of primary polls. The Texas governor soon found himself unable to shake off several dismal (abysmal?) debate performances, peculiar affectations, and occasional political tone deafness. While his position as governor of a major state (albeit one with a constitutionally weak executive), conservative record, and the fact that the previous Republican president, George W. Bush, used his position and name to catapult past challengers in 1999 en route to the nomination in 2000, should have solidified Perry's standing in the Establishment and beyond, some inside Republican power players expressed concern with the rhetoric, positions, and swagger of Perry.

One such figure who expressed doubts was A. B. Culvahouse, chairman of the powerful law firm O'Melvyny & Myers and former White House counsel in the Reagan White House. He also famously performed vice-presidential vetting duties for Sen. John McCain in 2008.[9] Culvahouse found Perry's style to be akin to the "tent revivalists" he knew growing up in rural Tennessee. At the same time, he found such populist, evangelical fervor preferable to other Tea Party candidates like Palin or Bachmann, given his experience as a state executive.

Soon out of the gate, however, despite Perry's entrance with great fanfare, and his conservative bona fides, he was stumbling—badly and irreparably. In a late September showdown with Romney in Orlando, Florida, for example, the conservative *Weekly Standard* characterized his debate performance as "marked by misstatements of fact, missed opportunities, and general incoherence."[10] One particular piece of Perry's performance—what was meant to be a blistering attack on Mitt Romney's shifting views on fundamental issues—was especially intriguing to the media and late-night comedians, and left some rank-and-file conservatives in the audience baffled or unimpressed:

> I think Americans just don't know sometimes which Mitt Romney they're dealing with. Is it the Mitt Romney that was on the side of against the Second Amendment before he was for the Second Amendment? Was it was before he was before the social programs from the standpoint of he was for standing up for *Roe v. Wade* before he was against *Roe v. Wade*? Ah, he was for Race to the Top. He's for Obamacare, and now he's against it. I mean we'll wait until tomorrow to see which Mitt Romney we're really talking to tonight.[11]

An enthusiastic Perry supporter in the Florida debate audience opined, "When he was talking to Mitt Romney there was a part of that—if you printed it, I don't think it even made sense."[12] Another prominent Republican who produced debates in 2004 and 2008 and was present for the Perry performance asserted "that the energy and enthusiasm for Perry in the debate hall disappeared when he flubbed his attacks on Mitt Romney."[13] In addition, Perry seemed to misread the conservative fervor for stronger anti–illegal immigration policies in the debate hall when he defended providing in-state college tuition rates to children of illegal (i.e., undocumented) immigrants. "I don't think you have a heart," he said, if you opposed the policy.[14] Needless to say, this went over about as well as a call for privatizing Social Security and Medicaid or banning all reproductive rights at a Democratic primary debate. In an infamous debate moment a few weeks later, Perry again stumbled terribly, failing to remember which three federal agencies he would eliminate if elected president. When pressed after his initial forgetfulness, he was again unable to name the third department, uttering an "oops" heard 'round the political world. In the words of an old commercial, Perry was falling, and he could not, and did not, get up, exiting the primary stage with one of the worst and most perplexing primary performances in recent history. The *Atlantic*'s James Fallows effectively summarized the cumulative and calamitous consequences of Gov. Perry's failure to deliver on the debate stage:

Perry had money, swagger, more than a decade's worth of governing experience in his big-state base, plus most of the proper policy positions for this year's Republican electorate. What he did not have was the presence of mind to remember which three federal agencies he wanted to abolish, as revealed in his excruciating brain-freeze moment on live TV.... Nor was he able to explain away in several debates his only unpopular-with-the-base position, a relatively soft line on illegal immigrants, as effectively as Mitt Romney has contained the damage from his support of "Obamneycare" in Massachusetts.... When I asked campaign veterans from both parties for names of other candidates who, like Perry, had been eliminated solely because of a few disastrous debates, no one could come up with a comparable case.[15]

He did try self-deprecation and acknowledging his limitations—noting that he was neither "the slickest candidate or the smoothest debater."[16] Yet even as Perry reflected, as the *Weekly Standard*'s Stephen Hayes correctly asserted, both "temperamentally and ideologically, the energy of the base of the Republican party," his major flubs in a number of debates, frequent inability to articulate his positions or coherent criticisms of others, and a bizarre New Hampshire appearance dominated by an odd exuberance the candidate later blamed on the effects of back medication, among other odd appearances and political miscues, caused him irreparable harm.[17] He could not master his lines, and his stage direction zigzagged. Even governors can be bumbling mechanicals under the bright lights of the national political stage; the spell of the primaries was too great.

Herman Cain: Motivational Speaker, Businessman, Book Buyer, Candidate

The polls are inaccurate in my opinion based upon anecdotal evidence ... based upon people that I know.
—Herman Cain, on the *Daily Show*, August 29, 2012

Successful businessman (CEO of Godfather's Pizza), former president of the National Restaurant Association, and popular conservative motivational speaker/ radio host, Herman Cain knew how to make a point and woo audiences. His clear, unvarnished, folksy and direct, not-put-through-twenty-focus-groups approach to political rhetoric was refreshing to many in the dominant antitax, antigovernment, antipolitics fiscal conservative wing of the party. This wing, of course, had greater sway in many of the primary states, where activists often have disproportionate electoral influence—such as Iowa and South Carolina.

Whether wearing a cowboy hat with a big grin, or proudly telling the audience at the 2011 Americans for Prosperity conference that the conservative-libertarian antiregulation Koch brothers were his metaphorical siblings—"I am their brother from another mother," he told the adoring crowd of activists—Cain was finding political gold in the fall of 2011, when he began to skyrocket in the polls with his catchy slogan, or tax reform and economic growth platform, known as his "9-9-9 plan."[18] The plan, however, soon met with scholarly scrutiny, with a number of nonpartisan policy experts questioning if the plan was little more than a simple catchphrase rather than a serious policy proposal from a potential president.[19] The 9-9-9 plan was now coming under heavy scrutiny from policy experts, but its simplicity was clearly an asset for more ideological voters fed up with taxes, tired of mediocre economic recovery, and believing that government was the primary source of their, and the nation's, ills.

In addition, Cain made history—and not in a particularly good way—when Federal Election Commission reports revealed that his campaign purchased copies of his autobiography, *I Am Herman Cain!* from his own motivational speaking company.[20] And while candidates writing books for a campaign is a common occurrence, purchasing them *from your own company* with campaign funds generally is not. Thus, as his stock rose in the polls—even staunch conservative Hank Williams Jr. cited him as his favorite Republican candidate for president—more and more questions arose about whether he was waging a campaign for president or a well-orchestrated media blitz to benefit his private coffers and future speaking fees. Then there were a series of policy misstatements, or oddities, and salacious allegations that muddied his political future just as he was peaking.

Pro-Life and ... Pro-Choice

One prominent example of Cain having two seemingly incongruous positions involved abortion. Appearing on CNN for an interview with talk show host Piers Morgan, Cain's response to a question on abortion policy was, even for candidates of both parties who routinely parse words to appease core constituencies, remarkably contradictory. After unequivocally stating that he was pro-life, that he believed life began at conception and would not favor *any* legal exception for abortion—as in the case of rape or incest—he then stated, after prodding from Morgan,

> It comes down to ... it is not the government's role or anybody else's role to make that decision.... What I am saying is, it ultimately gets down to a choice that that family or that mother has to make. Not a president, not some

> politician, not a bureaucrat, it gets down to that family and whatever they decide, they decide. I shouldn't try to tell them what decision to make....[21]

In other words, Cain succeeded in making one of the more succinct, direct cases for the pro-choice position on abortion rights in recent history. The problem was he had just stated that he was pro-life, without any exceptions, and was running in the Republican Party primaries.

Sexual Harassment Allegations

The largest and final blow to Cain's meteoric media- and conservative electorate–driven rise and fall was not the merits of his tax reform plan or his pro-life without exception/pro-choice position on abortion rights, but allegations of past sexual harassment (or improper advances and/or language) that came to light. In late October 2011, reports surfaced detailing past settlements with women who claimed Cain had engaged in "sexually aggressive behavior" while they worked for him at the National Restaurant Association.[22] Both accusers received separation packages after bringing formal charges—according to *Politico*, the publication that first broke the story—in the "five-figure range."[23] The requisite media appearances ensued, but the free-fall was on. Cain never recovered and was essentially a nonfactor by the time the Iowa caucuses and New Hampshire primary commenced. Indeed, a second mechanical had exited the stage—not in midsummer but mid- to late fall.

From Candidate to Court Jester

Yet the fairy Puck's (read: the presidential primary's) spells can take quite a while to shake off. Once the primaries are in your blood, it can be tough to leave the stage without making curious remarks or appearances, ala Bottom in the Bard's masterpiece. Such was the case with Cain. After his campaign died, he appeared with faux conservative (read: liberal satirist) Stephen Colbert on the South Carolina ballot—after Cain had essentially ended his race and was "standing in for comedian Stephen Colbert's exploratory committee for the presidency of the United States of South Carolina."[24] Indeed, here one can make the case that Cain was perhaps transformed into the master jester himself, dabbling in some of Puck's own bag of tricks. Now freed from the illusions of real primary victories, Cain the one-time Republican candidate became Cain the faux candidate, providing fodder for Colbert's satirical scathing critique of primary politics, campaign finance, and influence peddling in the post–*Citizens United* world. The Cain/Colbert team came in fifth in South Carolina, ahead of Rick Perry and close to fourth-place finisher Ron Paul. Several months later, on the August 29, 2012, episode of the *Daily Show* airing from Tampa, Florida, during the Republican National Convention, Cain provided this rationale for why more African Americans were not showing up as favoring Mitt Romney in the polls: "They were working, so they didn't answer the phone when they took the poll ... believe it or not some black people have jobs and careers and they run businesses. They didn't take that into account, Jon."[25]

Rep. Michele Bachmann: You Say Chutzpah, She Says Choots-Pa

On an appearance on Fox News in June 2011, on Greta Van Susteren's *On the Record*, Michele Bachmann, US Representative from Minnesota—Tea Party favorite, one-time IRS tax attorney-collector, school board activist, state senator, conservative populist firebrand (she once used a bullhorn from the US Capitol to address a crowd gathered to protest the Affordable Care Act, or "Obamacare"), and now candidate for the Republican nomination—was criticizing Barack Obama's spending and economic policies, when she stated that the President had "choots-pa."[26] Not *chutzpah* as in *"hoots-pah,"* the Yiddish phrase, but her version, *choots-pa.*

Obviously one minor mispronunciation should not automatically classify the congresswoman (or anyone) an amateur auditioning for the lead role on the biggest stage—the presidency. Even stating that Lexington and Concord were in New Hampshire, rather than Massachusetts, however unfortunate or inaccurate, should not (by itself) relegate Bachmann to the rank of bumbling mechanical on the primary stage. Yet the verbal gaffes are emblematic of other questionable statements, historical inaccuracies, and intellectually suspect ideas emanating from the candidate's mouth over the course of her primary performance and the period leading up to her national stage debut. The never-shy Chris Matthews once famously asked her on election night in 2010 if she was "hypnotized"—yet more than likely, she was merely under the spell of the political process and her own central place in the Tea Party movement between 2009–2011.[27] Far more serious than *choots-pa* would be the contention in a Fox News primary debate that citizens should not pay any federal taxes, or her suggestion that a vague notion of "anti-Americanism" in Congress be investigated.[28]

Investigate Anti-Americanism (Or ... Liberalism ... Leftists)

Rep. Bachmann arrived on the presidential primary stage with a variety of notorious statements and actions that called into question her ability to be a serious candidate for president. In 2008 during an infamous appearance on

Chris Matthews's MSNBC staple *Hardball,* she expressed concern that liberals or "leftists" in government, such as Nancy Pelosi, Harry Reid, and perhaps Sen. Barack Obama (the Democratic nominee for president)—possessed "far leftist" and "anti-American" views, adding that "the news media should do a penetrating expose.... At the views of people in Congress and find out if they are pro-America or anti-America."[29] Using the terms *liberal, leftist,* and *anti-American/America* interchangeably, Bachmann had appeared ostensibly to criticize Obama's real and alleged connections to his pastor, Rev. Jeremiah Wright, and former Weather Underground activist William Ayers, whom she found to be "over-the-top anti-American" individuals.[30]

The Founders as Ardent Abolitionists

Leader of the Tea Party Caucus since 2009, Bachmann had engaged in somewhat innocent if politically grandiose gestures such as giving away pocket Constitutions with her autograph, and she also supported a congressional resolution that would "bar the dollar from being replaced by any foreign currency"—later asking Treasury Secretary Tim Geithner to "categorically renounce the United States moving away from the dollar."[31] That there was zero likelihood of the United States actually doing such a thing did not deter her. But perhaps the most famous bouts of her inaccuracy or fantasy came in the form of Bachmann's unequivocal statement that the nation's founding fathers fought tirelessly against slavery.[32] Speaking before the Iowans for Tax Relief in late January as speculation about her presidential candidacy was increasing, Bachmann stated,

> We know we were not perfect. We know there was slavery that was still tolerated when the nation began. We know that was an evil and it was scourge and a blot and a stain upon our history. But we also know that the very founders that wrote those documents worked tirelessly until slavery was no more in the United States. And I think it is high time that we recognize the contribution of our forebears, who worked tirelessly, men like John Quincy Adams, who would not rest until slavery was extinguished in the country.[33]

Though she correctly noted John Quincy Adams's anti-slavery sentiments and activity, he is hardly considered a founding father. Of course, presidents Washington and Jefferson possessed slaves at different points in their lives, as did other significant political civic leaders of the age, and the Constitution—the foundational document of rights, responsibilities, and governmental structure—did not abolish slavery. Later in the same address, Bachmann stated that Barack Obama has amassed more debt in his first year in the White House than all presidents from George Washington to George W. Bush combined—another whopper, one deemed "mathematically impossible" and worthy of "Four Pinocchio" status by the *Washington Post*'s impartial, nonpartisan fact checker, Glenn Kessler.[34]

The Primary Spell Lingers ...

While some observers, including award-winning liberal *Rolling Stone* editor and commentator Matt Taibbi, viewed Bachmann's campaign as a "holy war" that was no laughing matter, warning of her deep grassroots support among evangelical conservatives in exurban and rural America, in the end Bachmann could not appeal beyond a very narrow base and was quickly overcome by other flavors-of-the-month, like Cain, and longtime electoral survivors, like former Speaker of the House, Newt Gingrich.[35] Yet, as it was with Herman Cain, the Puck-like spell placed on Michele Bachmann during the primary stage was powerful. As such, several months after her primary campaign officially ended, Bachmann continued down the path of unfounded fear and accusation as one of six members to sign a letter asking for an investigation of the alleged infiltration and undue influence of the Muslim Brotherhood in the US State Department, even citing the State Department's deputy chief of staff, Muslim immigrant, and longtime Hillary Clinton aide (and wife to former US Rep. Anthony Weiner, D-NY), Huma Abedin, in her letter.[36] A few conservative House members— such as Trent Franks (AZ), Louie Gohmert (TX), Tom Rooney (FL), and Lynn Westmoreland (GA)—joined her, sending letters to "several inspector generals in the State Department, Department of Homeland Security, the Department of Defense, the Department of Justice and the Office of National Intelligence as to whether the Muslim Brotherhood could be infiltrating the US government."[37]

Using words such as "extreme," "dishonest," "vicious," "outrageous," and "false" to characterize her baseless suggestions regarding infiltration of the Muslim Brotherhood and disparaging the reputation of Huma Abedin, Bachmann's former presidential campaign advisor Ed Rollins, mastermind of Ronald Reagan's 1984 reelection, denounced the letter and the insinuations and allegations.[38] Likewise, Sen. John McCain, in a speech on the Senate floor, derided the letters, especially Bachmann's, asserting that the "ugly and unfortunate attacks" on Abedin had "no logic, no basis, and no merit," and praising Abedin's "abiding commitment to the American ideals that she embodies so fully."[39] Coupled with her past call for investigating un-American activity and her rewrite of American history, perhaps Bachmann's abrupt exit from the Republican primary stage after a horrible performance in her native Iowa, like her rise from school board activist to Congress, is as *Rolling Stone*'s Taibbi found it: "almost certainly the funniest thing that has ever happened to American presidential politics"—more akin to a brief 1970s children's show called *Far Out Space Nuts* (starring Bob Denver as an inept NASA repairman) than an exercise in seriousness.[40]

Curtain Call: Mechanicals Exit the Stage, Only Romney Remains

In Shakespeare's brilliant play, Bottom, Quince, Snug, and Snout et al. were never really forced to leave the stage, no matter how clueless, incompetent, or fitted with an ass's head. In the electoral version of the Bard's play, the media elite, the primary voters, and the curious utterances, missteps, and occasional oddities of the aforementioned candidates served as chief removal mechanisms. With each remark, debate, or allegation of scandal, they found themselves one step closer to electoral oblivion and political irrelevance, and none were seriously considered to be vice presidential or even major surrogate material after Mitt Romney secured the nomination. Moreover, neither Perry, Cain, nor Bachmann was granted *any* significant speaking time at the Republican convention in Tampa. Indeed, watching and listening to the RNC proceedings in Tampa, you would be hard-pressed to know there were any challengers whatsoever in the primaries. Only one of Romney's primary cohorts, former senator Rick Santorum, was given a coveted evening speaking slot.

As the other political actors flamed, bumbled, stumbled, and burned, one-by-one exiting the primary stage after entering with great fanfare and early signs of electoral support, one person was left standing: Gov. Mitt Romney. Romney, the safe if uninspiring choice for movement conservatives and many others in the party, was a fairly standard Republican Establishment candidate in nonstandard, ultra-ideological times. As such, the 2012 Republican nominee, who chose conservative rising star Paul Ryan of Wisconsin as his running mate, stands in the long line of "next-in-line" nominees who finally won the nomination after one or more previous runs (e.g., McCain in 2008; Dole in 1996; George H. W. Bush in 1988; Reagan in 1980; Nixon in 1968).

Puck, Primaries, and the Parties: Casting Spells in the Forest ... of the Future?

While this brief application of Shakespearean realities to the 2012 presidential primary theater asserts that the not-ready-for-prime-time candidates act strangely as the spell of the primaries is cast upon them, this is hardly to suggest that every ounce of the American electorate is weighed down with erudition, sophistication, and attention to data and context. Barriers to political thinking abound, from the unwillingness of Americans to do the "heavy lifting" of citizenship, sifting through substantive information and analysis, to the prevalence of cable news, talk radio, and blogs that make it harder to discern reality, dissect policies, and make informed choices.[41] And for-profit media outlets often employ a horse race and conflict-driven coverage that speaks to the business model, not the citizenship model.[42]

Although ideological hubris, bizarre behavior, comical missteps, Bachmann-esque "choots-pa," absence of serious policy proposals and deliberation, and electoral dysfunction may have found a home in the quixotic 2012 primary campaigns of Rick Perry, Herman Cain, and Michelle Bachmann, amateur hour in the forest of American politics certainly need not be confined to one political party or set of candidates. A spell of ideological recalcitrance and pandering can infect any candidate or party. And while this brief application of Shakespeare to the recent American electoral stage does not deal with governance, and focuses on inept or ideologically extreme campaigning, as the title of this chapter suggests, polarization (not partisanship, an organic and often healthy aspect of representative democracy) can indeed be a nightmare. With their temperament and worldview, would the country have been well-served with a president Bachmann, Perry, or Cain? Yet, one way to identify and deal with the exploits of primaries, which can breed candidates, ideologies, and policies ill-suited to practical governance in a diverse, pluralistic society, is to first find the humor and absurdity in the condition and process. Shakespeare found the humor and absurdity in his play by his clever juxtaposition of elites, average working stiffs, and magical fairies. By looking to *A Midsummer Night's Dream*, we can in some small measure see the amateur actors on our biggest stage, sense the spells that affect them, and, like the fairies and lovers in Shakespeare's play, be able to shake it off and start anew.

Notes

1. William Shakespeare, *A Midsummer Night's Dream*, Mario Digangi, editor (New York: Barnes & Noble, 2007), pp. 43–44.

2. James Fallows, "Slugfest," *Atlantic*, September 2012, p. 68.

3. Matt Bai, "Does Anyone Have a Grip on the GOP?" *New York Times Magazine*, October 16, 2011, p. 50.

4. Ibid., p. 49.

5. Ibid., p. 50.

6. For Perry's treasonous comments regarding Federal Reserve Chair Bernanke, see www.cbsnews.com/8301-503544_162-20093433-503544.html. Perry's comments, as presented in the CBS article: "If this guy prints more money between now and the election, I dunno what y'all would do to him in Iowa but we would treat him pretty ugly down in Texas. Printing more money to play politics at this particular time in American history is almost treasonous in my opinion."

7. Rachel Weiner, "Rick Perry Almost Alone in Military Service," *Washington Post*, August 16, 2011, www.washingtonpost.com/blogs/the-fix/post/rick-perry-almost-alone-in-military-service/2011/08/16/gIQALjjEJJ_blog.html.

8. Fallows, "Slugfest."

9. Bai, "Does Anyone Have a Grip on the GOP?" p. 51. For Culvahouse's role in vetting Sen. John McCain's eventual running mate, Gov. Sarah Palin (AK), see John Heilemann and Mark Halperin, *Game Change* (New York: HarperCollins, 2010), especially chapter 20, "Sarahcuda."

10. Stephen F. Hayes, "The Frontrunner Stumbles," *Weekly Standard*, vol. 17, no. 3, October 3, 2011, www.weeklystandard.com/articles/frontrunner-stumbles_594141.html.

11. Perry's comments as reported and transcribed by Stephen F. Hayes, ibid.

12. Ibid.

13. Ibid.

14. Ibid.

15. Fallows, "Slugfest."

16. Hayes, "The Frontrunner Stumbles."

17. Video of Rick Perry New Hampshire speech, October 28, 2011, www.youtube.com/watch?v=21z30aNO3cA.

18. Cain at Americans for Prosperity conference clip, www.youtube.com/watch?v=NJkk8ysMnRk&feature=related.

19. Ron Scherer, "Herman Cain's '999 Plan': Long Overdue Tax Reform or Job Killer?" *Christian Science Monitor*, September 30, 2011, www.csmonitor.com/USA/Elections/President/2011/0930/Herman-Cain-s-999-plan-long-overdue-tax-reform-or-job-killer.

20. Jonathan D. Salant and Joshua Green, "Cain Used Campaign Funds to Buy Autobiography from His Company," Bloomberg.com, October 18, 2011, www.bloomberg.com/news/2011-10-18/cain-used-campaign-funds-to-buy-autobiography.html.

21. Morgan's interview with Cain, www.youtube.com/watch?v=OPKYYDefMV4.

22. Jonathan Karl et al., "Herman Cain Accused by Two Women of Inappropriate Behavior," *Politico*, October 31, 2011, www.politico.com/news/stories/1011/67194.html.

23. Ibid.

24. Cain was a stand-in for Stephen Colbert on the 2012 Republican primary ballot (they placed fifth—ahead of Rick Perry); see Jason Linkins, "Stephen Colbert, Herman Cain Take Fifth Place in South Carolina," *Huffington Post*, January 23, 2012, www.huffingtonpost.com/2012/01/21/stephen-colbert-herman-cain-south-carolina-primary_n_1221483.html.

25. The August 29, 2012, episode of *The Daily Show*, www.thedailyshow.com/watch/wed-august-29-2012/herman-cain.

26. Natasha Leonard, "Michele Bachmann Can't Pronounce Chutzpah," July 14, 2012, *Salon*, www.salon.com/2011/07/14/bachmann_yiddish_chutzpah/. For an

actual video clip of Bachmann's "choots-pah" pronunciation of chutzpah, see, among many others, www.youtube.com/watch?v=9_mWlXvKnq8.

27. See the video of the "hypnotized" exchange on midterm election night, November 3, 2010, www.huffingtonpost.com/2010/11/02/chris-matthews-asks -miche_n_778010.html.

28. Bai, "Does Anyone Have a Grip on the GOP?" pp. 47–48.

29. "Bachmann Calls for McCarthyite Investigation into Anti-American Activities of Liberals," *Think Progress,* October 17, 2008, http://thinkprogress.org /politics/2008/10/17/30892/bachmann-anti-american/?mobile=nc.

30. Ibid.

31. Pocket Constitutions with autographs—see Theda Skocpol and Vanessa Williamson, *The Tea Party and the Remaking of Republican Conservatism* (New York: Oxford University Press, 2012), p. 49. For the currency resolution and challenging Treasury Secretary Geithner, see Matt Taibbi, "Michele Bachmann's Holy War," Rolling Stone.com, June 22, 2011, p. 5, www.rollingstone.com/politics/news /michele-bachmanns-holy-war-20110622.

32. Glenn Kessler, "Bachmann on Slavery and the National Debt," *Washington Post*, January 28, 2011, http://voices.washingtonpost.com/fact-checker/2011/01 /bachmann_on_slavery_and_the_na.html. Video from C-SPAN's coverage of the event (and Bachmann's remarks) is embedded in Kessler's fact-checking article.

33. Ibid.

34. Ibid.

35. Taibbi, "Michele Bachmann's Holy War."

36. Arsalan Iftikhar, "Michele Bachmann vs. Huma Abedin: 'The Ramadan Conspiracy,'" *Washington Post*, July 19, 2012, www.washingtonpost.com/blogs/guest -voices/post/michele-bachmann-vs-huma-abedin-the-ramadan-conspiracy/2012 /07/19/gJQAFDAcvW_blog.html. For Sen. McCain's floor speech denouncing the letter, and for the other legislators that joined Rep. Bachmann, see also Lauren Fox, "Michele Bachmann Sticks to Accusations about Muslim Brotherhood," *US News*, July 19, 2012, www.usnews.com/news/articles/2012/07/19 /michele-bachmann-sticks-to-accusations-about-muslim-brotherhood.

37. Fox, "Michele Bachmann Sticks to Accusations about Muslim Brotherhood."

38. "Michele Bachmann's Vicious Smear Campaign," *US News*, July 19, 2012, www.usnews.com/opinion/blogs/susan-milligan/2012/07/19/michele -bachmanns-vicious-smear-campaign.

39. Ibid. To listen to portions of McCain's speech, see Brian Neely, "McCain Denounces Bachmann's Muslim Brotherhood Statement," Minnesota Public Radio, July 18, 2012, http://minnesota.publicradio.org/display/web/2012/07/18/politics /mccain-bachmann/.

40. Taibbi, "Michele Bachmann's Holy War."

41. Thomas Patterson, *We the People*, 9th edition (New York: McGraw-Hill, 2011).

42. See, for example, Alison Dagnes, *Politics on Demand* (New York: Praeger, 2010); and Thomas Patterson's classic, *Out of Order* (New York: Vintage, 1994).

INDEX

About the Editors and Contributors

Philip Abbott is Distinguished Professor of Political Science at Wayne State University, Detroit, Michigan. His most recent book is *Bad Presidents: Failure in the White House* (2013).

Bruce E. Altschuler is professor of political science at SUNY Oswego and the author or coauthor of five books, most recently *Acting Presidents: 100 Years of Plays about the Presidency* (2010). He has won both the SUNY Research Foundation and SUNY Chancellor's awards for outstanding scholarship. His political commentary is regularly featured on WRVO-FM and WSYR-TV.

Paul A. Cantor is Clifton Waller Barrett Professor of English at the University of Virginia, and has taught at Harvard in both the English and the government departments. He is the author of *Shakespeare's Rome: Republic and Empire* (1976) and the Hamlet volume in the Cambridge Landmarks of World Literature Series (1989, 2004), as well as many essays on Shakespeare's histories, comedies, and tragedies.

Thomas E. Cronin is McHugh Professor of American Institutions and Leadership at Colorado College and president emeritus of Whitman College. His recent writings have been on leadership, the American presidency, and politics. He is coauthor (with Robert Loevy) of *Colorado Politics and Policy: Governing a Purple State* (2012).

Michael A. Genovese is professor of political science and director of the Institute for Leadership Studies at Loyola Marymount University. He is the associate editor of the journal *White House Studies* and the author of thirty-one books, including *The Paradoxes of the American Presidency, Leadership Matters*, and *Encyclopedia of the American Presidency*.

Lilly J. Goren is professor of political science and global studies at Carroll University in Waukesha, Wisconsin. She teaches American government, the presidency, politics, literature and culture, gender studies, and political theory. Her published works include *Not in My District: The Politics of Military Base Closures* (2003); *You've Come a Long Way, Baby: Women, Politics, and Popular Culture* (2009); and *Women and the White House: Gender, Popular Culture, and Presidential Politics* (2012), coedited with Justin Vaughn.

Carol McNamara is the director of the Olene S. Walker Institute of Politics and Public Service at Weber State University. Her publications include articles on Shakespeare's political thought, Xenophon's Socrates, and Tom Wolfe, and an edited volume, *The Obama Administration in the Constitutional Order*. She is currently writing *A Political Companion to Tom Wolfe*.

Coyle Neal recently completed his PhD in political theory at the Catholic University of America. He teaches political philosophy in Washington, D.C.

John M. Parrish is associate professor of political science at Loyola Marymount University. He is the author of *Paradoxes of Political Ethics: From Dirty Hands to the Invisible Hand* (2007), coauthor (with Alex Tuckness) of *The Decline of Mercy in Public Life* (forthcoming), and coeditor (with Margaret Hrezo) of *Damned If You Do: Dilemmas of Action in Literature and Popular Culture* (2010) and (with Wayne Le Cheminant) of *Manipulating Democracy: Democratic Theory, Political Psychology, and Mass Media* (2011).

David Ramsey is assistant professor of government at the University of West Florida, where he teaches courses on constitutional law, jurisprudence, and political philosophy.

Sarah A. Shea is a PhD student in the Faculty of Religious Studies at McGill University in Montreal. Her work focuses on the writings of Albert Camus and French existentialism, along with political philosophy and ethics. Shakespeare remains, from the time of first exposure in high school, her guide for love and life.

Marlene K. Sokolon is associate professor of political science at Concordia University in Montreal. She specializes in political theory and focuses on questions concerning political emotions, politics and literature, and the interconnection of sociocultural and physiological processes. She is the author of several publications including the book *Political Emotions: Aristotle and the Symphony of Reason and Emotion* (2006).

Kevan M. Yenerall is professor of political science at Clarion University, where he teaches courses in American politics, popular culture, and public policy. He is the coauthor of *Seeing the Bigger Picture: American and International Politics in Film and Popular Culture* (2012) and serves as chair of the popular culture and politics section of the Northeastern Political Science Association.